# EMILY DICKINSON'S
## FASCICLES

DOROTHY HUFF OBERHAUS

# EMILY DICKINSON'S FASCICLES

## METHOD & MEANING

THE PENNSYLVANIA STATE UNIVERSITY PRESS
UNIVERSITY PARK, PENNSYLVANIA

Acknowledgment is made to the following:

Harvard University Press for material reprinted by permission of the publishers and the Trustees of Amherst College from *The Poems of Emily Dickinson,* ed. Thomas H. Johnson, Cambridge, Mass.: The Belknap Press of Harvard University Press, Copyright © 1951, 1955, and 1983 by the President and Fellows of Harvard College.

Little, Brown and Company for material reprinted by permission from *The Complete Poems of Emily Dickinson,* ed. Thomas H. Johnson, Copyright © 1929, 1935 by Martha Dickinson Bianchi; Copyright © renewed 1957, 1963 by Mary L. Hampson.

Houghton Library, Harvard University, for reproductions of poems reprinted by permission from Emily Dickinson's fortieth fascicle, MS Am 1118.3 (130) and (209–13).

Library of Congress Cataloging-in-Publication Data

Oberhaus, Dorothy Huff.
    Emily Dickinson's fascicles : method & meaning / Dorothy Huff
Oberhaus.
        p.        cm.
    Includes bibliographical references and indexes.
    ISBN 0-271-01337-0
    1. Dickinson, Emily, 1830–1886—Criticism and interpretation.
    2. Dickinson, Emily, 1830–1886—Criticism, Textual. 3. Manuscripts,
American—Facsimiles. 4. Bible—In literature. 5. Cycles
(Literature)  I. Title.
PS1541.Z5024    1995
811'.4—dc20                                                94-29805
                                                              CIP

It is the policy of The Pennsylvania State University Press to use acid-free paper for the first printing of all clothbound books. Publications on uncoated stock satisfy the minimum requirements of American National Standard for Information Sciences—Permanence of Paper for Printed Library Materials, ANSI Z39.48–1984.

*Title-page illustration:* Fringed gentian (*Gentiana crinita*) by Rick Pfanz, New York City. Emily Dickinson's opening sentence in the first fascicle's first poem is "The Gentian weaves her fringes." The fringed gentian, a significant emblem in four fascicle poems, blooms in Amherst from August until "just before the Snows."

*To Ed Oberhaus*
   *Ted Oberhaus*
   *Ann Huff Oberhaus Mackin*
*And in memory of*
   *Georgia Meadows Huff*
   *Harry Clifford Huff*

# Contents

# Acknowledgments

I am deeply grateful for the valuable suggestions of those who read and commented on my manuscript: Richard B. Sewall, Jack L. Capps, Edwin H. Cady, George Monteiro, and David Porter; my husband, Edward Oberhaus; and my copy editor, Keith Monley. Like all Dickinson readers and all readers of poetry, I am indebted to Ralph W. Franklin for reconstructing the fascicles. I am also grateful for the gracious aid of Dennis Marnon, Administrative Officer of the Houghton Library; Leslie A. Morris, Curator of Manuscripts of the Houghton Library; Elizabeth A. Falsey, Associate Curator of Manuscripts of the Houghton Library; and John Lancaster, Curator of Special Collections of the Amherst College Library. My thanks also go to Mercy College for granting me a sabbatical, a leave of absence, and reduced teaching assignments to enable me to write this book. Finally, I wish to thank Louis L. Martz, whose *Poetry of Meditation: A Study in English Religious Literature of the Seventeenth Century* provided an indispensable source; John T. Shawcross for his advice and encouragement; and Miriam K. Starkman, director of my 1980 dissertation, whose definition of the poetry of Christian devotion I have relied upon both then and throughout this book.

# Textual Note

Because this book concerns the importance of reading Emily Dickinson's poems in their fascicle context, I have emphasized the poems' numbering and order according to Ralph W. Franklin's 1981 *Manuscript Books of Emily Dickinson,* rather than their numbering according to Thomas H. Johnson's 1955 variorum. By Franklin's numbering I mean the numbers from 1 to 40 he assigns to the fascicles in *Manuscript Books,* and by order, the internal sequence in which the poems appear in each of the fascicles in *Manuscript Books.* Thus, for example, I refer to F-40-3, to the fortieth fascicle's third poem, or, in extended discussions of a particular fascicle, simply to poem 3 or the third poem. To further identify a poem, I often cite its first line and almost always, parenthetically, its Johnson number, preceded by J. Poems that Emily Dickinson did not include in the fascicles are cited by Johnson's numbering.

Since my book's primary focus is the fascicle that, according to *Manuscript Books,* is the fortieth and final fascicle Emily Dickinson copied and assembled, Appendix A is a transcript of F-40, and Appendix B, a reproduction of the F-40 manuscript. Line lengths, capitalizations, and punctuation in both Appendix A and the transcripts of individual poems throughout this book are, with a few exceptions, according to Johnson's variorum. In the transcript of F-40 and throughout, variant words and lines are in brackets on the line to which they refer, for variants are sometimes crucially important to comprehending F-40's poems, their relation to one another, and their relation to other fascicles.

# Introduction.
# The Fortieth Fascicle and the
# Poetry of Meditation

Although the poems of Emily Dickinson remained virtually unpublished during her lifetime, she did engage in a private kind of self-publication from about 1858 to 1864. During those years, she made copies of more than eight hundred of her poems, gathered them into forty groups, and bound each of these gatherings together with string to form booklets. While she sometimes sent a friend a copy of one of the poems from the booklets, there is no evidence that she showed them in their bound form to anyone. After her death in 1886, her sister, Lavinia—to whom she had willed all her earthly possessions—was astonished to discover the forty booklets among the poet's papers, as well as copies of nearly four hundred poems arranged in the manner of the booklets, but unbound; miscellaneous fair copies; semifinal drafts; and worksheet drafts written on odds and ends of paper—the backs of envelopes and discarded letters, bits of wrapping paper, and edges of newspapers.[1] Lavinia, who had known her sister wrote poems but had not suspected how many, was determined they be published. First she turned for editorial

help to her sister-in-law, Susan Gilbert Dickinson, who must have seemed—
and still seems—the logical choice. As the poet's surviving letters and holo-
graphs show, Emily Dickinson had shared a lively interest in literature with
Susan, sent her more poems and letters than those sent to any other single
recipient, and even on occasion sought her poetic advice.[2] When Susan
failed to take action quickly enough to suit Lavinia, she retrieved the poems,
then gave them to Mabel Loomis Todd, wife of an astronomy professor at
Amherst College (and mistress of the Dickinson sisters' brother, Austin),
who took on the enormous task of editing the manuscripts. With the help of
T. W. Higginson, a figure of some literary prominence with whom the poet
had corresponded, Todd selected and edited several hundred poems from the
mixed cache discovered by Lavinia, then saw them through their publication
in the three editions of the 1890s.

In these early editions and those that appeared in the following eighty or
so years, editors arranged the poems according to principles of their own that
did not reflect Dickinson's arrangement in her fascicles, as her booklets have
come to be known. Moreover, during the poems' complex publishing history
the fascicles were cast into disarray. Readers therefore knew that Emily
Dickinson had created them—both Lavinia Dickinson and Mabel Todd
referred to them as "volumes" or "fascicules"[3]—but without the fascicles
themselves, one could only wonder about their number, sequence, and even
precisely which poems were included. In his 1955 variorum, Thomas H.
Johnson attempted to identify the poet's original arrangement; then Ralph
W. Franklin in his 1967 *Editing of Emily Dickinson* and a series of subsequent
articles revised Johnson's ordering and added a number of missing poems.[4]
But the poet's original arrangement was not fully restored until 1981 with the
publication of Franklin's *Manuscript Books of Emily Dickinson*. Guided by
such evidence as stationery imperfections, smudge patterns, and puncture
marks where the poet's needle had pierced the paper to bind them, Franklin
returned the fascicles to their original state. For the first time, facsimiles of
the forty fascicles were made available to readers in the form Dickinson had
assembled them.[5]

By reconstructing the fascicles, Franklin introduced a new era in Dickinson scholarship and an important new question to be confronted by her
readers: what, if any, organizing principle or principles did the poet have in
mind when she created them? Because the forty fascicles include most of
Emily Dickinson's poetic production between 1858 and 1864, some have
proposed they are simply random gatherings, that as she wrote the poems,
she bound them chronologically to provide some degree of order to their

burgeoning number. Others have argued that one or all of the booklets focus upon a particular aesthetic or thematic principle.[6] Most recently Sharon Cameron, whose 1992 *Choosing Not Choosing* was published after I had completed this book, presented strong evidence that Emily Dickinson assembled the fascicles deliberately rather than chronologically. As Cameron points out, for example, some fascicles are composed of poems that Dickinson copied in different years. In some cases she later inserted an additional sheet into a fascicle she had already completed. In others she left a verso or half-sheet blank.[7]

My own response to the question implicitly posed by Franklin's work is the subject of this book. My primary focus is the booklet that, according to his *Manuscript Books*, is the fortieth and final booklet Dickinson assembled. Although at first this booklet appears to be simply a collection of unrelated poems in her late, dense style, in the process of grappling with these elliptical poems one discovers beneath their surface multiplicity a deep structural and thematic unity. The key to discovering this unity is in the poems' allusions to the Bible, their allusions to one another and to preceding fascicles, and their echoes of the Christian meditative tradition. This intertextuality forms a network of signals leading the reader to discover that the fortieth fascicle is a carefully constructed poetic sequence and the triumphant conclusion of a long single work, the account of a spiritual and poetic pilgrimage that begins with the first fascicle's first poem.

The centrality of the Bible and the Christian meditative tradition to the fortieth fascicle casts an important light on the whole Dickinson canon. Much of recent Dickinson criticism concerns her place as the first modern poet, her unique and forceful use of language, her problematic position as a woman poet writing in a tradition dominated by men, and the influences upon her of the nineteenth-century America in which she lived and wrote.[8] My study does not dispute these views of the poet. She may even have been, as some maintain, a victim of unrequited love. But a painstakingly careful, intertextual reading of this final booklet reveals that whatever else one may say about Emily Dickinson, her données, her forms, and many of her most arresting tropes place her within the tradition of Christian devotion.

As is well known, though she no longer attended church by the time she was thirty, Emily Dickinson was an avid reader of the Bible. Strong and persuasive evidence indicates she was also familiar with Christian meditative writings.[9] Books in the Dickinson libraries, now at the Houghton Library, include her own King James Version of the Bible, Cruden's biblical *Concordance*, and 1857 editions of Thomas à Kempis's *Imitation of Christ* and George

Herbert's *The Temple*. Her Bible shows extensive use, its condition so fragile that the library carefully monitors its use. Cruden's *Concordance* and the *Imitation of Christ* are similarly worn, so much so that each is precariously held together with a shoestring. Passages in the *Imitation*, which is inscribed "Emily Dickinson" in Susan Dickinson's hand, are marked with the light pencil strokes in the margin that are generally considered to be the poet's, and the Houghton catalog notes the markings are "possibly Emily's." Passages in *The Temple* are similarly marked, and though it is inscribed "S. H. Dickinson" (Susan's customary signature for the late 1850s), the catalog notes the markings are "probably Emily's."

Further evidence of the importance of the *Imitation* to the poet is provided by an 1876 edition, now at Beinecke Library. Inscribed "To Emily with love," the book was a Christmas gift from Susan Dickinson, suggesting she knew of the *Imitation*'s importance to the poet and thus supplied her with a more recent copy. Further evidence of Emily Dickinson's familiarity with Herbert's work is provided by the two stanzas from his "Mattens" found among her papers after her death. She had transcribed the stanzas into her own idiom of dashes and irregular capitals, and the result seemed so like Dickinson to Millicent Todd Bingham (who knew both Herbert and Dickinson well) that she assumed they were a poem by Dickinson and published them as such in her 1945 *Bolts of Melody*, an error soon discovered by *The New Yorker* magazine (see Figs. 1–4).[10] Still further evidence of Emily Dickinson's familiarity with Christian meditative writings is provided by a text required at Amherst Academy during the years she studied there: Thomas Upham's *Elements of Mental Philosophy*, which describes the meditative disciplines according to Ignatius Loyola, François de Sales, and Thomas à Kempis in a way that was palatable to nineteenth-century New England Protestants.[11] Moreover, as the fourteen-year-old Emily Dickinson wrote in a letter to Abiah Root, one of the subjects she was studying in 1845 was "Mental Philosophy."[12]

The evidence that she knew these texts provides a suggestive background for reading her fortieth fascicle, because, as the reader discovers, F-40 is a three-part meditation addressing in turn the three powers of the mind: first, sight and memory; then, understanding; and finally, will.[13] The speaker of the poems, a single dramatic character throughout, is represented as the meditator. The chief focus of her meditation is her present way of life as a Christian poet-pilgrim, an identity she reveals most specifically when she declares in F-40's first poem that she sees eternity and God as she "traverses"—versifies as she travels—the "Street" of "Existence," then in its final poem that through "Faith" she sees, though incompletely, the "New

# BOLTS OF MELODY

## NEW POEMS OF

## *EMILY DICKINSON*

✹ ✘ ✹

· 232 ·

MY GOD, what is a heart,
Silver, or gold, or precious stone,
Or star, or rainbow, or a part
Of all these things—or all of them in one?

My God, what is a heart,
That thou shouldst it so eye and woo,
Pouring upon it all thy art
As if that thou hadst nothing else to do'

Fig. 1.  Two stanzas from George Herbert's "Mattens" believed by Millicent Todd Bingham to be a poem by Emily Dickinson and published as such in Todd and Bingham's 1945 *Bolts of Melody*, first and second printings, p. 125. The stanzas appear as the final poem in a group Bingham titled "The Mob Within the Heart."

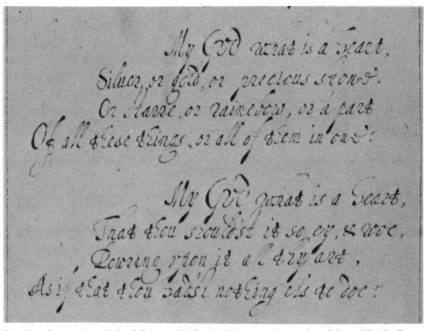

Fig. 2.   Stanzas 2 and 3 of George Herbert's "Mattens," reproduced from *The Bodleian Manuscripts of George Herbert's Poems: A Facsimile of Tanner 307*, by permission of the Bodleian Library and Scholars' Facsimiles and Reprints, Delman, New York.

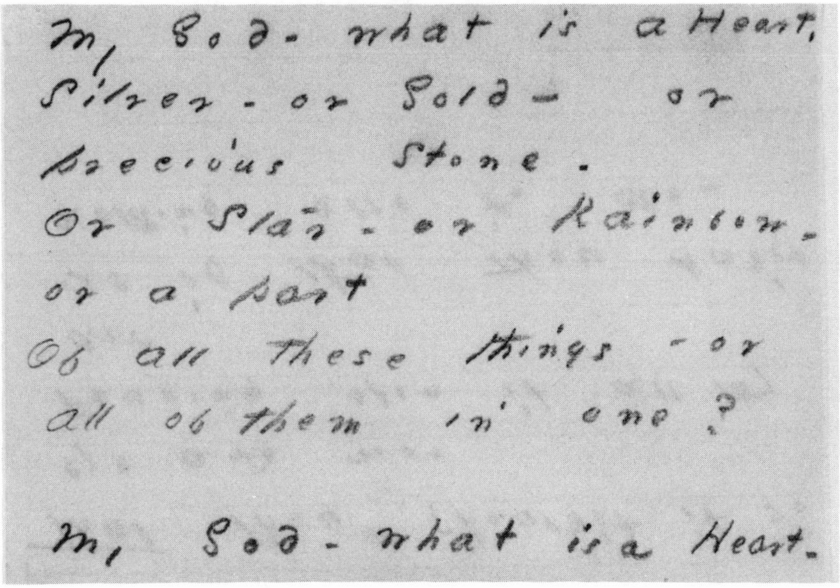

My God - what is a Heart,
Silver - or Gold -    or
precious   Stone .
Or   Star - or Rainbow -
or a part
Of all these things - or
all of them   in   one ?

My God - what is a Heart.

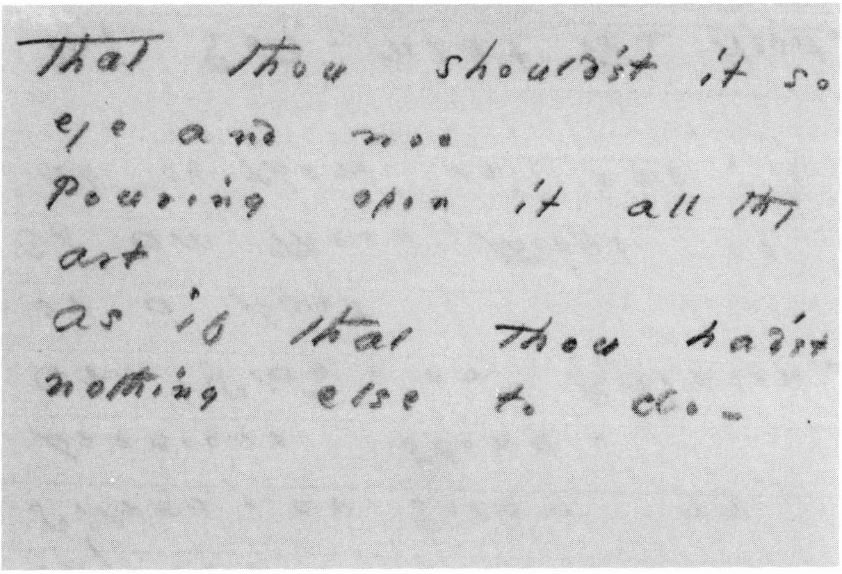

That   Thou   shouldst it so
eye and woo
Pouring upon it all thy
art
as if that Thou hadst
nothing   else   to   do -

Fig. 3.   Stanzas 2 and 3 of George Herbert's "Mattens" in Dickinson's handwriting.
Manuscript in the Emily Dickinson Collection (MS 890–890a), Amherst College Library,
Special Collections, reproduced by permission of the Trustees of Amherst College.

7

# THE TALK OF THE TOWN

## ✳✳✳✳

ONE of the poems in the new Emily Dickinson volume not only contains as clumsy a line as ever was penned but was not even written by Emily. It is the one beginning "My God, what is a heart?" The author is George Herbert, he of the seventeenth century. The clumsy line is "That thou shouldst it so eye and woo." (My God, what is a mouthful?) Emily presumably liked this poem, jotted it down, and tucked it away in that famous camphorwood chest, where it lay until Mrs. Bingham pulled it out with a glad cry and presented it to Harper & Brothers. We have no comment to make on this funny coincidence, except to point out to poets that it is dangerous to jot down any thought but your own, and sometimes inadvisable even to do that.

## JUNE 16, 1945

Fig. 4. *The New Yorker,* June 16, 1945, 15–16. Reprinted by permission; © 1945, 1973 The New Yorker Magazine, Inc.

Horizons" of eternity toward which she progresses.[14] One does not initially perceive that F-40 is a meditation, because it is a variation of the dramatic monologue. The poetic "I" addresses herself and another person who five times addresses her, and from what they say, the reader is asked to deduce that the "situation" is a meditation; that the poetic "I" is the meditator; that the fascicle's setting is her mind; and that the other person whom she repeatedly refers to and addresses and who himself addresses her is the fascicle's only person identified by name: the sixth poem's Jesus.

While the meditator and Jesus are F-40's only dramatis personae, the reader becomes a kind of third supporting character who is cast in the formidably demanding role of the text's decoder. The reader is specifically drawn into the text, beginning with the very first poem, in which Dickinson departs from the traditional dramatic monologue by causing her poetic "I" to interrupt her meditation to address the reader directly. This first poem, which begins with a proclamation—"The Only News I know / Is Bulletins all Day / From Immortality"—concludes with a promise: "If Other News there be . . . I'll tell it You." In other words, her "Bulletins" from "Immortality" are the "News" the following poems "tell." The challenge is that the text does not so much "tell" as "hide" its meaning and "fit" the reader with signals as in the game of hide-and-seek described in the following poem:

> Good to hide, and hear 'em hunt!
> Better, to be found,
> If one care to, that is,
> The Fox fits the Hound—
>
> Good to know, and not tell,
> Best, to know and tell,
> Can one find the rare Ear
> Not too dull—
>
> (J-842)

Since Dickinson's subject is often her poems, presumably this poem's subject is her cryptic verse. And since the poem, like the fortieth fascicle, is dated 1864 and its verbs "know" and "tell" appear in the fascicle's first poem, she may even have had in mind the enigmatic fortieth fascicle. Whether or not she did, the poem accurately describes the relation between the riddling fortieth fascicle and the reader: the poet is the sly "Fox" who hides, but "fits" the reader with signals, and the reader is the persistent "Hound" whose ear strains to be "Not too dull" to hear the news the meditator tells. As a result, reading F-40 is like reading a detective story, except there is no Sherlock Holmes to mediate between text and reader. Instead, the reader is pulled into the text and forced to enact the role of sleuth. By following the text's network of clues, the reader-sleuth makes a series of astonishing discoveries about F-40, about its relation to the preceding fascicles, and about the mind and art of Emily Dickinson.

## AN OVERVIEW OF F-40

F-40 is a work of great sophistication and artistic complexity, a rich tapestry of interwoven themes and structural principles. Although in 1862 Emily Dickinson wrote to Higginson, "[W]hen I try to organize—my little Force explodes" (L-271), either she was not leveling with Higginson, or else by the time she composed the fortieth fascicle she had overcome her earlier organizational problems, because F-40 is an architectural tour de force in which her poetic power, which is immense rather than little, never explodes—or even wavers. F-40 is a strange and idiosyncratic work that is unlike any other I know, though it bears some striking substantive and structural similarities to *The Temple* and is in some ways comparable to both *Ulysses* and *The Waste Land*. Like *Ulysses*, F-40 is an interior monologue that includes multiple puzzles and enigmas, though *all* F-40's action takes place within the meditator's mind. Like *The Waste Land*, F-40 is a long dramatic monologue composed of a series of poems whose relation to one another is not specifically stated, so that the reader must deduce how they relate to one another. Like *The Waste Land*, too, F-40 possesses epic dimensions and includes multiple literary allusions, though Dickinson's allusions are primarily to the Bible and to preceding fascicles, and she does not, like Eliot, ease the reader's way with explanatory notes. Nor did she, it is sobering to reflect, have the advice of an expert editor like Ezra Pound when she created this powerful and original work.

F-40 cannot be understood except in the context of the preceding fascicles. This final booklet is an apologia pro vita sua in which the meditator—who is represented as the author and protagonist of all forty fascicles, which she calls her "Experiment Toward Men" (poem 4)—celebrates the present way of life she has chosen. Because in the process of doing so she recollects events that took place in the preceding fascicles, the reader, too, must recollect them. As the meditator advises the reader in another direct address, "[you must] Question Memory!" (poem 4). F-40 is not only illuminated by the other thirty-nine fascicles, it also illuminates some of their most perplexing mysteries, including the numinous word "Circumference" and that much-debated series of poems, extending throughout the fascicles, in which the protagonist depicts and remembers a singularly momentous occasion when she received a stupendous gift; was identified, married, crowned; attained a new elevated state as "Wife" and "Woman"; and so forth.[15]

Understanding F-40 similarly depends upon the reader's seeing that none of its poems is fully able to stand alone as a self-sufficient, autonomous text, which may explain in part why many have received little or no critical attention. So interdependent are they that the referent for one poem's pronoun is frequently found in another. Often a poem introduces a subject that is then explained or further developed in a subsequent poem or poems. Some, like poem 4, the fascicle's most opaque, have little or no meaning outside their fascicle context. Even the more straightforward poems, like the ninth, a simple flower quatrain, and the eighteenth, a declaration of belief in the immortality of the soul, take on new and different meanings in their fascicle context. Because of their interdependence, each, when read separately, appears to be what Robert Weisbuch has called "sceneless" (*Emily Dickinson's Poetry* 16 and passim). But in their fascicle context, they do have a setting: the meditator's mind in the act of contemplation. When read separately, many have what Jay Leyda has called an "omitted center"—a subject hinted at, though never clearly stated (*Years and Hours* xxi). But when one reads them together in the context of their mutual code, one discovers their omitted centers in other F-40 poems, in preceding fascicles, and in the Bible.

While it is well known that the Bible was an important source of imagery for Emily Dickinson, F-40 shows that the Bible was not simply a rich tropic source, it was essential to her poetics, structure, and meaning. F-40's tropes and rhetorical figures are those of biblical writers: the metonym, the kenning, parallelism, the chiasm, the envelope structure, and key words to link related poems (Alter, *The Art of Biblical Poetry*). No F-40 poem is without biblical allusions, most of them to the New Testament, with particular emphasis on the Gospel of Matthew and Jesus' parables. But these allusions are far more than merely literary allusions. The reader must consult the passages Emily Dickinson alludes to because they are what F-40 is about. As one retrospectively sees after coming to some understanding of all its poems, the "News" the meditator knows and tells is Christ's good news, the gospel according to the New Testament, and how his scriptural "Bulletins" have transformed her own life. In a late poem Jesus is "the Man that knew the News" and in F-40 he is the man that knew the "Only News" she knows and tells (J-1492). She is, as she reminds him in an earlier fascicle, his "little 'John,'" a nineteenth-century American teller of the gospel (F-18-5, J-497). Moreover, she tells his news as a means of serving him, the "Brave Beloved," one of Dickinson's many original epithets for Jesus—"the Man that knew the News," "Tender Pioneer," "Largest Lover," "docile Gentleman," and so forth.[16]

The F-40 meditator is not only the Bible's "warbling Teller," she is also its "typic Teller" because, as F-40 shows, Emily Dickinson treats the Bible typologically—that is, she portrays biblical events as prefigurations of events that take place in the lives of Christ's followers (J-1545). This is most obvious in the poems in which she, as Chana Bloch writes of Herbert, paints the poetic "I" into the biblical scene (*Spelling the Word* 30). One such poem is the following dialogue, F-40's most overtly Christian poem, which is fore-grounded as the first of the fascicle's seven trochaic poems and its only poem that identifies Jesus by name:

> "Unto Me"? I do not know you—
> Where may be your House?
>
> "I am Jesus—Late of Judea—
> Now—of Paradise"—
>
> Wagons—have you—to convey me?
> This is far from Thence—
>
> "Arms of Mine—sufficient Phaeton—
> Trust Omnipotence"—
>
> I am spotted—"I am Pardon"—
> I am small—"The Least
> Is esteemed in Heaven the Chiefest—
> Occupy my House"—                    [House/Breast]

This dialogue between Jesus and the speaker is paradigmatic of the way F-40 asks the reader to deduce its poems' meanings from their fascicle con-text and biblical sources. Though the poem is in the present tense, its fascicle context and biblical analogues show it is a flashback to a time long before she utters her meditation, when Jesus persuaded her to occupy his

"House," an allusion to his parable of the house built upon a rock and one of F-40's recurring metonyms for his earthly kingdom.[17] One telling clue leading the reader to see this poem as a recollection is that although here Jesus urges her to "Occupy my House," throughout F-40 she identifies herself as an occupant of his earthly kingdom by means of other metonyms and kennings. Long before she utters F-40's meditation, her "Two" eyes (a synecdoche for herself) "leaned into Perfectness": Jesus who was made perfect and his earthly kingdom whose occupants strive for perfection (poem 3; Heb. 5.9; Matt. 5.48). She is now content to be his "Housewife" in the "Narrow Cottage," the grave of those who have died to the world—who have, like the "Son of God . . . put this World down, like a Bundle" (F-20-9, J-527)—and chosen the narrow way leading into life (poem 2; Matt. 7.14).

Another clue leading the reader to see their dialogue as a flashback is that throughout F-40 the meditator speaks in the mature tones of a woman, but here she is a foolish and sinful child—"small" and "spotted," the recurring child persona of preceding fascicles—whom Jesus implicitly addresses as a child by alluding to two biblical passages in which he takes up a child in his "arms" and to another in which he proclaims that in the kingdom of heaven a little child is the "greatest" (Mark 9.36, 10.16; Matt. 18.4). Moreover, the reader knows the occasion the meditator recollects has to do with her past conversion because its first two couplets echo Paul's conversion on the road to Damascus, when he, having seen a blinding light and heard a voice, asks, "Who art thou, Lord?" The Lord's response to Paul, "I am Jesus," is his exact response to the protagonist after she has said, "I do not know you," a variation of Paul's "Who art thou?" (Acts 9.5).

Here and throughout F-40 Emily Dickinson draws upon multiple biblical passages, which she varies, embellishes, and conflates, to depict events in the past, present, and future mental life of her protagonist. Obviously Jesus has initiated their debate by urging her to "Come unto me," his words in Matt. 11.28, and "Occupy my House," the house built upon a rock as opposed to the house built on sand she now occupies, because she responds, " 'Unto Me'?" then presents the first of a series of excuses why she cannot do so: she doesn't even know who he is or where his "House" is located. Ignoring her obtuseness and obvious reluctance to accept his proposal, Jesus responds by telling her his name, adding that he is both human and divine: "Late of Judea" and "Now—of Paradise." When Jesus identifies himself to Paul on the road to Damascus, Paul immediately asks, trembling and astonished, "Lord, what wilt thou have me to do?" But Emily Dickinson's protagonist, who is stubbornly unwilling to give in, next asks with silly literal-

mindedness how he could possibly transport her the very great distance from
"This," her present way of life in the house built on sand, to "Thence," his
house built upon a rock: would he carry her there in a "Wagon"? Once more
ignoring her fatuousness, he replies that his "Arms"—echoing the ninth and
tenth chapters of Mark, where he takes up children in his "arms"—are
sufficient "Phaeton," a witty verbal play on her homely wagon, then urges
her to trust "Omnipotence," himself, the all-powerful God.

In the final stanza their exchange becomes more rapid as her cavalier tone
evaporates and she begins to weaken. First she confesses she is "spotted" with
sin, to which he quickly responds, "I am Pardon," the Redeemer who died to
gain forgiveness for all (Isa. 59.20). When she finally confesses she is
"small," he quickly replies that in heaven the least is esteemed the
"Chiefest," echoing his biblical pronouncement that in the kingdom of
heaven a little child is the "greatest." Their debate concludes with his
reiteration of his initial proposal, "Occupy my House," to which she, having
been outdebated, presents no further argument.

This dialogue is not only paradigmatic of the way F-40's poems inform one
another, of the centrality of the Bible to this final fascicle, and of Emily
Dickinson's way of adapting, embellishing, and synthesizing biblical texts, it
is also central to solving many of F-40's mysteries. It provides crucial clues
enabling the reader to see that Jesus is the other person the meditator refers
to and addresses and who himself speaks to her throughout F-40. It draws
attention to F-40's echoes of *The Temple* and *The Imitation of Christ*. It leads
one to see that the meditation is both a self-examination and a contemplation of the merits of Christ in which the meditator contemplates her past,
present, and future relation to him. And it ultimately leads one to see that
embedded within F-40's complex architectural structure is a simple conversion narrative.

"'Unto Me'?" provides a touchstone enabling the reader to identify the
unnamed other speaker in four other F-40 poems because, when one reads all
five together, it becomes apparent that the other speaker who interrupts her
meditation in poems 4 and 10, who speaks the fourteenth poem, where she
imagines her own death, and who addresses her in eternity in poem 16 is the
same speaker as the sixth poem's Jesus. It may or may not be significant that
parts of the Book of Job's account of God's words from the whirlwind are
among several passages that have been cut out of Dickinson's Bible—
another passage is from the first two verses of Revelation's twenty-first chapter, which is of central import to F-40. Whether or not she was responsible
for this pious vandalism, Emily Dickinson does for Jesus something similar to

what Job's author does for God: she gives him an identifiable voice and characteristic speech patterns. In poem 6, as in poems 4, 10, 14, and 16, Jesus talks like a real person, carries on a true conversation, as Helen Vendler writes of Herbert's Jesus (*Poetry of George Herbert* 100–136). His lines are distinguishable from the meditator's because hers are often maddeningly obscure and convoluted but his are always clear and direct. As in poem 6, his diction and syntax are always simple, and many of his lines echo his biblical words. In poems 10 and 14, for example, he is concerned with the meditator's "industry," echoing the parable of the talents—a major text underlying all F-40's poems—whose lord rewards the industrious servants who multiplied their talents and castigates the one slothful servant who did not (Matt. 25.14–30). F-40's Jesus is always polite, but persistent, and in each poem where he speaks, it is he who speaks first, though in poem 4, as in poem 6, the reader must deduce what his lines are from the meditator's response. Moreover, Dickinson's Jesus, like the scriptural Jesus, is both a questioner and an answerer of questions. In poem 6 he answers the protagonist's questions, and in every other poem where he speaks, he asks her one or more questions.

The sixth poem's debate, in which Jesus calls himself by name and refers to himself as "I" and as "Pardon" and "Omnipotence," also draws attention to an important F-40 principle: he is specifically present in each of its poems but one, poem 15, a lament for those dark nights of the soul when he seems to be absent. In all the others, either he speaks, or else the meditator addresses him or refers to him pronomially or metonymically. When she refers to or addresses him pronomially, the reader knows he is intended not only because his is F-40's only proper name but also because of the poem's biblical analogue. In poem 2, for example, "Thou" signifies Jesus because the poem is a response to his parable of the sheep and goats, a response in which the meditator assures him that her poetic purpose is to be like the saved sheep, that is, to serve him by serving his brethren, her readers (Matt. 25.31–46). In poem 16 "Him" signifies Jesus because the poem echoes his parable of the ten virgins, as the meditator imagines herself as one of the prepared virgins—a "Fitter . . . Youth"—who enters the "Door" of the bridal chamber (Matt. 25.1–13). Similarly, in poem 17 "Himself" signifies Christ because here he is incapable of "Fraud"—the variant is "Lie"— echoing his own declaration in John 14.6, "I am . . . the truth," an antonym for "Lie."

When in poem 6 Jesus twice says "I am," he, of course, echoes the Gospel of John's recurring *ego eimi*, and when he calls himself "Pardon" and "Omnipotence," he echoes the many passages in the Bible where he is given and gives himself such metonymical titles as "bridegroom," "first and last," "Light," "life," "Master," "Redeemer," "the Sun of righteousness," "truth," "wisdom," and "witness." The meditator, who reveals in poem 13 that she "imitates" the beloved bridegroom, follows his example and the example of Scriptures by referring to him metonymically throughout F-40. Some of her metonyms are her own inventions, like the twentieth poem's "Brave Beloved" and the second poem's "Tenant of the Narrow Cottage." Others come directly from the Bible. In poem 7, for example, he is "Wisdom," and in poem 12, "Light" and "Witness" (1 Cor. 1.24, John 1.9, Rev. 1.5). Similarly, in the first poem he is "Immortality," echoing both his own proclamation, "I am the resurrection" (John 11.25), and Paul's description of him as the bringer of "immortality to light through the gospel," the "Only News" the meditator knows and tells.

Jesus is thus a major figure in F-40, as he is in the works of all Christian devotional poets, a group that includes the "Dream of the Rood" poet, the medieval lyricists, the seventeenth-century's school of Herbert, Dickinson's near-contemporary Hopkins, and Eliot and Auden in the twentieth century.[18] The sixth poem's dialogue between him and the protagonist is particularly reminiscent of the *Imitation*'s dialogues between the Disciple and Christ and of *The Temple*'s dialogues between Jesus and the poetic "I."[19] But it most strikingly resembles Herbert's "Dialogue," which is also a debate between Jesus and the speaker about whether he will lead the Christian life:

> Sweetest Savior, if my soul
> Were but worth the having,
> Quickly should I then controll
>     Any thought of waving.
> But when all my care and pains
> Cannot give the name of gains
> To thy wretch so full of stains,
> What delight or hope remains?
>
> *What, Child, is the ballance thine,*
>     *Thine the poise and measure?*
> *If I say, Thou shalt be mine;*
>     *Finger not my treasure.*
> *What the gains in having thee*
> *Do amount to, onely he,*     [no stanza break]

*Who for man was sold, can see;*
*That transferr'd th' accounts to me.*

But as I can see no merit,
    Leading to this favour:
So the way to fit me for it
    Is beyond my savour.
As the reason then is thine;
So the way is none of mine:
I disclaim the whole designe:
Sinne disclaims and I resigne.

*That is all, if that I could*
    *Get without repining;*
*And my clay, my creature, would*
    *Follow my resigning:*
*That as I did freely part*
*With my glorie and desert,*
*Left all joyes to feel all smart—*
    Ah! no more: thou break'st my heart.

* * * * * * * * * *

"Unto Me"? I do not know you—
Where may be your House?

"I am Jesus—Late of Judea—
Now—of Paradise"—

Wagons—have you—to convey me?
This is far from Thence—

"Arms of Mine—sufficient Phaeton—
Trust Omnipotence"—

I am spotted—"I am Pardon"—
I am small—"The Least
Is esteemed in Heaven the Chiefest—
Occupy my House"—        [House/Breast]

There are, of course, many differences between these two dialogues—
which is hardly surprising, since the unique voice of each poet is widely
acclaimed and since Herbert was a seventeenth-century English priest,

whereas Dickinson was a nineteenth-century American woman—but what I wish to discuss here are their formal and substantive similarities. Both dialogues tell essentially the same story. Both are debates with Jesus about whether the speaker will lead the Christian life. Both begin *in medias res* with the speaker's response to Jesus' unrecorded invitation. Because both speakers are reluctant to accept, both present a series of excuses why they cannot do so. But Jesus successfully counters each of their arguments and in the end wins both debates. The two dialogues are also stanzaically similar. Both poems underscore the initial separation between the speaker and Jesus by separating their alternating speeches with stanza breaks; then both underscore the outcome of their debates, the speaker's ultimate union with Jesus, in a concluding stanza in which both speak. Moreover, in both dialogues Jesus' lines, which Dickinson places in quotation marks and Herbert underlines, are a mixture of scriptural allusion and original invention. And although in the present tense, each is a flashback to a past time when Jesus persuaded the speakers to lead the Christian life they now lead, Herbert's in *The Temple* and Dickinson's in F-40.

The two portraits of both the poetic "I" and Jesus are also strikingly similar. Each poet depicts the poetic "I" as a child. Herbert's Jesus specifically addresses him as "Child," and Dickinson's Jesus does so implicitly by alluding to three biblical passages that focus upon a child. Each poem's child is initially smug and complacent, really a comic character, who is stubbornly unwilling to give up his or her old way of life and has to be persuaded. Moreover, two of the excuses Dickinson's speaker gives in order to avoid doing so are the same as Herbert's. As his speaker protests he is not "worth the having," so hers protests she is "small," meaning "unworthy." As his speaker protests he is "full of stains," so hers protests she is "spotted," a synonym for "stained."[20]

Despite their protests, neither is a match for Jesus, whom both poets portray as a skilled debater. Though he listens politely and patiently to their arguments, then responds kindly, he is also persistent and persuasive and won't take no for an answer. Quick with the rejoinder, he is witty and adroit with the pun. Herbert's Jesus instantly turns his speaker's "I resign" into an argument that the speaker follow the example of Jesus' "resigning," his freely parting with his "glorie and desert" for the sake of humankind. Similarly, Dickinson's Jesus instantly turns her "Wagon" to his advantage by assuring her that his arms are sufficient "Phaeton," not only a witty verbal play on her homely wagon but also, since "Phaeton" is the mythic "son of the sun," a pun on himself as the sun/Son, a recurring devotional figure the meditator herself echoes in other F-40 poems. Not surprisingly, both speakers ultimately lose their debates with this powerful adversary. As Herbert's gives in, heartbroken at Jesus' allusion to his willing sacrifice of himself, so Dickinson's, after Jesus' final "Occupy my House," presents no further argument. And in the context of the fascicle, the reader knows she has given in because all F-40's other poems are about what *has* happened, what now *is* happening, and what she hopes *will* happen as a result of his winning their debate.[21]

## F-40's NARRATIVE

As one ultimately discovers, when F-40's poems are arranged chronologically they form a simple conversion narrative. This sequential narrative begins in the recollected past with the sixth poem's debate, when Jesus persuaded her to occupy his "House," his earthly kingdom; extends through the fascicle's prevailing present time, when she affirms her chosen way of life as his "Housewife," an occupant of his earthly kingdom; and concludes in the anticipated future with the sixteenth poem's imagined meeting with him, when she enters the "Door" of his eternal house, his heavenly kingdom. The following paragraphs are a brief summary of this conversion narrative, which of necessity postpones many detailed explanations until Parts i, ii, and iii, where each poem is fully discussed.

There are five poems in which the meditator recollects the past—in chronological order, numbers 6, 3, 4, 7, and 10—all but number 6 in the past tense, and all in the meditation's first half. After Jesus persuaded her to occupy his house in the sixth poem's debate, she experienced a two-part spiritual and poetic conversion that transformed her mind, her way of seeing, and her art. She alludes to these two occasions in the final lines of poem 2, when she reminds him she had already "die[d]" for him even before she "saw" him, then recollects them more fully in poems 3 and 4. As the cryptic third and fourth poems reveal, on the first day of her conversion her "Two" eyes and therefore she herself "died" to the world and "leaned into Perfectness," a metonym for him and his earthly kingdom. It was at this "full, and perfect time" that she began to compose the fascicles, her "Experiment Toward Men." Then, on the second day of her conversion, she in some way "saw"

Christ, and their union became complete, a union she celebrates throughout
F-40 as their betrothal (e.g., in poems 2, 8, and 13). As a result of their
union, her "Experiment" began to become "tenderer," more like Christ, the
"Tender Pioneer," the bridegroom whom she "imitate[s]" (poem 13). In other
words, she began to become the single-mindedly Christian poet she is in F-
40, one whose "Only News" is from him.

Her transformation was not, however, without agonizing conflicts, though
these conflicts are in some way resolved at the time she utters her meditation. In poem 7 she recollects the pain she suffered when she renounced
her comfortable "Home" built upon the earth in order to occupy Christ's
"House" built upon a rock. Then in poem 10 she recollects a past time
when she smugly congratulated herself on the prosperity of her spiritual and
poetic business, only to have her meditation interrupted by Christ, who
reminded her she did not have "Me, nor Me," neither himself nor his
brethren, the readers she intends to serve as a means of serving him. This
was true, of course, and still is, in F-40's fictive present. The meditator is
an unpublished poet who longs for readers for her "Experiment Toward
Men" and cannot be certain if she will ever have them. Nor does she now
really "have" Christ, because their union will be complete only in eternity
(poem 16). Moreover, she cannot be certain if she will ever attain full
union with him, because that depends upon him, and his verdict is suspended until Judgment Day (poem 20).

Despite these uncertainties, in the fascicle's present time she has attained
a plateau of joy and confidence. She celebrates her betrothal even though it
has caused her previous "Home" to be "effaced" (poem 8). And even though
she does not know if she will ever have readers or gain full union with him,
she is content with her life as his "Housewife" (poem 2). As a result of their
union, she has gained freedom from poetic "Laws" (poem 5). She has also
acquired "Compound Vision," which enables her to see the eternal in the
sphere of time and also to see forward toward the "God of Him," the loving
God Jesus describes and personifies (poem 12). Though she sometimes suffers
from dark nights of the soul, when he seems to be absent, she acknowledges
that when she does not feel his presence, the fault lies with herself, because
he is always with her (poems 15 and 19).

Not surprisingly, the conversion narrative's future time takes place
through imagination. In poem 14 she imagines her own death, when he
will see that she has, in fact, labored industriously at her one poetic
talent—wedding the "Lily" to the "Bee"—until night came for herself and

she could no longer work. Then in poem 16 she imagines their meeting in eternity, when she hopes she will have become so "perfect" that he may well mistake her for someone else and ask, " 'The Other—She—is Where'?"—that is, where is the previously imperfect meditator? Their meeting in eternity is the conversion narrative's climactic conclusion, and though it is only a hope, the final five poems are the narrative's coda, in which she declares her firm faith in Christ and his promises both for the present and the future.

These final five declarations are linked by the word "Faith," which appears in poems 17 and 21 and is implied in poems 18, 19, and 20, as well as by the emphatic trochaic meter of all but number 19. In poem 17 she declares her belief in Jesus, who is "Himself" the "truth" and therefore incapable of "Fraud." In poem 18 she declares her belief in his promise that death is not final. In poem 19 she declares her belief in the bond of faith and love between them that is as strong as the gravitational pull between the moon and earth and will remain so until the end of time, doomsday, the "Mutual Day" they front (Matt. 28.20). In poem 20 she imagines Judgment Day, when she will defend her case to him, the almighty judge who will separate the saved sheep from the damned goats, by assuring him that in her lifetime she has "endured" in her service to him, the "Brave Beloved." Though she acknowledges that her ultimate salvation lies with him and that his decision is suspended until the Judgment, in poem 21 she declares her "Faith" in eternity's "New Horizons," which will be a "Revolution / In Locality" from the finite sphere, the "Street" of "Existence" she now traverses, to God's infinite sphere. Or as she expressed it in two earlier fascicles, she will progress from the "Circumference" of time to the "Circumference" of eternity (F-26-13, J-633; F-38-13, J-802).

These final five poems, like the sixth poem's dialogue, are of crucial importance to understanding F-40. They are the conversion narrative's triumphant coda. They provide another instance of the many resemblances between F-40 and *The Temple*: both works conclude with four of the "five last things"—death, doomsday, Judgment Day, and heaven—though Dickinson, like Herbert, omits hell, which is customarily the fourth of the "five last things." F-40's final five declarations, linked by the key word "Faith" and by their prevailing trochaic meter, also provide an important clue leading the reader to see that F-40 is a meditation that concludes with the meditator's summoning the faculty of will to declare her faith in Christ and his promises.

What Emily Dickinson has done in F-40 is to fashion a simple story, a conversion narrative, into the complex form of a meditation, which is the fascicle's plot, its arrangement of events.


## DISCOVERING F-40 IS A MEDITATION

One of the first clues leading the reader to suspect that F-40 is more than a random collection of poems is its verbal and tropic patterns. The verbal doubling back of its final two poems on its first two draws attention to F-40's envelope structure. The fascicle begins and ends with a pun on "I" and "eye." In the first poem the poetic "I"/eye sees the immanent God as she traverses the "Street" of "Existence," the finite sphere; then, in the twenty-first, her "Eye"/I sees, though incompletely, eternity's "New Horizons," the infinite sphere of the transcendent God. Similarly, the second poem's "endure" is repeated in the twentieth poem's "endured," both allusions to Jesus' words in Matt. 24.13, "he that shall endure unto the end . . . shall be saved." In the second poem she declares to "Sweet," the master/bridegroom, that she, his "Housewife," intends to "endure" in her service to him; then in poem 20 she imagines Judgment Day, when she will boast to him that she *has* "endured" in her service to him, the "Brave Beloved." The envelope's brackets are thus chiastic, parallel but with a reversal of order:

A.   Poem 1      the poetic "I"/eye sees the immanent God in the finite
                 sphere
B.   Poem 2      the "I" intends to "endure" in her service
B.   Poem 20     the "I" will have "endured" in her service
A.   Poem 21     her "Eye"/I sees, though incompletely, eternity's "New
                 Horizons," the infinite sphere of the transcendent God

Other verbal and tropic patterns provide the reader's first glimpse of the fascicle's meditational structure. In the process of deciphering these elliptical poems, one discovers that clusters of sequential poems are linked by a repeated word or trope. The word "Day" appears in poems 1, 2, and 4. Tropes of domiciles and neighborhoods appear in poems 5 through 8: the fifth poem's "Vicinity," "Suburb," and variant "rent"; the sixth poem's "House"; and the seventh and eighth poems' "Home." The sixteenth poem's trope for eternity, "the Door / I go—to Elsewhere go no more," returns to the fifth through eighth poems' "House"-"Home" imagery, but in between poems 8 and 16 are two other clusters, each linked by a word. The ninth poem's "flower" is repeated in the eleventh poem's "Flowers." The word "Time" appears in poems 12, 15, and 16. And, as I noted earlier, the final five poems are linked by the word "Faith."

These clusters of poems, each linked by a key word or words, form the outlines of the fascicle's meditational structure. Diagram 1 shows this structure and how Emily Dickinson has incorporated the conversion narrative's recollected time and imagined future time into the meditation's present time.

As Diagram 1 on page 24 shows, the poems in each of the three clusters of the poems of analysis are linked by two opposing key words rather than one. As the diagram also shows, time operates on two levels in F-40, one the conversion narrative's unspecified number of years from the recollected past to the imagined future, and the other the half hour or so in the fictive present when the meditator utters her meditation—presumably silently, since a meditation is a "mental prayer" (Martz, *Poetry of Meditation* 26). In the following pages I will give an overview of this meditational structure, then in Parts I, II, and III fill in the many gaps and provide the explanations an overview can only suggest.

In the first four poems, the meditation's composition of place, the meditator summons the powers of sight and memory to create a mental image of the place she intends to contemplate: her mind, or soul, which is filled with "Bulletins" from "Immortality"/Christ. As the key word "Day" draws attention to these poems' unity, so her explicit and implicit diction of sight and memory leads one to perceive that she is summoning these faculties. In poem 1, for example, she "sees" eternity and God in the everyday. Since poem 2 is a response to his sheep-and-goats parable, obviously she has seen and is now recollecting Jesus' scriptural words. In the second poem's final lines, she recollects when she died for him, then "saw" him. And then in the third and fourth she more fully "recollect[s]" these two singularly momentous occasions, which she still sees as vividly in memory as when they took place. The composition of place concludes with the words "Question Memory!"

Having created an image of her mind in F-40's first four poems and by doing so begun to reveal what she knows and therefore who she is, the meditator next summons the faculty of understanding to analyze her chosen way of life. The parameters of the poems of analysis are signaled by the architectural imagery of poems 5 through 8 and the sixteenth poem's "Door." Though the twelve poems of analysis are divided into three clusters, each

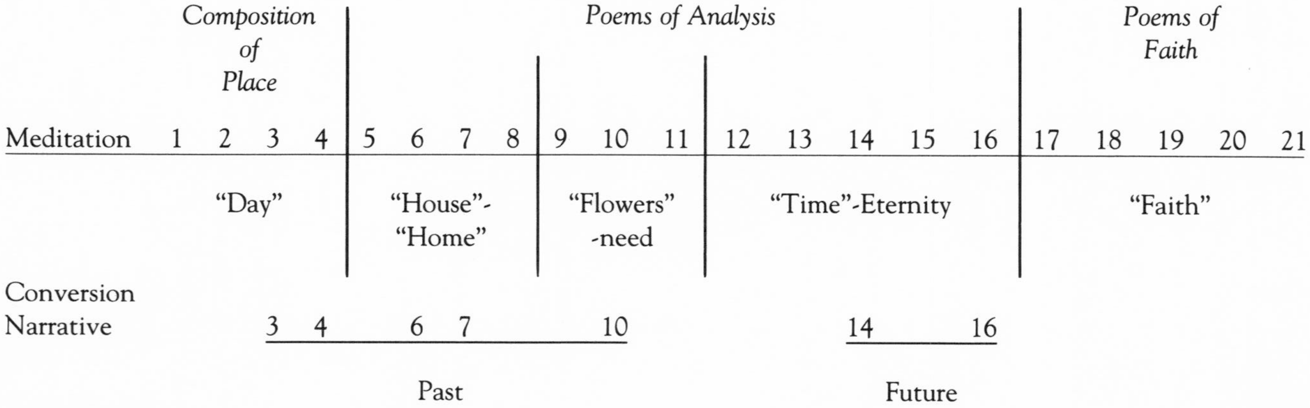

Composition of Place      Poems of Analysis      Poems of Faith

Meditation   1   2   3   4 | 5   6   7   8 | 9   10   11 | 12   13   14   15   16 | 17   18   19   20   21

"Day"     "House"-"Home"     "Flowers"-need     "Time"-Eternity     "Faith"

Conversion Narrative    3   4     6   7     10     14   16

Past      Future

Diagram 1.

with its own key words (perhaps echoing the Ignatian meditation's division of the long section of analysis into a series of "points" [Ignatius, *Spiritual Exercises* 55–56]), they are further linked by their recurring analytical and business diction—"procures," "accounted," "Estimate," "negotiate," "Station," "industry," "worth," "impute," "Wealth" and "Destitution," "prosperity" and "Reverse," "gain" and "loss," and so forth—as well as by a common pattern: in each cluster, the penultimate poem introduces a problem that is then resolved in its final poem. In poem 7 she recollects the pain she experienced when she renounced her "Home," her past way of life; but as poem 8 shows, she has now resolved this problem, because she returns to the present to celebrate their betrothal even though it means her "Home" has been "effaced." Similarly, in poem 10 she recollects a past time when Jesus reminded her of her "need" for him and his brethren, the readers she does not yet have; but as poem 11 shows, she has come to terms with her loneliness and need, because she again returns to the present to declare that her "Flowers"/poems are intended to negotiate the distance separating her from him and them. Finally, in poem 15 she laments the "Pain" of those dark nights of the soul when she does not feel his presence, but in the sixteenth she looks forward to their union in eternity, when her "Grief"—the variant is "pain"—will be ended.

Having assessed her chosen way of life and concluded that while it is not always easy, its joys far outweigh its sorrows, the meditator finally summons the faculty of will to declare her faith in Christ and his promises. The period following the twenty-first poem's final declaration both underscores the firmness of her faith and indicates the conclusion of her meditation. This final period, one of only three in F-40, also calls attention to F-40's system of punctuation, in itself a network of signals.

Because Dickinson's ubiquitous dash most often separates one F-40 poem from the next, departures from this norm are highly significant. The fascicle's only exclamation point concludes poem 4, thus signaling the conclusion of the composition of place. Its only concluding question mark follows poem 7, whose final rhetorical question, "What Comfort was it Wisdom—was— / The spoiler of Our Home?" she herself answers in poem 8 by celebrating her betrothal even though her "Home" has been "effaced." Of the fascicle's three strategically placed periods, the third concludes the meditation and the forty fascicles. The second concludes poem 11, which is the exact center of F-40's twenty-one poems, drawing attention to a shift in focus I will return to shortly. And the first concludes the first poem's first sentence:

> The Only News I know
> Is Bulletins all Day
> From Immortality.

By separating the poem's first tercet from its other three, this first period—a rare form of punctuation in Dickinson even at the ends of poems—draws attention to the import of this opening sentence to the entire meditation: it is the meditator's declaration of purpose (Martz, *Poetry of Meditation* 84). Her meditation will be a self-examination, a contemplation of what she now knows and therefore of who she has become. In the composition of place she contemplates what she knows through sight and memory; in the poems of analysis, what she knows through understanding; and in the final five poems, what she knows through faith. But since she states in this opening sentence that the "Only News" she knows is from Christ, and since in every F-40 poem but one he is referred to or addressed pronomially or metonymically or else himself speaks, her meditation will be more specifically a contemplation of her past, present, and future relation to him and his scriptural "Bulletins." And as one finds after having attained an overview of F-40, together its poems portray his character and their relationship with remarkable fullness.

# F-40's FIVE STRUCTURAL PRINCIPLES

An overview of F-40 (Diagram 2) also reveals four other structural principles embedded within F-40's meditation: a two-part structure signaled by the eleventh poem's period; a garland of praise composed of five artfully inter-woven clusters of flowers/poems; a letter addressed to the reader, in which she tells Jesus' news as a means of serving him; and, concealed beneath this architectural superstructure, the chronological conversion narrative.

As Diagram 2 shows, through a series of signals I describe fully in my discussion of poems 4 and 5, this strange, idiosyncratic text invites the reader to deduce and insert two omitted but implicit poems, which I have called 3b and 5b. I do not, of course, propose that these two poems be included in future printings of the F-40 poems. But as I will demonstrate, just as Dickinson readers must often deduce and insert implicit but omitted words in order to comprehend her tightly compressed poems, so the reader must deduce and insert two implicit but omitted poems in order to comprehend F-40. As this diagram also shows, F-40's center cluster is foregrounded because it is pivotal

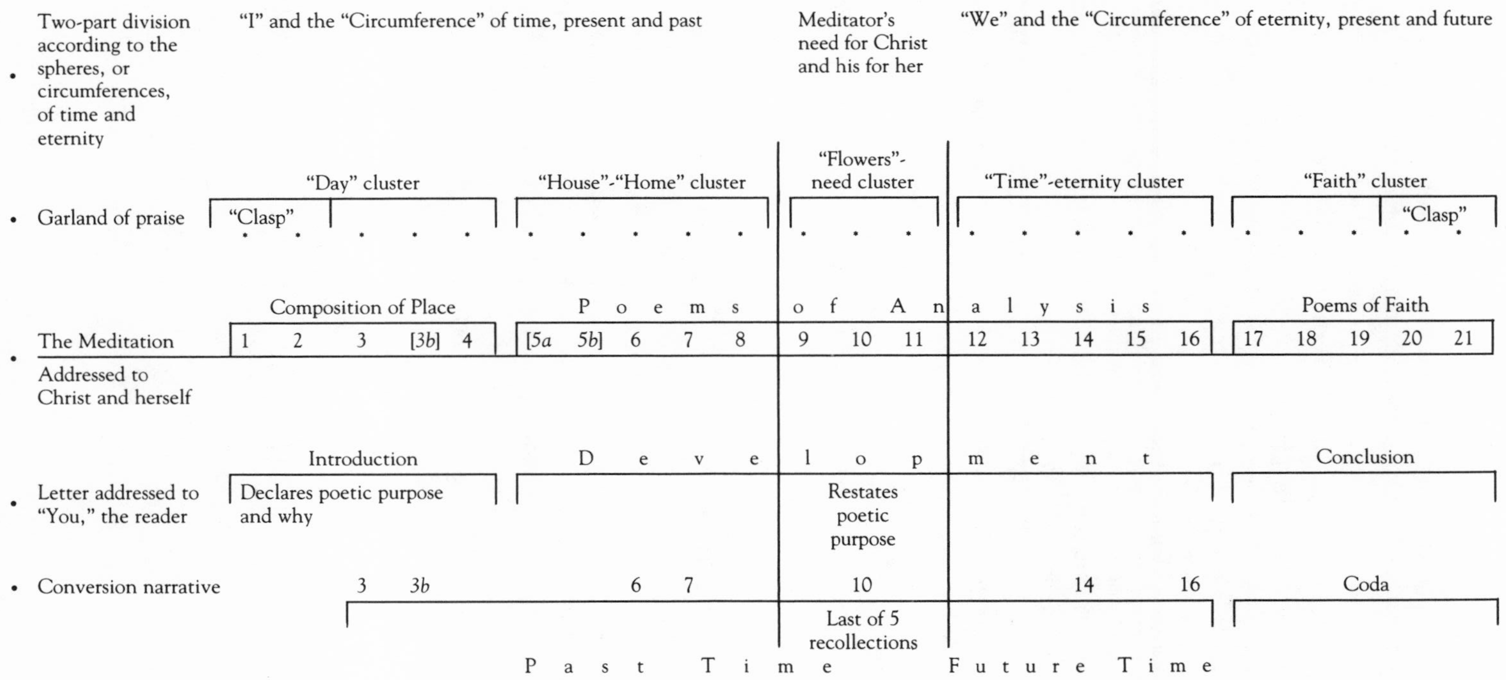

Diagram 2. F-40's five structural principles

**Five structural principles (column heading groups):**

- Two-part division according to the spheres, or circumferences, of time and eternity
- "I" and the "Circumference" of time, present and past
- Meditator's need for Christ and his for her
- "We" and the "Circumference" of eternity, present and future

**Clusters (across the top):**

| "Day" cluster | "House"-"Home" cluster | "Flowers"-need cluster | "Time"-eternity cluster | "Faith" cluster |
|---|---|---|---|---|
| "Clasp" | | | | "Clasp" |

**Poem numbers:**

| 1 | 2 | 3 | [3b] | 4 | [5a | 5b] | 6 | 7 | 8 | 9 | 10 | 11 | 12 | 13 | 14 | 15 | 16 | 17 | 18 | 19 | 20 | 21 |
|---|---|---|---|---|---|---|---|---|---|---|---|---|---|---|---|---|---|---|---|---|---|---|

**The five principles (rows) with their labels:**

- **Garland of praise** — "Clasp"
- **The Meditation** (Addressed to Christ and herself):
  - "Clasp"
  - Composition of Place
  - P o e m s   o f   A n a l y s i s
  - Poems of Faith (17 18 19 20 21)
- **Letter addressed to "You," the reader:**
  - Introduction — Declares poetic purpose and why
  - D e v e l o p m e n t — Restates poetic purpose
  - Conclusion
  - Coda
- **Conversion narrative:**
  - 3   3b
  - 6   7
  - 10 — Last of 5 recollections
  - 14   16
  - Coda

**Timeline (bottom):**  Past Time | Future Time

Diagram 2. F-40's five structural principles

to each of the four structural principles embedded within F-40's meditation. Because here the meditator focuses upon her need for Christ and also upon his need for her to be his poet/psalmist—a recurring theme in F-40, as it is in the Psalms (e.g., Ps. 30.9)—this center triad suggests that their mutual need is what connects the finite sphere she focuses upon in her meditation's first half to the infinite sphere she focuses upon in its second half. Because one of its key words is "Flowers"—here and often in Dickinson a trope for poems—this center triad provides one of the clues leading the reader to perceive that F-40's five clusters of flowers/poems form a garland. It is in this center cluster that the meditator restates the poetic purpose she has declared in poems 1 and 2. And it is here that she concludes her recollections of the events that took place before F-40's meditation began.

Long before one sees F-40's garland, letter, or two-part division, it becomes apparent that each of its five clusters is an artfully constructed unit of meaning and that all five share a pattern: the first poem in each introduces its cluster's key word or words, though sometimes in an oblique way; each cluster's poems are linked not only thematically and by a key word or words but also by other formal properties, such as meter, repeated words, or alliteration; and each cluster's final poem is transitional—that is, it both concludes its cluster and foreshadows the following one, thereby linking its cluster to the next. These clusters of interwoven flowers/poems, which replicate the progression of the meditator's mind as she focuses upon one subject and through association moves on to the next, are then "clasped" by F-40's envelope structure whereby the final two poems double back on the first two.

I have called this structure a garland because in F-40's center cluster "Flowers" signifies poems and because, as Diagram 3 shows, this series of interwoven clusters foregrounding poems 9, 10, and 11 and "clasped" by the meditator's return in poems 20 and 21 to the subjects she began with in poems 1 and 2 looks like a garland, a crown of flowers/poems. I have called it a garland of "praise" because the meditation is not only a self-examination but also a contemplation of the merits of Christ, in which the meditator views his character from a different perspective in each poem. In the composition of place, for example, he is first "Immortality," her sacred Muse and the bringer of life and immortality through the gospel (poem 1); then he is the master/bridegroom whom she serves (poem 2); then he is the "Perfectness"—he who was made perfect—into whom she leaned (poem 3); and then he is the inner voice that interrupts her meditation to ask her two questions (poem 4).

F-40's first four poems are thus the garland's first cluster as well as the

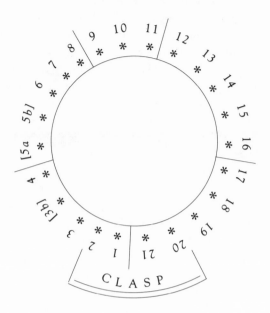

Diagram 3.

meditation's composition of place, in which she summons the faculties of sight and memory to create a mental image of her mind, or soul, the place she intends to contemplate in the poems of analysis and faith. But as Diagram 2 shows, these first four poems serve simultaneously as the introduction to the letter addressed to the reader. Though F-40 is primarily a spoken text in which the meditator is represented as addressing Christ and herself, it is at the same time a written text in which, as she declares in poems 1 and 2, she tells his news to "You," the reader, as a means of serving him. In these first four poems she introduces her letter by declaring (in the first two poems) her poetic purpose, then explaining (in poems 3 and 4) why her purpose is as it is: her purpose is to tell his news to the reader as a means of serving him because, as she explains in poems 3 and 4, she has experienced a two-part spiritual and poetic conversion that has transformed her mind, her way of seeing, and therefore her art.

I have called this structural principle a "letter" for several reasons. One is that in an earlier fascicle she herself calls her poems a "letter" to the world that is intended for readers she cannot see (F-24-14, J-441). Another is that by telling Jesus' news to the reader of F-40, she does, in effect, what the New Testament epistolary writers have done. The F-40 meditator repeatedly refers to these New Testament letters, most often to those the King James Bible attributes to Paul, and in several cases she compares herself to Paul, who, in a much later poem dated 1880, "knew the Man that knew the News" (J-1492). Although the meditator, like Paul, never met the historical Jesus, she, like Paul, knows and tells his "News" in a written text—a letter—addressed to readers.

As Diagram 2 also shows, the meditator's focus shifts midway through her meditation. In its first half, poems 1 through 11, she focuses upon the sphere of time, her own present experience of time in relation to the past: her child's life, her transforming conversion, and the conflicts she subsequently experienced and has now resolved. Then in the meditation's second half, poems 12 through 21, she focuses upon the sphere of eternity and its present and future relation to herself as one of "Us," which, as she explains in poem 21, means those of "Us" who have faith. The period following the eleventh poem draws attention to this shift in focus. Before this period, she uses the first-person-singular pronoun in every poem but three, but after the eleventh poem's period she uses "I" in only three poems. Beginning with poem 12, her pronouns are more often "We," "Us," and "our," meaning the faithful, or "you" and "He," meaning one of the faithful—"you" who are betrothed to Christ (poem 13) and "He" who believes in him and his promises (poem 17). Moreover, before the eleventh poem's strategically placed period (the second of the three in F-40), her departures from the meditation's prevailing present tense are to the past; but after this period, there are no flashbacks, only flashforwards. This shift from "I" to "We" and from flashbacks to flash-forwards is underscored by the twelfth poem's concluding lines: "We" see both "Back—toward Time," which she does in the meditation's first half, and "forward— / Toward . . . God," which she does in its second half.


## F-40 AND "CIRCUMFERENCE"

The eleventh poem's period also indicates an important tropic shift. With the twelfth poem's "Convex—and Concave," the meditator begins to use tropes of circularity: the fifteenth poem's "Circumference / Of a single Brain"; the nineteenth poem's implicit moon and earth, tropes for Christ and herself; and the twenty-first poem's spherical "Eye" and "Horizons" of eternity. These circular and spherical tropes draw attention to the relation between F-40 and Emily Dickinson's use of the word "Circumference" throughout the canon. By doing so, they show that even though the word actually appears only once in F-40, this final fascicle is about "Circumference" in the sense that Dickinson uses this word in at least six of the seventeen poems in which the word appears.

In the Dickinson canon, "Circumference" means what her lexicon says it means: a circle or sphere.[22] But she uses the word as a metonym for different kinds of circles or spheres. In some poems "Circumference" signifies the sphere of the brain. In others it signifies an elevated sphere as opposed to a lower one. In one poem "Circumference" signifies the sphere of time, and in another, the sphere of eternity. The F-40 meditator contemplates all four of these spheres—her brain, her elevated poetic and spiritual sphere, the spheres of time and eternity—but in most cases her metonyms are different. In other words, F-40 is about what "Circumference" elsewhere signifies, but most of its signifiers are different.

In F-40-15 "Circumference" signifies the brain's sphere, as it does in J-1663 ("His mind of man, a secret makes"), where the "Circumference" of each person's "mind" is a secret to everyone else. Throughout F-40 the meditator contemplates her mind's "Circumference," that is, what she knows through sight and memory, understanding, and faith. But in F-33-12 ("I should have been too glad, I see—") and F-38-8 ("She staked her Feathers—Gained an Arc—") "Circumference" signifies an elevated sphere as opposed to a lower one. In the former, the speaker contrasts her "new . . . lifted . . . Circumference" life to her past "little Circuit" life (J-313). In the latter, the bird—often Dickinson's trope for the poet or soul—ascended into the height of "Circumference" where she is now as at home as she once was on the lowly bough where she was born (J-798). The F-40 meditator has similarly ascended into what she calls in poem 12 a "Hight," an elevated poetic and spiritual sphere, where she is now as content as she once was with her past lower sphere; but her metonyms for these two spheres are more often nuptial and architectural: in F-40 she is even more content with her elevated "Hight," her life as Christ's "Housewife" in the house built upon a rock, than she once was as a foolish child in the inferior house built on sand, what she calls the "Home" she has renounced.

To complicate matters, in F-38-13 "this Circumference" signifies the sphere of time, what the F-40 meditator calls in its first poem the "Street" of "Existence." And in F-26-13 "that . . . Circumference" signifies the sphere of eternity, what she calls in F-40's final poem eternity's "New Horizons":

Time feels so vast that were it not
For an Eternity—
I fear me this Circumference
Engross my Finity—

To His exclusion, who prepare
By Processes of Size
For the Stupendous Vision
Of His Diameters—

(J-802)

When Bells stop ringing—Church—begins—
The Positive—of Bells—
When Cogs—stop—that's Circumference—
The Ultimate—of Wheels.

(J-633)

The implicit emblem heading both these meditations is a figure composed of two adjacent circles or spheres that meet at death (Diagram 4). These two poems are like mirror images of one another. In the former, "this Circumference" signifies the sphere of time, and "His Diameters" is a synecdoche for the sphere, or circumference, of eternity. But in the latter, "that . . . Circumference" signifies the infinite sphere, while "Cogs," a synecdoche for a watch or clock, signifies the finite sphere, or circumference, what she calls

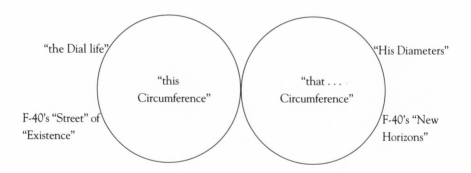

Diagram 4.

elsewhere the "Dial life" (F-11-6, J-287). Each of these poems is a single long sentence. In the former, the circumference of time feels so vast to the speaker that were it not for the circumference of eternity, "this Circumference" of time would engross her finite "I"/eye to the exclusion of God, who prepares one by processes of size for the stupendous vision of his diameters. And in the latter, an extended simile, just as the cessation of church bells means the beginning of church, so the cessation of one's dial life means the beginning of eternity, "that . . . Circumference."[23]

Since F-40, too, is about the relation between the finite and infinite spheres—or, more specifically, about the relation between the meditator as representative of the finite sphere and Christ, who is "Now—of Paradise," as representative of the infinite sphere—it seems likely that there is also an implicit emblem heading her meditation and that this emblem is a variation of the one heading the two earlier cognate poems (Diagram 5). Whether or not these two linked circles are the meditation's emblematic focus, they illustrate its two-part structure. In its first half, poems 1 through 11, the meditator focuses upon her own present and past experiences in the sphere of time. In poems 9 through 11, which conclude her meditation's first half and also introduce its second half, she focuses upon the mutual need between humans and Christ. Then in its second half, poems 12 through 21, she focuses upon the sphere of eternity and its present and future significance for those of "Us" who have faith.

The assumption that such a figure heads F-40's meditation is strengthened by the startlingly vivid, emblematically visual nature of Emily Dickinson's

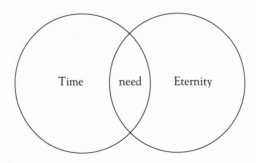

Diagram 5.

imagination.[24] As she sometimes included a flower, a dead bee, a literary passage, or a picture along with a poem on the subject, so she implies still further variations of the finite and infinite circles in F-40's poems 12, 13, 15, 19, and 21. This is most obvious in poems 19 and 21. In the former, she as the earth and Christ as the moon are held together by a bond of faith and love as strong as the gravitational pull between the earth and moon (Diagram 6). Similarly, in poem 21 her terrestrial "Eye"/I perceives through faith, though incompletely, eternity's "New Horizons" (Diagram 7).

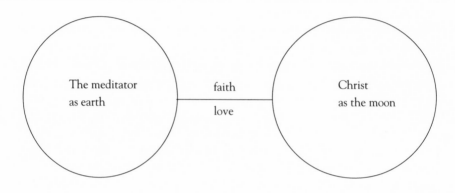

Diagram 6.

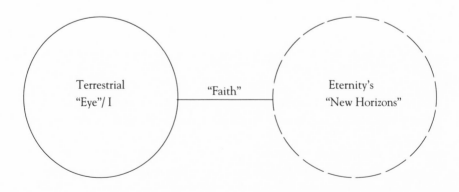

Diagram 7.

## F-40's PENTOLOGY

F-40's five structural principles provide one of many instances of the fiveness the reader encounters again and again in this final fascicle, a pentology that is far too pervasive to be coincidental. Jesus speaks five times, in poems 4, 6, 10, 14, and 16. The meditator alludes quite specifically to circles or circumferences in five poems, numbers 12, 13, 15, 19, and 21. The garland is composed of five clusters of flowers/poems. The conversion narrative begins with five recollections. And F-40 concludes with five declarations of faith. Moreover, a close reading of F-40 will reveal other instances of fiveness. Poem 5, for example, includes five metonyms for Christ, and in five poems the meditator describes her union with him as a betrothal. This recurring fiveness, which surely must be as deliberate as it is in *Sir Gawain and the Green Knight*, echoes the pentology of the Bible and of Christian tradition. There are five books of Moses and five parts to the Book of Psalms. Chapters 5 through 25 of the Gospel of Matthew, which is F-40's most frequently echoed source, include the five great discourses of Christ; and the eschatological fifth discourse concludes with five parables, often called the parables of preparedness or the "household" parables (Drury, *Parables in the Gospels* 10 and passim)—the parables of the householder and the thief, the trusty servant, the ten virgins, the talents, and the sheep and goats—all five of them re-created in F-40. Though Emily Dickinson was not a member of the Roman Catholic Church—or a member in good standing of any church—it seems worth noting that there are five decades, fifty-five beads, on the little rosary, or chaplet, which are intended as aids to contemplating the five joyful mysteries, the five sorrowful mysteries, and the five glorious mysteries.[25] There are also the five wounds of Christ, the five joys of the Virgin, and the Pentangle, the sign of Solomon.

According to T. W. Higginson, Emily Dickinson told him, "When I read a book [and] feel as if the top of my head were taken off, then I know *that* is poetry" (L-342a). By her own standard, F-40 works as true poetry, though not in the way her comment suggests. Her definition appears to imply an affective theory of poetry, that true poetry appeals to the emotions, as many of her poems do—"There's a certain Slant of light," for example, and "Because I could not stop for Death." But F-40's poems do not create this same kind of response, because their impact is cerebral rather than emotional. As one is drawn ever more deeply into this strange, absorbing text, one is dazzled by Emily Dickinson's power over language, by her powers of organization, by her technical versatility, and by the "Truth" she so "slant[ly]" and "gradually" reveals (J-1129). But most of all, one is stunned by her text's powerful control over the reader. Though F-40 demands that the reader participate in a way that is, as far as I know, unprecedented, the reader remains in its firm grasp.[26] The reader is manipulated by this uncanny text, forced to enact a specific role, the role of sleuth, of the "Hound" whose ear must strain to hear what the "Fox"/poet causes the meditator to tell.

Though the F-40 reader makes one astonishing discovery after another, there are, of course, questions that remain, chief among them, how close is F-40's meditator to Emily Dickinson herself? Did the poet, like her protagonist, experience a two-part spiritual and poetic conversion? Did she, too, attain her meditator's firm faith in Jesus' promises—at least at the time she wrote and assembled F-40's poems? Did she, too, long for readers for the forty fascicles' "Experiment Toward Men"? The comments of those closest to the poet are of little help because they contradict one another. While Lavinia maintained that her sister's poems were no more autobiographical than Shakespeare's plays, Susan Dickinson's obituary for the poet portrays an Emily Dickinson who resembles F-40's meditator. As Susan wrote, the poet's life was "all aglow with God and immortality."[27] Dickinson's comments about the relation between herself and her poems are similarly contradictory. While she wrote to Higginson that her poems' speaker was not herself but "a supposed person," she wrote to Elizabeth Holland, "[A] Book is only the Heart's Portrait, every Page a Pulse" (L-268; L-794).

Because the meditator, like her creator, is an unpublished poet and the author of all forty fascicles, she is to some extent autobiographical. But there are other resemblances between Emily Dickinson and F-40's meditator. Both, for example, died to the world to devote their lives to their poetic vocations. Whether or not the poet, like her meditator, attained a firm faith in Jesus and his promises, he is a major figure in the Dickinson canon who is explicitly named in at least seventy poems and the implicit subject and addressee of many others.[28] F-40 also presents evidence that at the time she composed the fascicles Emily Dickinson, like her meditator, longed for readers for her long lyric cycle. She must have intended F-40 to be read by someone, at some time, because this final fascicle clearly implies a reader. Not only does the meditator directly address this implied reader four times (poems 1, 2, 4, and 9), but F-40's complex of riddles implies readers who will solve them. Moreover, because F-40's riddles can only be solved if one recollects the preceding fascicles, presumably she wished that all the fascicles be read together as a single oeuvre.

Two letters dated 1862 reveal further similarities between the meditator and her creator. In one, Emily Dickinson wrote to Higginson, "My Business is Circumference" (L-268), which is also the business of F-40's meditator, who contemplates the circumference of her own single brain, her own elevated spiritual and poetic circumference, and the circumferences of time and eternity. In the other 1862 letter, she wrote to the Hollands, "My business is to love" (L-269), which is echoed in the meditator's declaration in the final lines of poem 2 that she lives the "Life" that means "Love." Dickinson's letter to the Hollands concludes with a parable about a bird she supposedly found on a little bush at the foot of her garden. When the poet asked the bird why she sings, "since nobody *hears*," the bird replied, " 'My business is to *sing*,'—and away she rose!" The poet then added, "How do I know but cherubim, once, themselves, as patient, listened, and applauded her unnoticed hymn?" One can hardly doubt that this bird parable is about Emily Dickinson herself, but it also describes the F-40 meditator, who, having risen into the circumferential height, perseveres in her poetic vocation even though she does not know if she will have readers for her "Experiment" and will not know until eternity whether her poems have been applauded by her ultimate addressee, who is "Now—of Paradise."

# Part I

# The Composition of Place:
# Poems 1 Through 4,
# "Bulletins From Immortality"

F-40's first four poems are proleptic, though the reader sees this only retro-spectively after having attained an overview of the fascicle. As the medita-tion's composition of place, these introductory poems reveal F-40's setting, the "Circumference" of the meditator's mind. As the introduction to the letter addressed to the reader, they disclose her poetic purpose, then explain why it is as it is. As the garland's first cluster, they establish the principles that will govern each of the following clusters. These first four poems also introduce F-40's prevailing tone of affirmative resolution and its three pre-vailing forms: the emphatically spoken monologue, the meditation, and the dialogue. In addition, by demonstrating that fascicle context, the preceding fascicles, and the Bible are essential to comprehending F-40's poems, and by initiating the reader into the rigorous complexities of his or her role as decoder, poems 1 through 4 implicitly but forcefully tell the reader how to read F-40:

The Only News I know
Is Bulletins all Day
From Immortality.

The Only Shows I see—
Tomorrow and Today—
Perchance Eternity—                    [Three—with Eternity—
                                       /And some Eternity—]
The Only One I meet
Is God—The Only Street—
Existence—This traversed                [traversed/traverst]

If Other News there be—
Or Admirabler Show—
I'll tell it You—                      [I'll Signify—/I'll testify—]

_____

Wert Thou but ill—that I might show thee
How long a Day I could endure
Though thine attention stop not on me
Nor the least signal, Me assure—                [Me/Mine]

Wert Thou but Stranger in ungracious country—
And Mine—the Door
Thou paused at, for a passing bounty—           [passing/doubtful]
No More—

Accused—wert Thou—and Myself—Tribunal—
Convicted—Sentenced—Ermine—not to Me
Half the Condition, thy Reverse—to follow—      [Condition/
Just to partake—the infamy—                      distinction]

The Tenant of the Narrow Cottage, wert Thou—
Permit to be
The Housewife in thy low attendance
Contenteth Me—

No Service hast Thou, I would not achieve it—    [achieve/attempt]
To die—or live—
The first—Sweet, proved I, ere I saw thee—    [proved I/That was]
For Life—be Love—          [be Love/is—Love—/means—Love—]

_____

Midsummer, was it, when They died—
A full, and perfect time—
The Summer closed upon itself
In Consummated Bloom—

The Corn, her furthest kernel filled
Before the coming Flail—
When These—leaned into Perfectness—        [When These Two—
Through Haze of Burial—                              leaned in—Perfectness—]

---

The first Day that I was a Life
I recollect it—How still—
The last Day that I was a Life
I recollect it—as well—

'Twas stiller—though the first
Was still—
'Twas empty—but the first
Was full—

This—was my finallest Occasion—
But then
My tenderer Experiment
Toward Men—

"Which choose I"?
That—I cannot say—
"Which choose They"?
Question Memory!

Like each of the garland's following four clusters, this first cluster is both a unit of meaning and an artfully arranged grouping of poems whose diverse formal properties create poetic interest and display Emily Dickinson's stunning technical virtuosity. With its four crisp, concise tercets, the first poem itself resembles a "Bulletin," while the five quatrains of the second poem's response to Jesus' parable of the sheep and goats are far more discursive and metrically irregular, extending from pentameter to monometer. The third is a pseudo-elegy of two stanzas whose mortuary and seasonal tropes are mostly from Jesus' two "corn" parables, the corn of wheat that must die in order to bear fruit and the full corn in the ear ready for harvest (John 12.24; Mark

4.26–29), while the fourth, a riddle asking the reader to determine the identities of the two days she compares, suddenly and startlingly concludes with the fourth stanza's dialogue. Like the final poem of each of the other four clusters, poem 4 is transitional in that its final dialogue about choice both concludes the composition of place and introduces the subject of the twelve poems of analysis, the meditator's chosen way of life.

The arrangement of these diverse poems forms an envelope structure, whereby the first and fourth poems bracket two poems centering upon biblical texts:

| Poem 1 | Poem 2 | Poem 3 | Poem 4 |
|--------|--------|--------|--------|
| "Bulletins" from "Immortality" | sheep-and-goats parable | two "corn" parables | Concludes with a dialogue |

This envelope structure draws attention to the progression of the meditator's thoughts as she creates an image of her mind. First she declares the "Only News" she knows is her "Bulletins" from "Immortality." Then in poems 2 and 3 she recollects Jesus' scriptural words, thus revealing that he is the sender of her "Bulletins." Finally, in poem 4, as she recollects and compares the two days of her conversion, he interrupts her meditation, thus retrospectively explaining why the "Only News" she knows is from him: because of their union, he has become a voice within her mind, or soul.

These four poems are linked not only by their key word, "Day," and their recurring diction of sight and memory, but also by repeated words linking each poem to the next. In the first, for example, the meditator witnesses God's "Shows"; then in the second she wishes to "show" thee. In the final lines of the first she tells her news to "You," the reader; then in the second "You" becomes "Thou," as she explains that she tells "You" because you are "Thou," that is, one of the brethren Jesus proclaims in the sheep-and-goats parable one must serve as a means of serving him. In the final lines of the second poem, she tells him she would "die" for him and, in fact, already has done so; then in the third she recollects the occasion when she "died" to the world. In the third she describes the time of her death as "full"; then in the fourth she describes the first of the two days she recollects as "full," providing one of several clues leading the reader to realize that the fourth poem's recollected "first Day" is the death she recollects in poems 2 and 3.

This pattern of verbal repetition, which points to the cluster's role as the introduction to the letter addressed to the reader, is reinforced by the poems' formal, alliterative, and tonal pattern: the first two poems are paired, as are the third and fourth, and these two pairs are linked by the final stanza of poem 2. The first two poems, in which she declares her poems are both from Christ and intended to serve him, are exuberant monologues whose *ee* rhyme and assonance extend through both almost as though they were a single poem. Then in the second poem's final lines this exuberant *ee* modulates into the third and fourth poems' mellifluous *L* as the meditator's tone shifts from declaration to pensiveness and her tense shifts from the present to the past of poems 3 and 4, both recollective meditations in which she reveals why her poems are both from Christ and intended to serve him:

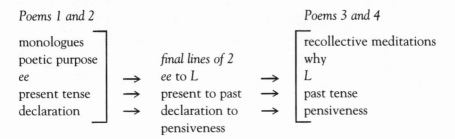

*Poems 1 and 2*                                             *Poems 3 and 4*

| monologues | | recollective meditations |
| poetic purpose | *final lines of 2* | why |
| ee | → ee to L → | L |
| present tense | → present to past → | past tense |
| declaration | → declaration to → | pensiveness |
| | pensiveness | |

# POEMS 1 AND 2

The ars poetica the meditator declares in these first two monologues bears some striking similarities to Herbert's in his "Dedication" to *The Temple*:

> Lord, my first fruits present themselves to thee;
> Yet not mine neither: for from thee they came,
> And must return. Accept of them and me,
> And make us strive, who shall sing best thy name.
> Turn their eyes hither, who shall make a gain:
> Theirs, who shall hurt themselves or me, refrain.

As poetic texts, Herbert's "Dedication" and Dickinson's first two poems are, of course, very different, but their substantive similarities remain. Both speakers declare their poems are not only from Christ but also intended for him. As Herbert's speaker declares his poems are "from thee"/Christ, so Dickinson's declares in the first poem that her poetic news is "From Immortality"/Christ. As Herbert's presents his poems "to thee," so Dickinson's declares in the second poem that hers are intended to serve "thee." Moreover, both speakers express the hope that their poems will be a means of their salvation. As Herbert's asks God to "Accept" him as well as his poems, so Dickinson's demonstrates that she is like the parable's saved because her poems are intended to serve Christ's brethren, her readers, as a means of serving him.

An important difference between the two is their treatment of readers. Whereas Herbert's speaker mentions readers only in the final two lines, when he asks that only the eyes of those "who shall make a gain" be turned to his poems, Dickinson's meditator democratically begins by addressing the reader as "You," whoever may be reading her poems, then explains in poem 2 that by "You" she means "Thou," the reader as one of Christ's brethren. Another difference between the two is that Herbert challenges other poets to engage in a kind of contest to "strive, who shall sing best thy name," whereas Dickinson presents no such challenge. The many resemblances between F-40 and *The Temple*, however, suggest that she, like Henry Vaughan, Richard Crashaw, and others, including her American predecessor Edward Taylor, may have accepted Herbert's challenge.

Whether or not she did, these first two monologues are the culmination of a series of poems, extending throughout the fascicles, in which the protagonist comments on her poems' source and intended audience. In "Publication—is the Auction / Of the Mind of Man," as in F-40-1, her poetic "Thought" is from "the White Creator" (F-37-16, J-709). Although in that poem she repudiates publication, elsewhere, as in F-40, she intends her poems to be read by someone, at some time. In "This is my letter to the World," for example, the "News" her poems tell is intended for readers she cannot see (F-24-14, J-441). In "My nosegays are for Captives," dated 1859, her poems intended for those who are imprisoned, as are her poems in F-40-2's third stanza (F-3-8, J-95). Interestingly, according to Dickinson's lexicon, always an indispensable aid to deciphering her poems, "nosegay" is a synonym for "fasciculus," or "fascicle," a division of a book. Since, according to Dickinson herself, her lexicon was for some years her "only companion," and since, according to her niece, Martha Dickinson Bianchi, she read her dictionary "as a priest [reads] his breviary—over and over, page by page," it seems likely that the earlier poem's "nosegays" signifies not simply poems but, more specifically, fascicles (L-261; Bianchi, *Life and Letters* 80). This would mean that even in the early years of composing the booklets, Emily Dickinson considered them to be fascicles, that is, divisions of a single book.

F-40's second poem is also one of a series of poems, extending throughout the fascicles, that center upon Christ. Though in F-40 Dickinson causes only Jesus himself to use his name, in preceding fascicles the protagonist often refers to or addresses him as Jesus or as Christ, Savior, Redeemer, Rabbi, Lord, or Son (see note 28 in the notes to the Introduction). In preceding fascicles, as in F-40, she sometimes creates original titles for him—"Largest Lover," "Tender Pioneer," "Brave Beloved"—or else refers to him pronomially or metonymically, leaving it to the reader to deduce from the poem's biblical sources that he is intended (F-28-17, J-573; F-35-13, J-698; F-40-20). In an earlier meditation on the Resurrection, for example, he is not named, but Jesus is obviously "He [who] gave away his Life / To Us," then "Broke—perfect—from the Pod" (F-28-6, J-567). Similarly, in an undated meditation on the Crucifixion, his is obviously the "highest head" that wore the crown of thorns (J-1735).

Some of these poems on Christ are specifically Trinitarian. In "Only God—detect the Sorrow," for example, Deity is both the singular "God" and the plural "Jehovahs," including Father, "Son," and "Spirit" (F-32-13, J-626). In a late meditation God sent his "Son" to test the bridge of faith, and he pronounced it firm (J-1433). In "Given in Marriage unto Thee," which is also dated 1864 but not included in a fascicle, the speaker is not only Jesus' spouse, as in F-40, but "Bride" of the Trinity, "of the Father, . . . the Son, . . . [and] the Holy Ghost" (J-817). In others Jesus is her model for imitation, as she says he is in F-40-13 and shows he is throughout F-40. In "To put this World down, like a Bundle," she, like "the Son of God," has renounced the world (F-20-9, J-527). In "Perhaps you think me stooping," she follows the example of Christ, who "stooped until He touched the Grave" (J-833). Similarly, in "The Test of Love is Death," she attempts to imitate him, the "Largest Lover," though she does so imperfectly because, as she apologetically tells him, she is only "Dust" (F-28-17, J-573).

Poem 2 also introduces the importance to F-40 of the Gospel of Matthew, particularly of the five parables concluding Matthew's account of Jesus' final discourse before his arrest and execution. In this final eschatological discourse Jesus describes the perilous events that will precede his second coming, then tells his disciples, "he that shall endure unto the end . . . shall be saved" (24.13). He concludes by warning them to "Watch . . . for ye know not what hour your Lord doth come" (24.42), then illustrates his point by telling the five "household" parables of preparedness. Emily Dickinson recreates each of these parables in F-40, but in each case she conflates the parable with other biblical texts and casts the meditator in the role of protagonist. Poem 7 echoes the parable of the householder, whose home was "broken up" by a thief, but it is the meditator whose circuit "Home" was broken up by Christ, "the spoiler of Our Home." Poem 14 is a conflation of the parable of the talents and the parable of the trusty servant, but the meditator herself is the faithful servant, the "Little Maid," who has been industriously perfecting her one poetic talent until her death. Poem 16 echoes the parable of the ten virgins, but it is the meditator who is one of the prepared virgins, a "Fitter . . . Youth" who enters the "Door" of the bridal chamber. And poem 2, in which she identifies herself as Christ's "House-wife," is a response to the fifth "household" parable, the parable of the sheep and goats, though the parable of the talents is also an important source, as it is for all F-40's poems.

As Jesus conflates the creative and spiritual life in the parable of the talents, whose lord rewards the servants who multiplied their talents and castigates the one servant who did not, so Emily Dickinson conflates the meditator's poetic and spiritual life throughout F-40. Her recollected two-part conversion was both poetic and spiritual. Jesus is both her sacred Muse and the Redeemer who died to gain pardon for all (poems 1 and 6). She prepares herself both poetically and spiritually in order to be "Fitter" to meet the master/bridegroom (poem 16). Both her life and art are dedicated to glorifying the "Brave Beloved" (poem 20). As she declares in poem 2, he has "No Service," poetic or spiritual, she would not achieve.

## Poem 2

To comprehend F-40's second poem, the reader must not only see that it is a response to the sheep-and-goats parable, a response in which Emily Dickinson draws upon several other biblical sources including the parable of the talents, one must also have come to some understanding of the following poems, especially poems 10 and 20. In poem 10 the meditator reveals she is an unpublished poet who longs for the readers she does not yet have and cannot be certain she will ever have. In the same poem and in poem 20 she acknowledges that she cannot be certain she will be among the saved sheep, because that depends upon Christ, and his decision, as in the parable, is suspended until Judgment Day. What she does in poem 2, then, is to declare what her poems are intended to do if and when she has readers, and to declare her contentment with her present life as his "Housewife" even though she does not know for certain what the ultimate outcome of her life of service will be.

In the sheep-and-goats parable Jesus predicts that at the Judgment the "Son of man shall come in his glory," "shall" separate the saved sheep from the damned goats, and then "shall" say to the saved,

> . . . I was an hungred, and ye gave me meat: I was thirsty, and ye gave me drink: I was a stranger, and ye took me in:
> Naked, and ye clothed me: I was sick, and ye visited me: I was in prison, and ye came unto me.

When the saved, puzzled because they do not recall having served him in this way, ask when they did so, he will reply, "Inasmuch as ye did it unto one of the least of these my brethren, ye have done it unto me" (Matt. 25.35–40). Retrospectively, then, hearers or readers of the parable realize that by using "I" and "me" to mean both himself and one of his brethren, Jesus has indirectly proclaimed that serving him means serving his brethren.[1]

In the second poem's first three stanzas the meditator follows Jesus' example by using "Thou" and "thee" to mean both him and one of his brethren, the readers of her poems:

Wert Thou but ill—that I might show thee
How long a Day I could endure
Though thine attention stop not on me
Nor the least signal, Me assure—                    [Me/Mine]

Wert Thou but Stranger in ungracious country—
And Mine—the Door
Thou paused at, for a passing bounty—               [passing/doubtful]
No More—

Accused—wert Thou—and Myself—Tribunal
Convicted—Sentenced—Ermine—not to Me
Half the Condition, thy Reverse—to follow—          [Condition/
Just to partake—the infamy—                          distinction]

The Tenant of the Narrow Cottage, wert Thou—
Permit to be
The Housewife in thy low attendance
Contenteth Me—

No Service hast Thou, I would not achieve it—       [achieve/attempt]
To die—or live—
The first—Sweet, proved I, ere I saw thee—       [proved I/That was]
For Life—be Love—            [be Love/is—Love—/means—Love—]

The meditator responds to each of the parable's afflictions, though she
varies them, reorders them, and substitutes her own ministrations for his. To
his "I was sick," she responds, "Wert Thou but ill"; to his "I was a stranger,"
she responds, "Wert Thou but Stranger"; to his "I was in prison," she responds, "wert Thou . . . Accused . . . Convicted—Sentenced." In these
first three stanzas she addresses both Christ and the reader as "Thou" and
"thee," but with the fourth she begins to address Christ alone. In stanza 4 she
wittily responds to the parable's three other afflictions and ministrations by
portraying herself as his "Housewife," who is content to administer to his
hungry, thirsty, and naked brethren. Then in stanza 5 she sums up her wish
to serve him: he has "No Service" she would not achieve—including, but
not limited to, the services to his brethren he names in the parable—
whether it be to die or live. After parenthetically reminding him she had
already proved the first—that she would die for him—even before she "saw"
him, she explains her willingness both to die and to live for him: it is because
the "Life" she presently leads and began to live when she died for him means
"Love" for him and therefore for his brethren, her readers, echoing Jesus'
proclamation that the first great commandment is to love God and that the
second is like it, to love one's neighbor as oneself (Matt. 22.36–40).

Her declarations in the final stanza—that he has *no* service she would not
achieve and that she *would* die for him and, in fact, *has* already done so—are
among several clues leading the reader retrospectively to see that in this poem
she not only declares her poetic intentions, she declares that *all* her intentions and actions, both poetic and spiritual, are directed to his service.[2]
Among the other clues leading one to see that the poem concerns her actions
as well as her intentions is that in the following poems, which are spoken
only moments afterward, she reveals that she now *is* doing or *has* done what
she appears to say here she intends to do. Another clue is the meditator's shift
from the subjunctive to the indicative. Whereas in the first three stanzas her
verbs appear to be subjunctive—if "Thou" *were* ill, then what she *could* or
*would* do—in the fourth stanza her verbs are clearly indicative: being Christ's
housewife "Contenteth"—*contents*—her. This means that the sentence's first
clause, too, must be indicative because it would make no sense to say, "If you
were the tenant of the narrow cottage, then the permit to be the housewife in

thy low attendance *contents* me." Besides, Christ *was*, in fact, the original tenant of the narrow cottage, the grave of those who have renounced the world, the grave she shares with him both here and in "The grave my little cottage is" (J-1743). The fourth stanza's "wert," then, is not the subjunctive but the second-person-singular past indicative, and its subject and verb are inverted:

Thou . . . wert . . . The Tenant of the Narrow Cottage     [, and my]
Permit to be
The Housewife in thy low attendance
Contenteth Me—

The fourth stanza's indicative as well as the fifth stanza's mixture of the subjunctive and indicative—she *would* die or live for him, and she *has* already died for him and *now* lives for him—call into question the verbs in the second and third stanzas' main clauses, which are omitted and must be supplied by the reader:

Wert Thou but Stranger in ungracious country—
And Mine—the Door
Thou paused at, for a passing bounty—     [passing/doubtful]
No More—

Accused—wert Thou—and Myself—Tribunal—
Convicted—Sentenced—Ermine—not to Me
Half the Condition, thy Reverse—to follow—     [Condition/
Just to partake—the infamy—                      distinction]

Should these verbs be subjunctive, like the first stanza's "could endure," or indicative, like the fourth stanza's "Contenteth"? Should the second stanza read, "[Thou wouldst be a stranger] No More" or "[Thou art a Stranger] No More"? Should the third stanza read, "Ermine [would] not [be] to Me" or "Ermine [is] not to Me"? As the reader finally figures out, the answer is both, because the whole poem is a strange mixture of the subjunctive and indicative, of what the meditator intends and what she now does and has done.

Retrospectively one sees that this poem's verbal and pronominal ambiguity begins in its first stanza, as the meditator continues her address to the reader begun in the first poem's final stanza:

The Only News I know
Is Bulletins all Day
From Immortality.

The Only Shows I see—
Tomorrow and Today
Perchance Eternity—                        [Three—with Eternity—
                                           /And some Eternity—]
The Only One I meet
Is God—The Only Street—
Existence—This traversed                   [traversed/traverst]

If Other News there be—
Or Admirabler Show—
I'll tell it You—                          [I'll Signify—/I'll testify—]

---

Wert Thou but ill—that I might show thee
How long a Day I could endure
Though thine attention stop not on me
Nor the least signal, Me assure—           [Me/Mine]

After declaring in poem 1 that the only news she knows is from immortality, that she sees eternity in the everyday, and that she meets only God as she traverses the street of existence, the meditator turns from general declaration to address the reader directly. Once she has traversed the street of existence, if she finds other news to compare with her bulletins or admirabler show than those she describes in stanzas 2 and 3, then she will tell "You," the reader. Meantime, what she knows and sees is what her poems tell. Though she does not explain why she sees the eternal in the finite until poem 12, when she explains it is because she possesses "Compound Vision," in the second poem's variation of Jesus' parable she begins to tell her news from him. The subjunctive of the first poem's final stanza—which is, of course, a false subjunctive because she does not really expect to find better "News" or "Admirabler Show"—continues into the second poem's first two lines, which, along with the two stanzas' *ee* rhyme ("be"-"thee"-"me") and their repeated words ("Shows"-"show," "I'll"-"ill," "Signify"-"signal," "You"-"Thou") draw attention to the continuity between the two stanzas.

Having established that what she knows and sees is what she tells "You," the reader of F-40, she then in the second poem's first stanza tells "Thou,"

Christ and the reader, as one of his brethren, what she intends her poems to do. The problem is that until one sees that this poem mixes the subjunctive with the indicative, its first stanza makes no sense. First she declares that if the reader were ill, then it is her intention to show "thee," Christ and the reader, that she—that is, her poems in which, as she reveals in poem 9, she hides herself—could endure in her service for an indefinitely long period of time. But then she adds that she could do so even if the reader's attention did not "stop" on her, which is impossible: how, if the reader's attention did not "stop" on her poems, could her poems possibly administer to the reader?

As one finally sees, lines 3 and 4 allude to poems 10 and 20, in which she reveals that *at the present time* she receives no attention from the readers she longs for, or any assurance she will be among the saved sheep. Lines 3 and 4, then, are in the present indicative, and they apply to the whole poem:

> [Even] Though thine [the reader's] attention [does] not
> [now] stop on me
> Nor [does] the least signal assure Me [that I will be among
> the saved sheep]

Although the reader's attention does not now stop on her, it is her intention that when and if she does have readers, her poems will administer to them in the way she describes in this poem. And although she has no assurance she will be among the saved sheep, the intentions and actions she declares show not only that she is a pretty impressive candidate for salvation but also that she is content to serve as Christ's "Housewife" no matter what the ultimate outcome will be.

In the poem's first two lines, then, she states her poetic intentions in general terms. By substituting the more general "ill," meaning to suffer misfortune as well as to be "sick," as in the parable, she introduces all the misfortunes she then describes more specifically in the following lines. If "Thou," the reader, suffered any of these misfortunes, it is her intention to show "thee," Christ and the reader, how long a day she could endure in her poetic service. Whereas these first two lines are subjunctive and the third and fourth are indicative, the second and third stanzas operate simultaneously on two separate but interwoven levels, one subjunctive and the other indicative. On one level, she addresses "Thou," Christ and the reader, about what she intends her poems to do; and on the other level, she addresses "Thou," Christ alone, about what she has done and now does to serve him.

Insofar as the second stanza is about her poetic intentions, it is in the
subjunctive. If the reader were a stranger and stopped at her door for a
"passing bounty"—the freely bestowed gift of her poems—then it is her
intention that her poems cause the reader to feel like a stranger "No More."
But insofar as this stanza is addressed to Christ alone, it is in the indicative
and has an inverted subject and verb:

> Thou . . . Wert but [a] Stranger in ungracious country
> And Mine [was] the Door
> Thou paused at, for a passing bounty—
> [And you are a Stranger] No More—

These lines are in the indicative because they are about what *has*, in fact,
happened. According to the Bible, Jesus *was* a stranger in an ungracious
country—"He was in the world . . . and the world knew him not" (John
1.10); and according to poem 8, he *is* the "Stranger" who already *has* paused
at her door, requesting the passing bounty—the freely given gift of her
imperfect self. And she has not only taken him in, as in the parable; she has
forsaken all to accompany him.

The third stanza further blurs the distinction between her intentions and
actions. Insofar as it is addressed to Christ and the reader and concerns her
poetic intentions and actions, it is both subjunctive and indicative. If the
reader were imprisoned and she were the judge, then she would gladly
renounce her judicial "Ermine" to share the reader's infamy. What makes this
stanza indicative as well as subjunctive is that, as F-40's eighth poem shows,
she already *has* acted as judge and chosen to renounce the world to perfect
her "One" poetic talent in the hope that she will one day have readers. But
insofar as it is addressed to Christ alone about her spiritual actions, it is
definitely in the indicative:

> Thou . . . wert . . . Accused . . . Convicted—Sentenced
>     and Myself [was] Tribunal [;]
> Ermine [is] not to Me
> Half the Condition, thy Reverse—to follow—
> Just to partake—the infamy—

Once more, this stanza is about what *has* happened and *is* happening. Jesus
*was*, in fact, accused, convicted, sentenced, then infamously executed; and

according to poem 5, the meditator *has* acted as judge by choosing to share his "Agony" and "Affliction."

Retrospectively one sees that in this poem's strange mixture of indicatives and subjunctives there are only three true subjunctives, meaning contingencies. One is, will she ever have readers for her "Experiment"? The second is, if she has readers, will her poems serve them as she intends? The third is, will she be among the saved at the Judgment? Whatever the answer to the third contingency, the reader who, of course, knows the answers to the first two is struck by the eerie feeling that this is F-40's only instance in which the reader knows more than the poet-pilgrim. Retrospectively one also sees that by blurring the distinction between "Thou," meaning Christ, and "Thou," meaning the reader, the meditator makes the point Jesus makes in the sheep-and-goats parable, that serving him *means* serving his brethren. By blurring the distinction between the subjunctive and indicative, she declares that both her intentions and her actions are dedicated to Christ's service (see note 2). And by blurring the distinction between her spiritual and poetic service, she makes the point Jesus makes in the parable of the talents when he conflates the spiritual and creative life: "Themself are One," as her companion in the grave says of "Truth" and "Beauty" in "I died for Beauty" (F-21-9, J-449).

Poem 2 is of enormous import to F-40's structural totality. Because it concludes the ars poetica begun in poem 1 and introduces the meditator's recollections of her two-part conversion in poems 3 and 4, poem 2 is the linchpin of the composition of place. Because it directly alludes not only to poems 3 and 4 but also to poems 5, 8, 9, and 10, as well as to poem 20, with which it is paired to form F-40's envelope structure, poem 2 also introduces many of the following poems' most important subjects. Whether or not the ars poetica the meditator declares in poems 1 and 2 echoes Herbert's "Dedication" to *The Temple,* she expands upon it in poems 3, 4, 5, 9, and 10, then restates her poetic intentions in poem 11. And whether or not poem 2 echoes the Ignatian preparatory prayer and second prelude (see note 2), in poem 20 the meditator repeats her declaration that all her intentions and actions are directed toward Christ's service, as well as her request to be among the saved at the Judgment.

As F-40's most heavily freighted poem, poem 2 draws attention to the question, how did Emily Dickinson go about composing this final fascicle? Because its poems are so intricately interwoven and its structural principles so complex, she obviously did not simply write twenty-one separate poems, then stitch them together. Nor does it seem likely that she initially wrote the poems in their present sequence and interdependent state. Since, as the following discussion of poems 3 and 4 shows, F-40's conversion narrative summarizes events that took place in the preceding fascicles, it seems likely that she began with the conversion narrative, then fashioned this sequential story into F-40's plot, its arrangement of events according to the meditation. If she began with the conversion narrative, this would not necessarily mean that she wrote each of its poems specifically for F-40's sequential story. Poem 9, "I hide myself—within my flower," for example, is a variation of F-3-14, dated 1859. But it would mean that she had composed all or most of the narrative's poems, at least in rough form, before she began to rearrange the poems according to the meditation. As she rearranged them, she would then have modified some to suit her structural and aesthetic purposes, probably rejected others, and written some specifically to fit into the meditation.

What must probably remain unknown is which are the modified poems and which are those she wrote specifically for F-40's meditation. Is the heavily freighted second poem, for example, a poem, like number 9, that she wrote earlier, then modified? Or is it a poem that she wrote with the conversion narrative in mind, then modified to serve all the structural functions it presently serves? Or did she write the poem specifically to serve all these functions? That is, when she wrote poem 2, did she set herself the task of writing a poem whose first stanza would be a continuation of poem 1 and whose fifth stanza would introduce poems 3 and 4? A poem that would also introduce poems 5, 8, 9, 10, and 11 and be paired with poem 20 to form F-40's envelope structure? A poem that at the same time would be of considerable poetic interest, in which the meditator would request that she be among the saved and declare that her poetic and spiritual intentions and actions are dedicated to Christ's service?

Whatever the answer to these questions, the following discussion of poems 3 and 4 provides further evidence of the conversion narrative's centrality.


# POEMS 3 AND 4

F-40's third and fourth poems are the culmination of a series of poems, extending throughout the fascicles, in which the protagonist depicts, celebrates, and contemplates two singularly important occasions that led to her elevated state as "Czar," "Woman," and "Wife!" (e.g., F-9-21, J-119). F-40's third and fourth poems directly allude to the earlier occasional poems, and unless one recalls those poems, neither of these is decipherable. Conversely, poems 3 and 4 retrospectively explain the earlier occasional poems. Reading this series of cognate poems sequentially shows that they form a narrative thread that proceeds from the earlier poems' depictions, commemorations, and allusions to the thirty-eighth and fortieth fascicles' explanations.

Though in the earlier occasional poems it is not really clear whether the protagonist alludes to one occasion or several, she specifies in the thirty-eighth fascicle's tenth poem that there were, in fact, *two* occasions when her "Two . . . Eyes," a synecdoche for herself, experienced eternity in time:

> Two—were immortal twice—
> The privilege of few—
> Eternity—obtained—in Time—          [Eternity in Time obtained]
> Reversed Divinity
>
> That our ignoble Eyes
> The quality conceive          [conceive/perceive—]
> Of Paradise superlative—
> Through their Comparative.

In the final stanza of the fortieth fascicle's second poem, she again recollects *two* occasions, but here she reveals what they were. On the first, she died to the world and began to lead the life that means love. Then, on the second, she in some way "saw" Christ:

> No Service hast Thou, I would not achieve it—          [achieve/attempt]
> To die—or live—
> The first—Sweet, proved I, ere I saw thee—          [proved I/That was]
> For Life—be Love—          [be Love—/is—Love—/means—Love—]

In F-40's third poem she then recollects more fully the occasion when her "Two" eyes—echoing F-38-10's "Two . . . Eyes"—died to the world and leaned into perfectness, the second poem's life that means love ("means" is a variant in F-40-2, and "Two" is the variant in F-40-3; as I observed in my Textual Note, variants are often important to comprehending F-40's poems):

Midsummer, was it, when They died—
A full, and perfect time—
The Summer closed upon itself
In Consummated Bloom—

The Corn, her furthest kernel filled
Before the coming Flail—
When These—leaned into Perfectness—          [When These Two—
Through Haze of Burial—                      leaned in—Perfectness—]

Finally, in poem 4 she compares the two occasions she has commemorated in the preceding fascicles, then explained in F-40-2:

> The first Day that I was a Life
> I recollect it—How still—
> The last Day that I was a Life
> I recollect it—as well—
>
> 'Twas stiller—though the first
> Was still—
> 'Twas empty—but the first
> Was full—
>
> This—was my finallest Occasion—
> But then
> My tenderer Experiment
> Toward Men—
>
> "Which choose I"?
> That—I cannot say—
> "Which choose They"?
> Question Memory!

Verbal repetitions confirm that the two days she compares in F-40-4 are the two occasions she alludes to in the final lines of F-40-2. In poem 2 she reminds Christ that she "first" died for him and began to live the "Life" that means love, then "saw" him. In poem 3 she then describes the day when she died as a "full" time. Because in poem 4 she then describes the "first" day she was a "Life" as "full," the fourth poem's "first" day is the second poem's "first" occasion, the occasion she describes in greater detail in poem 3 as a "full" time. Moreover, because she specifies in poem 2 that she saw him after she died for him, and because in Dickinson, as in the Bible, "last" often means latter, the fourth poem's last, or latter, day is the second poem's later occasion when she saw him (see, e.g., "I know lives, I could miss," F-25-6, J-372, in which "last" signifies "latter," and Cruden, *Complete Concordance* 368):

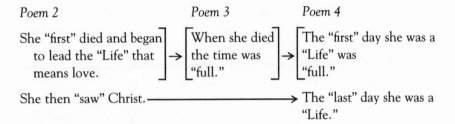

Poem 2

She "first" died and began to lead the "Life" that means love.

→ When she died the time was "full."

→ The "first" day she was a "Life" was "full."

She then "saw" Christ. ⟶ The "last" day she was a "Life."

As the following discussions of poems 3 and 4 show, the second day she recollects in poems 2 and 4, the day she "saw" Christ, is the occasion she begins to celebrate in the eighth and ninth fascicles, then celebrates in nearly every fascicle thereafter: the occasion when she was "identified," made royal, and became a "Wife!" (F-8-11, J-174; F-9-16, J-195; F-9-21, J-199). As the following pages also show, the first day she recollects in F-40-2, -3, and -4, the day when she died for Christ, is the event she depicts in the first fascicle's first poem:

> The Gentian weaves her fringes—
> The Maple's loom is red—
> My departing blossoms
>     Obviate parade.
>
> A brief, but patient illness—
> An hour to prepare,
> And one below, this morning
> Is where the angels are—
> It was a short procession,
> The Bobolink was there—
> An aged Bee addressed us—
> And then we knelt in prayer—
> We trust that she was willing—
> We ask that we may be.
> Summer—Sister—Seraph!
> Let us go with thee!

> In the name of the Bee—
> And of the Butterfly—
> And of the Breeze—Amen!

Although customarily read as a mock-elegy for summer, when read in its fascicle context one sees that this poem's central focus is the protagonist's own vow to die, as the summer has done. Like F-40, this poem is a three-part meditation. In its first stanza, Emily Dickinson creates the poem's setting, the close of summer, when the "Gentian" blooms and the "Maple" turns red. Then, in the second stanza's first ten lines, she contemplates what has taken place in a fanciful little parable. Because the summer has died, summer's creatures, including herself, have held a funeral in which they prayed they might be as willing to die as they trust the summer was. Then, in an apostrophe to summer, she declares her—and their—intention to die, as the summer has done: "Let us go with thee!" Her concluding benediction echoes Jesus' words in the final two verses of the Gospel of Matthew, in which he charges his disciples to go and teach all nations, though she substitutes summer's "Bee" for his powerful Father, summer's "Butterfly" for his resurrected Son, and the summer "Breeze" for his Holy Ghost, then closes, as he does, with a firm "Amen!"—so shall it be.

## Poem 3

In the third poem, Emily Dickinson draws upon three biblical passages about Christ's earthly kingdom—his corn parables in Mark and John as well as Paul's letter to the Colossians—to create her own parable of the meditator's death to the world and entry into his kingdom of "Perfectness." Initially this is not apparent, because the poem appears to be an elegy for two unidentified persons who died in midsummer:

> Midsummer, was it, when They died—
> A full, and perfect time—
> The Summer closed upon itself
> In Consummated Bloom—
>
> The Corn, her furthest kernel filled
> Before the coming Flail—
> When These—leaned into Perfectness—        [When These Two—
> Through Haze of Burial—                     leaned in—Perfectness—]

The poem defeats the reader's attempts to read it as a true elegy because there are incongruities in the text that operate in much the same way as the surface incongruities in many of Jesus' parables. As John Drury explains, the hearer or reader of Jesus' parables is often meant to see a parable's incongruities, realize it is not a realistically accurate story, then search for its deeper figurative meanings (*The Parables* 58). One is meant to ask, for example, why in the parable of the talents the lord entrusted such vast sums to his servants, and why in the parable of the ten virgins the wedding takes place at midnight. Similarly, in poem 3 one is apparently meant to ask how this can be a true elegy—like those Emily Dickinson wrote for Elizabeth Barrett Browning and her nephew Gilbert, for example—when the meditator's felicitous tone remains uninterrupted by even the slightest expression of grief, when she pays no tribute to those who died, and when she devotes fewer lines to the fact that they died than to the season when they did so. The season she describes is in itself problematic because it is not realistically coherent. First their deaths are represented as having taken place at "Midsummer," June 21, then at the end of summer, when "The Summer closed upon itself" and the "Corn" was ripe. The image of the corn and flail is similarly puzzling because a "Flail" is an instrument for threshing grain, like wheat or barley, not for shelling the Indian corn that grows in North America.

These seeming incongruities are among the clues leading the reader to see that the variant "Two" who died are her "Two . . . Eyes," as in F-38-10, and that the poem's natural images are a mixture of the figurative and the literal. But before one can deduce which are figurative and which literal, one must make some sense of the poem's ambiguous syntax. While the first line is a complete sentence, it is not initially clear how the following lines fit together. After much trial and error, one sees that the poem is a single compound sentence composed of two complex sentences, and that these two complex sentences are chiastic, parallel but with a reversal of order:

A. when They died [,]
B. it was Midsummer [, that is,
B. it was] A full, and perfect time [when]
B. The Summer closed upon itself / In Consummated Bloom[;]
B. The Corn [stood with] her furthest kernel filled / Before the coming Flail[,]
A. When These Two—leaned in—Perfectness / Through Haze of Burial[.]

In other words, the first compounded sentence begins with a "when" clause and follows with a main clause describing the season, while the second compounded sentence begins with a main clause describing the season and follows with a "when" clause.

These two "when" clauses are parallel in the way that Robert Alter describes the dynamic parallelism of the biblical poetic line: the second does not simply restate the first, it elaborates and expands upon it (*Art of Biblical Poetry* 3–26 and passim). To the first line's "when They died," the final two lines add that "Through [this] Burial" they "leaned into Perfectness." The first two seasonal descriptions are similarly parallel:

> it was Midsummer [, that is,
> it was] A full, and perfect time.

And so are the second two, which begin with an article, then continue with a subject and a verb followed by two prepositional phrases:

> The Summer closed upon itself / In Consummated Bloom
> The Corn [stood with] her furthest kernel filled / Before
>       the coming Flail.

While Alter describes the Bible's parallelism as most often progressing from the literal or the prosaic to the figurative, Dickinson's seasonal lines begin with the figurative "Midsummer," then progress to the prosaic "full, and perfect time," then to the literal summer's close, and then to the figurative "Corn."

Though the poem itself does not specify which images are literal and which figurative, one assumes that "Midsummer" is figurative, because in the only other place the word appears in Dickinson, it signifies mental felicity, "Midsummer—in the Mind" (F-34-2, J-646). Moreover, according to Dickinson's lexicon, the synonym for "midsummer" is "solstice," which in Dickinson often signifies "turning point," as in an earlier occasional poem, "There came a Day—at Summer's full," her soul passed the "Solstice" (F-13-15, J-322). By declaring that when she died it was "Midsummer," then, she declares it was a supremely felicitous time and a turning point in her life. As she adds, it was a "full, and perfect time" for herself, but it was also a full and perfect season when the "Summer closed upon itself / In Consummated Bloom." One does not see that the image of summer's close is literal until one has deciphered poem 4, in which the meditator reveals that on the day she died she began to compose the fascicles. Only then does it dawn on the reader that the first fascicle's first poem, when she vowed to die and actually *did* begin to compose the fascicles, took place at summer's close, when the "Gentian" blooms. The occasion she recollects in F-40-3, then, is the occasion she depicts in the first fascicle's first poem.

The following image of the corn returns to the figurative. The corn with *her* furthest kernel filled is an apt metonym for the meditator herself. Since in Dickinson "furthest" is sometimes "inmost" (F-30-12, J-543) and "kernel" always mind, or soul (e.g., J-1039), a paraphrase of this second stanza is as follows:

> The Corn/meditator [stood with] her inmost soul filled
> Before the coming Flail
> When These Two—leaned in—Perfectness—
> Through Haze of Burial—

Because North American corn, meaning maize, is not threshed with a flail, and because in the Bible "corn" signifies "grain," which *is* threshed with a flail, this corn is biblical corn, that is, grain (Cruden, *Complete Concordance* 110). The "Corn" trope thus asks the reader to remember Christ's two corn parables of the kingdom of heaven, as "Perfectness" asks one to remember the only place in the Bible where the word occurs, Paul's letter to the Colossians, in which he, too, comments at length on Christ's earthly kingdom.

Mark's parable, often called the parable of the "seed growing secretly," focuses upon how the soul becomes ready for "harvest," entry into the kingdom:

> . . . So is the kingdom of God, as if a man should cast seed into the ground;
> And should sleep, and rise night and day, and the seed should spring and grow up, he knoweth not how.
> For the earth bringeth forth fruit of herself; first the blade, then the ear, after that the full corn in the ear.
> But when the fruit is brought forth, immediately he putteth in the sickle, because the harvest is come. (4.26–29)

Mark's parable, in which Christ is both the sower and the reaper who wields the sickle, begins with sowing and concludes with harvest, entry into the kingdom. But John's perspective and figuration are very different.

His trope for entry into the kingdom is planting rather than harvest. Here Jesus begins with a corn, or seed, of wheat that must be planted and concludes with the effect of its having been planted—the plant will bear fruit: "Except a corn of wheat fall into the ground and die, it abideth alone: but if it die, it bringeth forth much fruit." After telling the parable, which he did, according to John, shortly before his own arrest and death, he explains and expands upon it:

> He that loveth his life shall lose it; and he that hateth his life in this world shall keep it unto life eternal.
> If any man serve me, let him follow me; and where I am, there shall also my servant be. (12.24–26)

Only if one dies, as Jesus was soon literally to do, does one gain eternal life and union with him.

Paul's perspective is different from that of either parable. Both parables concern what *does* in general terms happen, but Paul's letter to the Colossians concerns what *has* happened, what it means, and what therefore *should* happen. After telling the Colossians that God has already "translated us into the kingdom of his dear Son" (1.13), he describes this realm in the language of fullness and perfection and with images of death and burial echoed in Dickinson's poem: "ye are complete in [Christ]"; "may [ye] stand perfect and complete in the will of God"; "[ye are] Buried with him, . . . dead with Christ." After declaring in chapter 3, "ye are dead, and your life is hid with Christ in God," he urges the faithful to put off sins and put on Christian virtues, but above all to put on love, "the bond of perfectness" that binds all the other virtues together.

By drawing upon all three biblical texts and conflating them, Emily Dickinson creates a tableau depicting the "full, and perfect time" when the meditator was "harvested," as in Mark; planted, as in John; and "buried" or "hid with Christ," as in Colossians. Reading the poem in the context of these three biblical texts shows how they illuminate the first stanza and explain the second:

> Midsummer, was it, when They died—
> A full, and perfect time—
> The Summer closed upon itself
> In Consummated Bloom—

The Corn, her furthest kernel filled
Before the coming Flail—
When These—leaned into Perfectness—      [When These Two—
Through Haze of Burial—      leaned in—Perfectness—]

The first line's "died," like the preceding poem's "die," echoes John's corn of
wheat, which must "die" in order to bear fruit. The second line's "full, and
perfect time" not only further explains the preceding line's "Midsummer"
and the following line's summer's close, it also echoes Paul's "stand perfect
and complete in the will of God," thus further explaining the meditator's
mental state at the time her death took place. The fifth line's "Corn" is not
only a coherent metonym for the meditator, it also echoes John's corn of
wheat, which must die in order to bear fruit. "The Corn, her furthest kernel
filled / Before the coming Flail" echoes even more closely Mark's "full corn in
the ear," ready for the "sickle" and "harvest." In Mark, Christ is the reaper,
the wielder of the "sickle," and in Dickinson he is the thresher, the wielder
of the "Flail," but in both cases he is the soul's cultivator, a recurring biblical
and devotional trope (see, e.g., Dickinson's "A Solemn thing within the
Soul / To feel itself get ripe," F-22-12, J-483, and Herbert's "Paradise").

Dickinson's entire second stanza echoes Mark's concluding sentence, but
she reverses his subordination. According to him, when the corn is ripe it is
harvested, and according to her, the corn was ripe when it "leaned into
Perfectness." She thus substitutes for his "harvested" her own "leaned into
Perfectness," a fusion of John's "fall into the ground," Paul's "perfectness," and
"leaned," in its biblical sense. In Proverbs one is advised to "lean not unto
thine own understanding" but to trust in the Lord (3.5), and in the Gospel of
John the beloved disciple is twice described as "leaning" on Jesus' breast
(13.23; 21.20). By leaning into perfectness, then, the meditator leaned in
both these ways into Christ, who was made perfect. But "Perfectness" also
alludes to Paul's urging the Colossians to put on love, "the bond of perfectness." When she leaned into perfectness, then, she leaned not only into
Christ, the essence of perfection, but into his kingdom, the preceding poem's
"Life" that means "Love." Through what Northrop Frye calls the "royal meta-
phor," king and kingdom are one—as they are in poem 6, whose variant line
for "Occupy my House" is "Occupy my Breast" (Great Code 87–90).

Her lean into Christ and his earthly kingdom was "Through Haze of
Burial," a return to the first line's juxtaposition of seasonal and mortuary
tropes and a fusion of this poem's Dickinsonian and biblical tropes. Elsewhere Dickinson associates the hazy atmosphere of summer with the season

itself, as "Haze" is a synecdoche for summer in "Besides the Autumn poets sing" (F-6-11, J-131). "Burial" echoes Paul's "Buried with Christ" and also, because Webster's synonyms for "bury" are "to hide" and "to plant," Paul's "hid with Christ" as well as John's "fall into the ground," be planted. Because "Haze of Burial" alliteratively echoes the sixth line's "Flail," and because a flail is an instrument for "thrashing," Webster's preferred spelling of the word, and because, according to Webster, "Haze" is etymologically a blow, it appears that "Haze of Burial" also alludes to the violence of her translation from her past way of life—a trauma she describes more fully in F-40's seventh poem. If "Haze of Burial" is, as it appears to be, an allusion to the violence of her transformation, then the phrase follows the poem's pattern of dynamic parallelism by repeating the poem's seasonal and mortuary diction while adding new information.

The pyrrhic and dash with which the poem concludes signal that her burial was not a conclusion but a beginning, whose outcome is revealed in poem 4. There is, then, in this single tableau an implicit three-part narrative. At some unrecorded time before the poem's recollected present, a seed, as in Mark, was planted in the meditator's soul, where it secretly grew and flourished. At the time of the poem's recollected present, the corn was fully ripened and harvested, as in Mark; planted, as in John; and buried or hid with Christ, as in Colossians. Thereafter she did, as in John, bear fruit, for as poem 4 reveals, it was on this first full day that she began to compose the fascicles.

## Poem 4

The fortieth fascicle's fourth poem is composed of a series of interwoven riddles that draw the reader into the text in a way that, as far as I know, is unprecedented. While Dickinson readers are accustomed to having to deduce and insert omitted words in order to comprehend her tightly compressed poems, this strange, idiosyncratic poem asks the reader to deduce and insert both an omitted poem, which I have called 3b, and an omitted stanza, which I call 2b. I do not, of course, propose that this implicit stanza and poem be included in future printings of the F-40 poems. Nevertheless, in order to understand poem 4, which is of crucial importance to understanding F-40, the reader must first recognize that there are these two ellipses and must then, by following the text's clues, determine what these omitted components are. After one has identified and inserted this omitted stanza and poem, one discovers not only that each fits into the text both tropically and verbally but also that each reveals crucially important information. Stanza *2b* reveals that on the first day of her spiritual-poetic conversion the meditator began to compose the fascicles. And poem *3b* re-creates the second day of her conversion, the event she alludes to and celebrates throughout F-40 and throughout the preceding fascicles beginning with fascicles 8 and 9: the occasion when she was "identified," made royal, and became a "Wife."

Though these two ellipses are not initially apparent, it *is* initially apparent that poem 4 poses a riddle: what are the two days the meditator recollects and compares?

> The first Day that I was a Life
> I recollect it—How still—
> The last Day that I was a Life
> I recollect it—as well—
>
> 'Twas stiller—though the first
> Was still—
> 'Twas empty—but the first
> Was full—
>
> This—was my finallest Occasion—
> But then
> My tenderer Experiment
> Toward Men—
>
> "Which choose I"?
> That—I cannot say—
> "Which choose They"?
> Question Memory!

The relation between text and reader is far more complex in this poem than in the preceding one. In poem 3 the meditator recollects a singularly momentous occasion; in the process of recollecting it, she in effect re-creates the occasion by describing it quite fully, though cryptically; and the reader is invited to deduce what the occasion is. By contrast, in this poem she recollects two singularly momentous occasions, but she does not fully describe either of them. All she reveals about these two days is that she recollects them equally vividly ("How I recollect the first day still," "I remember the last day as well"); that the first day was "still" and "full," whereas the last was "stiller" and "empty"; that the last day was her "finallest" occasion and resulted in her "tenderer Experiment Toward Men"; and that she cannot say which of these two stupendously important days she prefers.

If this poem were read outside its fascicle context, one would simply have to throw up one's hands and conclude that it has an "omitted center," that the speaker alludes to two days and does not disclose what they were. But when read in its fascicle context, there are strong and telling clues to the two days' identities. Poem 4 is, after all, one of that series of cognate poems that form a narrative thread, extending throughout the fascicles, in which the protagonist celebrates two transforming occasions. The fourth poem's "first Day" is thus the event she depicted in the first fascicle's first poem, then recollected in the fortieth fascicle's second and third poems, the day she died to the world. And its "last Day" is the occasion she began to celebrate in fascicles 8 and 9, then recollected in nearly every fascicle thereafter, the occasion when she was "identified," acquired a "Crown," and became a "Wife." Poem 4's fascicle context thus solves its chief riddle, the identities of the two days she compares. But at the same time, its fascicle context, and particularly the narrative segment beginning with F-40-2, introduces another riddle: if poem 3 re-creates the first occasion she alludes to in poems 2 and 4, then where is the poem re-creating the later occasion she alludes to in poems 2 and 4? As this narrative segment shows, there is a disparity between the progression of the meditator's mind and what the reader sees in the text. Because in the fourth poem's first stanza she declares that she recollects both days with equal vividness, *she* obviously has both days in her mind's eye, but all the reader sees in the narrative segment is the re-creation of the first day:

| *Progression of the meditator's mind:* *what she recollects* | *Progression of the narrative:* *what the reader sees* |
|---|---|
| 1. Reminds Christ that she died for him before she saw him | Poem 2—Re-creates her reminder |
| 2. Recollects when she died for him | Poem 3—Re-creates her recollection of her death |
| 3. Recollects when she saw him | • • • • • • • • • • |
| 4. Compares the two days, which she recollects with equal vividness | Poem 4—Re-creates her comparison |

This gap in the narrative sequence is one of several strong indications that there is, in effect, an implicit poem between poems 3 and 4, in which the meditator re-creates the day she "saw" Christ, as in the third poem she re-creates the day she "died" for him. This implicit but omitted poem 3b is something like a literary "black hole." Everything in the text points to its existence, yet it is not actually visible in the place where it should be seen. It simply does not make narrative sense that she would allude to both days in F-40-2, then re-create the first day in poem 3, and then, without further describing the second day, refer specifically to both days throughout poem 4. Nor does it make sense that in her meditation's composition of place she would summon the powers of sight and memory to create an image of her mind, but leave out one of the two most important occasions of her life, the second day that she has repeatedly celebrated in nearly every fascicle, beginning with F-8. Moreover, she alludes to the second day throughout the following F-40 poems. In poem 13, "Till Death—is narrow Loving," for example, she declares that she began to imitate the bridegroom "Thenceforward," from that day onward, that is, beginning with the day of their betrothal. In poem 16, "Fitter to see Him, I may be," she remembers when she was "chosen" and directly alludes to that "One Day."

Furthermore, since the fourth poem's "first Day" alludes to a specific poem, F-40-3, it makes sense to suppose that the same poem's "last Day" also alludes to a specific poem. And because the fourth poem expects the reader to deduce the first day's identity by looking backward to a preceding occasional poem, F-40-3, it makes sense to suppose that the same poem also expects the reader to deduce the last day's identity by looking backward to a preceding occasional poem. The problem is that while the poem re-creating the first day is relatively easy to determine because it is the poem immediately preceding, there is no preceding F-40 poem that re-creates the last day as the third poem re-creates the first day. This must mean, then, that the reader is meant to look backward through the preceding fascicles' occasional poems to find the poem re-creating the last day as F-40-3 re-creates the first day.

Since in the fourth poem the meditator describes this second day/poem quite specifically, thereby providing significant clues to its identity, the reader's task is to determine the identity of this implied but omitted poem 3b by following the clues the meditator provides as she compares the two days. But in the process of following these clues, which are themselves riddles, the reader discovers there is also an implicit stanza one must deduce and insert before one can make sense of poem 4. The chief clue leading one to see there is a missing stanza and then to deduce what it is lies in the poem's recurring rhetorical figures. Not only is the poem in the rhetorical mode of comparison and contrast, it is also like the rhetorical figure of aposiopesis, as defined in Dickinson's lexicon: it "aggravates what [it] pretends to conceal by uttering only a part," hinting at the identities of the two days, "and leaving the rest," their identities, "to be understood" by the reader. This poem's figurative language, too, is rhetorical rather than tropic. Both "The first Day that I was a Life" and "My tenderer Experiment Toward Men" are kennings, a form of the rhetorical figure of circumlocution, or periphrasis. The poem is paronomastic throughout in that the meaning of a single word shifts; in the first stanza, for example, "still" signifies "yet," but in the second stanza "still" signifies "quiet." The fourth stanza's two questions, as I will show, are rhetorical, and its final line, "Question Memory!" is an apostrophe to the reader.

Most important, because the poem's first two stanzas' sentences are parallel, as are the final stanza's two questions, the third stanza is foregrounded as the poem's only nonparallel stanza:

> This —was my finallest Occasion—
> But then
> My tenderer Experiment
> Toward Men—

This foregrounded third stanza is in itself a riddle because the superlative "finallest" and comparative "tenderer" show it is a continuation of the first two stanzas' comparison. But where, then, is the standard to which it is being compared? The poem's emphasis upon the rhetorical leads the reader to see that this third stanza is an enthymeme, the rhetorical counterpart of a syllogism, in which one proposition is omitted. The standard to which this stanza is compared, then, is omitted and must be supplied by the reader.

This is a problem similar to the problem of the implicit poem 3b except that 3b actually exists in a preceding fascicle and the reader is invited to deduce which poem it is by following the text's clues. By contrast, the reader is asked to deduce what the implicit stanza 2b must be, judging from the explicit stanza's comparison and the poem's recurring parallelism: if "This" was her "finallest Occasion," which resulted in her "Experiment's" becoming "tenderer," then "That" must have been her "final Occasion," which resulted in her "tender Experiment." The implicit stanza, then, is as follows:

That—was my final Occasion—
But then
My tender Experiment
Toward Men—

When this stanza is inserted into the poem, it not only provides the omitted standard for the third stanza's comparison, it also complements the poem's pattern of parallelism, corrects its grammatical error, and refers specifically to the variant reading of the second poem's final lines:

The first Day that I was a Life
I recollect it—How still—
The last Day that I was a Life
I recollect it—as well—

[It, the last day, was] stiller—though the first [day]
Was still—
[It, the last day, was] empty—but the first [day]
Was full—

[That (the first day) was my final Occasion—
But then
My tender Experiment
Toward Men—]

This [the last day] was my finallest Occasion—
But then
My tenderer Experiment
Toward Men—

"Which choose I"?
That—I cannot say—
"Which choose They"?
Question Memory!

The implicit stanza 2b complements the explicit stanzas' parallelism by adding a new variation: the poem begins with two stanzas, each composed of two nearly identical parallel sentences; these two stanzas are now followed by two nearly identical parallel stanzas; and the poem concludes with a stanza that includes two nearly identical parallel questions. The implicit stanza 2b also corrects the poem's grammar fault. Without the implicit stanza, the referent for the third stanza's "This," meaning the last, or more recent, day, is the noun immediately preceding, which is the second stanza's "first" day. But after one inserts the implicit stanza between stanzas 2 and 3, the referent for stanza 2b's "That" becomes, correctly, the second stanza's "first" day. Most astonishingly, the implicit stanza's "That," the first day, directly refers to the variant reading of the second poem's final lines, in which "That" is also the "first" day:

> No Service hast Thou, I would not achieve it—
> To die—or live—
> The *first*—Sweet, *That* was ere I saw thee—
>                    (emphasis added)

Thus in both poems "That" is the first day, the more distant occasion, while in the fourth poem's third stanza "This" is the last day, the more recent occasion.

The first stanza introduces the terms of the comparison between "That" day and "This" day, which will be maintained throughout the poem: the two days were descriptively different, but they were of equally momentous import, an equality underscored here and throughout by the poem's parallelism:

> The first Day that I was a Life
> I recollect it—How still—
> The last Day that I was a Life
> I recollect it—as well—

Although the first day occurred before the last, both were equally memorable, and both were equally important turning points. Whereas in poem 3 the meditator expressed the liminality of the first day metonymically with "Midsummer"/solstice, meaning turning point, here she expresses both days' equal liminality with two double trochees, each signaling a turn:

> The fírst Dáy that Í wăs ă Lífe
> The lást Dáy that Í wăs ă Lífe

Each of these lines is a kenning, and as a kenning it is, as Robert Alter demonstrates, a riddle that has been transformed from the interrogative to the declarative (*Art of Biblical Poetry* 15–16). As "fruit of one's loins" signifies child, so "The first Day that I was a Life" signifies the day of her death and entry into "Perfectness," the second poem's "Life [that] means Love."

But as the biblical kenning amplifies child by drawing attention to the close physical bond between parent and child, so Dickinson's kenning amplifies the day of the meditator's death: it was on the first day that she began to live "Life" with a capital *L*, as opposed to the child's life she had led at the time of her debate with Christ in F-40-6. "The last Day that I was a Life" is similarly a kenning/riddle whose simple answer is the second poem's occasion when she "saw" Christ, but precisely how this kenning amplifies the later occasion becomes clear only after the reader has discovered the implicit poem *3b*.

The second stanza gives further clues to poem *3b*'s identity by describing how it was descriptively different from poem 3:

> 'Twas stiller—though the first
> Was still—
> 'Twas empty—but the first
> Was full—

Her description of the first day as "still" and "full" asks the reader to remember that in poem 3 the meditator described the day of her death and rebirth with images of fullness and that while her tropes were seasonal, it was "still"—that is, there were no sounds, no buzzing bees or singing birds. More important to the reader in search of clues to poem *3b*'s identity, her description of the last day reveals that the implicit poem's imagery is of emptiness rather than fullness and of a stillness even greater than the silent third, a highly significant clue enabling the reader to determine which of the occasional poems *3b* is.

In the implicit stanza *2b* she then reveals what the first day occasioned:

> That—was my final Occasion—
> But then
> My tender Experiment
> Toward Men—

The first day was her "final Occasion," the ultimate, decisive day when she began her "tender Experiment Toward Men." Since the meditator is a poet, and since "Experiment" elsewhere signifies the bird's song (J-1084), often in Dickinson a metonym for the poet's song, or poem, the simple answer to this kenning/riddle is poems. But "tender Experiment Toward Men" also amplifies poems. These are poems with a particular aim. They are "tender," loving, and directed "Toward Men." These are the "nosegays"/fascicles that she began to compose when she died to the world—as she vowed to do in the first fascicle's first poem—and began to lead the life that means love for Christ and his brethren, her readers.

As she then reveals in the explicit third stanza, on the second day her "Experiment" became even "tenderer":

> This—was my finallest Occasion—
> But then
> My tenderer Experiment
> Toward Men—

Though the reader will not know precisely why her experiment became "tenderer" until deducing the implicit poem *3b*, this stanza's superlative "finallest" appears at first to compare the first day to the last and to give the last greater significance. This would subvert the terms of the comparison insisted upon throughout the poem, that the two days were equally important. But as the reader at last sees, what "finallest" shows is that the last day, when she saw Christ, was not a new and different experience, but an intensification of the first "final" day when she died to the world and began to compose the fascicles. The terms of the comparison thus remain the same. The superlative "finallest" makes the last day in one sense the most important and decisive occasion in her life. But because the last day was an intensification of the first, the first day was in another sense the most important and decisive occasion in her life: the last day, when she saw Christ, could not have taken place without the first day, when she died to the world and began to compose the fascicles—just as the explicit third stanza describing the last day cannot be comprehended until the reader deduces and inserts the implicit stanza *2b* describing the first day.

It is hardly surprising, then, that when Jesus, her inner voice, interrupts her meditation to ask which day she prefers, she replies, after repeating his question, "That—I cannot say":

> "Which choose I"?
> That—I cannot say—
> "Which choose They"?
> Question Memory!

His first question is rhetorical because he has obviously overheard her meditation and therefore knows she does not prefer one day over the other. His second question is puzzling until one sees that the referent for "They" is the poem's only plural noun, "Men," the readers toward whom her experiment is directed. As one of these "Men," the reader realizes with a start that he or she is suddenly being drawn into the conversation. But if Christ's question is, which do readers choose? then it cannot be, which *day* do they *prefer?* because the reader is in no position to judge; the meditator has repeatedly stressed that both days were incomparably important, and the reader must accept her judgment. The meaning of "choose," then, has paronomastically shifted from "prefer" to "select," and Jesus' second question is, Which two poems does the reader select as those being compared in this poem? In other words, has the reader deduced which poems re-create the two occasions? The question is rhetorical because the questioner assumes the answer to be obvious. The reader, too, has overheard the meditator's comparison and should therefore know which poems they are. But since the meditator does not know if the reader has deduced their identities, she turns his question back upon the reader: "[If you do not know which poems re-create the occasions being compared, then you must] Question [your] Memory!"

Jesus' second question thus straightforwardly states the chief riddle the poem poses: What are the two days/poems the meditator recollects and compares? And her response makes explicit the directive implicitly given throughout poems 3 and 4: to solve their riddles, the reader must "Question Memory!"—that is, the reader must look backward to the preceding fascicles' occasional poems. Even before realizing that "Question Memory!" is an apostrophe to him- or herself, the reader has already been questioning memory in order to decipher poems 3 and 4. Unless one remembered poems 2 and 3 as well as the preceding fascicles' occasional poems, one would not be able to determine the identities of the two days compared in poem 4. To determine the identity of the "Two" who died in poem 3, one must look backward both to poem 2, where the meditator specified that she herself died, and to the thirty-eighth fascicle's tenth poem, where the "Two" who obtained eternity in time were her "Two . . . Eyes," a synecdoche for herself. Nor would one know which of the third poem's seasonal images are figurative and which literal unless one remembered the first fascicle's first poem, where she vowed to die and began to compose the fascicles at summer's close.

## Poem 3b

The reader's challenge is now to assemble the clues given in poems 2 and 4, then to look backward through the preceding fascicles' occasional poems to find which one re-creates the second day the meditator recollects. As poem 2 specifies, this second day was when she in some way "saw" Christ. And as poem 4 specifies, the implicit poem depicts an occasion that is in some way the last day she was "a Life." It was her "finallest Occasion" and caused her experiment to become "tenderer." It caused their union to become complete: while in the third poem she leaned into him and his kingdom, in the fourth he has become a voice within her mind, or soul. Most important, the fourth poem's second stanza gives clues to the implicit poem's imagery, which she describes as "empty" rather than "full," and even "stiller" than the silent third poem. Another clue to the implicit poem's figuration is provided by F-40's recurring nuptial tropes. After referring to herself as Christ's "Housewife" in poem 2, the meditator describes their union as a betrothal in three subsequent F-40 poems. In poem 8, echoing the wedding vows' "forsaking all others," she declares she has "forsook . . . All" to accompany this "Stranger." In poem 13, echoing the marriage vows' "until death us do part," she observes that loving only "Till Death" is a "narrow" kind of loving but that her own love for the divine bridegroom will last through death and into eternity. And in poem 16, echoing the parable of the ten virgins, whose prepared virgins enter the "door" of the bridal chamber, she imagines the happy conclusion of her lifelong betrothal: her full union with the bridegroom, when she, "A Fitter . . . Youth," will enter that "Door." In view of F-40's recurring nuptial tropes, then, the implicit poem 3b must be one of the preceding occasional poems whose tropes are nuptial.

In searching through the preceding fascicles' nuptial poems, one finds that although the protagonist repeatedly refers to herself as a wife and as wed, there are only two that actually re-create the event itself in the way that F-40-3 re-creates the earlier occasion. One is the thirteenth fascicle's fifteenth poem, which begins, "There came a Day—at Summer's full" (J-322). The other is the twenty-fifth fascicle's fifth poem, which begins, "It was a quiet way" (J-1053). Since the meditator specifies in the fourth poem's second stanza that the imagery of the poem depicting the last day is "stiller" than the silent third poem and "empty" rather than "full," "There came a Day—at Summer's full" cannot be the implicit poem 3b, because it describes the day as "full." The day/poem the meditator recollects must therefore be "It was a quiet way" because in this poem she describes the occasion as both "quiet" and empty:

> It was a quiet way—
> He asked if I was His—
> I made no answer of the Tongue,
> But answer of the Eyes—

And then he bore me high
Before this mortal noise
With swiftness as of Chariots—
And distance—as of Wheels—

The World did drop away
As Counties—from the feet
Of Him that leaneth in Balloon—
Upon an Ether Street—

The Gulf behind—was not—
The Continents—were new—
Eternity—it was—before
Eternity was due—

No Seasons were—to us—
It was not Night—nor Noon—
For Sunrise—stopped upon the Place—
And fastened it—in Dawn.

This nuptial poem satisfies all the clues given in F-40-2 and 4. The second poem's later occasion, when the meditator "saw" Christ, was when she first saw or knew him as bridegroom and spouse. It was therefore, as she declares in the fourth poem's first stanza, the last day she was "a Life"—a single, solitary life—because with their betrothal the two became one: though the implicit 3b begins with "He" and "I," it concludes with "us." Because they became one, he became her inner voice, her better self, as he is in the fourth poem's final stanza. Their betrothal was her "finallest Occasion" because it was permanent, irrevocable; as F-40's thirteenth poem explains, their union will extend through death and into eternity. This finallest occasion caused her experiment to become "tenderer," more like Christ, the "Tender Pioneer" (F-35-13, J-698), because, as F-40-13 also explains, their betrothal caused her "Thenceforward" to imitate her divine spouse. "It was a quiet way" satisfies and explains not only the second and fourth poems' clues to the occasion and its results but also the latter's clues to its diction and imagery. Her description of the implicit poem as "stiller" than the third poem and "empty" rather than "full" sums up the differences between the two poems' diction and figuration. While the third is "still" because there are no aural images, this poem is "stiller" because its silence—more remarkable in a dramatic scene between two characters—is explicitly stated: his proposal

was "quiet"; she replied only with her "Eyes"; and after her silent assent he
bore her high above this "mortal noise." Similarly, while the third poem's
imagery is of fullness, this poem's imagery is of emptiness, of timelessness and
spacelessness: as he bore her high into empty air, the world of time dropped
away, and they entered an eternal height where there were "No Seasons" and
it was neither "Night, nor Noon."

As well as solving the fourth poem's riddle, poem 3b fills in the gap in F-
40's narrative segment. After one has placed 3b between poems 3 and 4,
there is no longer a disparity between what the meditator recollects and what
the text re-creates. In the second poem's final lines she alludes to both days;
in the third poem she recollects the first day; in poem 3b she recollects the
last day; and in poem 4 she compares the two days and reveals what they
occasioned. While this is hardly surprising, since the gap in the narrative
segment was one of the chief clues leading the reader to deduce the implicit
poem's existence in the first place, it is surprising that when one inserts poem
3b between poems 3 and 4, it fits into the composition of place with astonishing coherence:


The Only News I know
Is Bulletins all Day
From Immortality.

The Only Shows I see—
Tomorrow and Today—
Perchance Eternity—                          [Three—with Eternity—
                                             /And some Eternity—]
The Only One I meet
Is God—The Only Street—
Existence—This traversed                     [traversed/traverst]

If Other News there be—
Or Admirabler Show—
I'll tell it You—                            [I'll Signify—/I'll testify—]

_____

Wert Thou but ill—that I might show thee
How long a Day I could endure
Though thine attention stop not on me
Nor the least signal, Me assure—            [Me/Mine]

Wert Thou but Stranger in ungracious country—
And Mine—the Door
Thou paused at, for a passing bounty—                [passing/doubtful]
No More—

Accused—wert Thou—and Myself—Tribunal—
Convicted—Sentenced—Ermine—not to Me
Half the Condition, thy Reverse—to follow—              [Condition/
Just to partake—the infamy—                              distinction]

The Tenant of the Narrow Cottage, wert Thou—
Permit to be
The Housewife in thy low attendance
Contenteth Me—

No Service hast Thou, I would not achieve it—     [achieve/attempt]
To die—or live—
The first—Sweet, proved I, ere I saw thee—       [proved I/That was]
For Life—be Love—              [be Love/is—Love—/means—Love—]

Midsummer, was it, when They died—
A full, and perfect time—
The Summer closed upon itself
In Consummated Bloom—

The Corn, her furthest kernel filled
Before the coming Flail—
When These—leaned into Perfectness—        [When These Two—
Through Haze of Burial—                       leaned in—Perfectness—]

[It was a quiet way—
He asked if I was His—
I made no answer of the Tongue,
But answer of the Eyes—

And then he bore me high
Before this mortal noise
With swiftness as of Chariots—
And distance—as of Wheels—

The World did drop away
As Counties—from the feet
Of Him that leaneth in Balloon—
Upon an Ether Street—

The Gulf behind—was not—
The Continents—were new—
Eternity—it was—before
Eternity was due—

No Seasons were—to us—
It was not Night—nor Noon—
For Sunrise—stopped upon the Place—
And fastened it—in Dawn.]

---

The first Day that I was a Life
I recollect it—How still—
The last Day that I was a Life
I recollect it—as well—

'Twas stiller—though the first
Was still—
'Twas empty—but the first
Was full—

[That—was my final Occasion—
But then
My tender Experiment
Toward Men—]

This—was my finallest Occasion—
But then
My tenderer Experiment
Toward Men—

"Which choose I"?
That—I cannot say—
"Which choose They"?
Question Memory!

Poem 3b completes the composition of place because without it the meditator would have summoned the faculties of sight and memory to create an image of her mind and left out one of her two most vivid and important memories, the finallest occasion of her life, when she was betrothed to Christ. Poem 3b also completes her letter's introduction by explaining that because they are one, a betrothed pair, her "Only News" is his news, and her poems are intended primarily for him. In addition, poem 3b complements this first cluster's formal, alliterative, verbal, and tropic patterns. Because poem 3b's chief biblical analogue is, as I will show, Rev. 21, the cluster still has an envelope structure, though now the first and fourth poems bracket three, rather than two, poems centering upon biblical texts. Similarly, the cluster still begins with two monologues paired by their assonant *ee*, though now it concludes with three, rather than two, recollections linked by their consonant *L*. Moreover, each poem is still linked to the next by a repeated word or words. The third poem's "leaned" and "was it" are repeated in poem 3b's "leaneth" and "It was." The third poem's "was it" and 3b's "It was" are then repeated in the fourth poem's " 'Twas," and so are the third poem's "full" and 3b's "quiet" repeated in the fourth poem's "full," "still," and "stiller." These three recollections are further linked by their insistence upon the liminality of the occasions, though each expresses this liminality in a different way. In poem 3 "it was Midsummer," her solstice. In the fourth poem, they were the first and last "Daý[s] thăt Í wăs ă Lífe." And in poem 3b it was when the "Sunrise—stopped," echoing the third poem's implicit "solstice": etymologically, when the sun stands still.

Poem 3b also adds significant variations to the cluster's recurring pun on "I" and "eye," to its key word, "Day," and to F-40's recurring metonyms for Christ. In the first poem the meditator declares that "I"/eye "see . . . Eternity" and "meet . . . God"; in the second, that "I"/eye "saw" Christ; in the third, that her eyes/I "died"; and in the fourth, that "I"/eye "recollect." In poem 3b this pun on "I" and "eye" becomes a pun on "eye" and "aye": the meditator responded to Christ's proposal with her "Eyes"/ayes, a silent but resounding "yes," whose result is summed up in the poem's final two lines:

> . . . Sunrise—stopped upon the Place—
> And fastened it—in Dawn.

"Sunrise," another of F-40's several variations of the devotional pun on Jesus as the sun/Son, adds another metonymical title for him, as "Dawn," the break of day, adds another variation to the cluster's key word "Day." But what really takes off the top of one's head is that 3b's "Place" directly alludes to what has now become the poem's context. Now that the reader has inserted the implicit 3b between poems 3 and 4, this nuptial poem is, in effect, in F-40's composition of *place*, in which the meditator creates a mental image of the *place* she intends to contemplate, her mind, or soul; and as 3b explains, it was at their betrothal that Christ as "Sunrise" stopped upon that "*Place*" and became her soul's permanent illuminator (emphasis added).

In the implicit 3b, as in F-40-2 and -3, Emily Dickinson paints the meditator into a biblical scene she creates by conflating several biblical passages. The Jesus she depicts in its first stanza resembles the persistent suitor of Rev. 3.20: "Behold, I stand at the door, and knock: if any man hear my voice, and open the door, I will come in to him." As she re-creates this verse's first sentence in "Just so—Christ—raps" (F-11-12, J-317), so in 3b's first stanza she echoes its second sentence by representing the meditator as having heard his "voice" and replied "yes":

> It was a quiet way—
> He asked if I was His—
> I made no answer of the Tongue,
> But answer of the Eyes—

Immediately after her assent, he became the powerful bridegroom who did "come in" to her in a stunning consummation scene whose chief biblical analogue is John's account in Rev. 21 of how he was borne high and shown the holy city, the New Jerusalem arrayed as a bride for her husband:

> And then he bore me high
> Before this mortal noise
> With swiftness as of Chariots—
> And distance—as of Wheels—

This stanza's first line echoes Revelation's "And he carried me away in the spirit to a . . . high mountain," but beginning with line 2, she departs from Revelation by describing what she left behind as well as the speed and distance of their ascent. Though in this stanza their recollected ascent was as swift and far as though she were being carried in Elijah's chariot, in the following stanza she compares her sensation, as they left the world behind, to the giddy sensation of ascending in a modern balloon:

The World did drop away
As Counties—from the feet
Of Him that leaneth in Balloon—
Upon an Ether Street—

"The World did drop away" echoes Revelation's "the earth . . . passed away," but the following simile—so vivid it almost makes one feel queasy—alludes not only to Revelation but also to F-40's first and third poems. Neatly reversing the third poem's juxtaposition of the standard "leaned" with the biblical "Perfectness," this poem juxtaposes the biblical "leaneth" with the modern "Balloon." From this height, the first poem's "Street" of "Existence" looked like an "Ether Street," as Revelation's "street" was like transparent glass.

After the second and third stanzas' breathtaking ascent, the final two stanzas describe what this new height was like. In the fourth,

The Gulf behind—was not—
The Continents—were new—
Eternity—it was—before
Eternity was due—

This stanza's first two lines echo Rev. 21.1, whose final clause is one of the passages that have been cut out of Emily Dickinson's Bible: "And I saw a new heaven and a new earth; for the first heaven and the first earth were passed away; and there was no more sea." But she reverses the first and third clauses' order and varies Revelation's tropes. "The Gulf behind—was not," the first of the final two stanzas' three litotes, is a variation of "there was no more sea," the first of Rev. 21's recurring litotes. On the day of their betrothal, the two were no longer separated by what she calls elsewhere the "Sea— / Between Eternity and Time" (F-33-15, J-644). "The Continents—were new" is similarly a witty variation of Revelation's "new heaven and new earth," in which one of Dickinson's "Continents" is a synecdoche for "earth," which is in turn a metonym for the finite meditator, while the other continent is a metonym for "sun"—as in *Twelfth Night* the sun is an "orbed Continent" (act 5, scene 1, line 271)—and "sun" is in turn both a synecdoche for Revelation's "heaven" and a metonym for Christ, the sun/Son.

This stanza's concluding sentence, "Eternity—it was—before Eternity was due," like the third poem's "Two" eyes, alludes to F-38-10's description of both days of her conversion as when her "Two . . . Eyes . . . obtained . . .

Eternity . . . in Time." But in poem *3b*'s final stanza she further describes this eternal state:

> No Seasons were—to us—
> It was not Night—nor Noon—
> For Sunrise—stopped upon the Place—
> And fastened it—in Dawn.

This final stanza echoes Rev. 21.25, "there shall be no night" in the holy city, as well as Rev. 21.23, "And the city had no need of the sun, neither of the moon, to shine in it: for the glory of God did lighten it, and the Lamb is the light thereof" (a verse Emily Dickinson re-creates in "The Sun and Moon must make their haste . . . For in the Zones of Paradise / The Lord alone is burned," J-871, also dated 1864). As Revelation's city had no night and no sun or moon, "*for*" God and the Lamb were its lights, so to Dickinson's "us" there were no seasons and no night or noon, "*For* Sunrise—stopped upon the Place— / And fastened it in Dawn" (emphasis added). For Revelation's "city" she thus substitutes "Place," the meditator's soul. And for Revelation's "Lamb" and "light," she substitutes "Sunrise" and "Dawn," thereby echoing Jesus' words in Rev. 22.16, "I am . . . the bright and morning star."

On the day of their betrothal, the meditator's soul became a "Place" occupied by Christ, as in the devotional trope of *anima* as *ecclesia*, *The Temple*'s central trope. On that day her soul attained a new height, a new elevated "Circumference" in which "He" and "I" became "us." The sequential progression of the two days of her conversion is thus from the third poem's death and rebirth to poem *3b*'s union. This sequence of events not only resembles the progress of the soul as described by Thomas à Kempis and others— whereby the soul begins by renouncing the world, then gains illumination, and then attains union with Christ—it also recapitulates the sequence of events depicted in the forty fascicles' first six occasional poems:

> Fascicle 1, dated 1858
>   F-1-1:
>     The Gentian weaves her fringes—
>     The Maple's loom is red—
>     My departing blossoms
>       Obviate parade.

A brief, but patient illness—
An hour to prepare,
And one below, this morning
Is where the angels are—
It was a short procession,
The Bobolink was there—
An aged Bee addressed us—
And then we knelt in prayer—
We trust that she was willing—
We ask that we may be.
Summer—Sister—Seraph!
Let us go with thee!

In the name of the Bee—
And of the Butterfly—
And of the Breeze—Amen!


F-1-9:
As if I asked a common alms,
And in my wondering hand,
A Stranger pressed a kingdom—
And I—bewildered stand—
As if I asked the Orient
Had it for me a Morn?
And it sh'd lift it's purple dikes
And flood me with the Dawn!


Fascicles 8 and 9, dated 1860
F-8-11:
At last, to be identified!
At last, the lamps upon thy side
The rest of Life to *see!*

Past Midnight! Past the Morning Star!
Past Sunrise!
Ah, What leagues there *were*
Between our feet, and Day!

F-8-20, first eight lines:
As if some little Arctic flower
Upon the polar hem—
Went wandering down the Latitudes
Until it puzzled came
To continents of summer—
To firmaments of sun—
To strange, bright crowds of flowers—
And birds, of foreign tongue!

F-9-16, first stanza:
For this—accepted Breath—
Through it—compete with Death—
The fellow cannot touch this Crown—
By it—my title take—
Ah, what a royal sake
To my nescessity—stooped down!

F-9-21:
I'm "wife"—I've finished that—
That other state—
I'm Czar—I'm "Woman" now—
It's safer so—

How odd the Girl's life looks
Behind this soft Eclipse—
I think that Earth feels so
To folks in Heaven—now—

This being comfort—then
That other kind—was pain—
But why compare?
I'm "Wife"! Stop there!

As in the fortieth fascicle's third poem, a pseudo-elegy, the protagonist remembers the day at summer's close when she died to the world and began to compose the fascicles, so in the first fascicle's first poem, also a pseudo-elegy, she *does* vow to die at summer's close—underscoring her vow with a firm "Amen!" so shall it be!—and *does*, in fact, begin to compose the fascicles. Since in F-40-3 she recollects this as the occasion when she leaned into "Perfectness," retrospectively one sees that her apostrophe to summer in F-1-1, "Let us go with thee!" echoes Heb. 6.1, "let us go on unto perfection," glossed in the Oxford Bible as "let us give ourselves over to perfect consecration to God's service." In F-1-9, she then reflects upon her new state: it is as if a "Stranger"—Christ is the "Stranger" not only in F-40-2 and -8 but also in L-243—has given her a kingdom; it is as if she has been flooded with dawn, blinding illumination. In both the first and final fascicles, then, her vision is transformed.

In both the earlier and fortieth fascicles, too, her death and rebirth lead to a second transcendent occasion and an even more elevated state. Though in both F-9-21 and F-40 she portrays this second state with nuptial tropes, the eighth and ninth fascicles' occasional poems show that from the beginning Emily Dickinson enlisted a variety of tropes to signify her protagonist's union with Christ. In the first of these 1860 poems, she is "At last . . . identified"—as her owner "identified" her in "My Life had stood—a Loaded Gun" (F-34-9, J-754)—and for the rest of her life will see the lamps upon "thy side" of what she calls elsewhere the "Vail" separating eternity from time (F-12-9, J-263). In F-8-20, it is as though a "little Arctic flower"—the "little Gentian"/poet that bloomed just before the snows (F-24-15, J-442)—has entered into "firmaments of sun," as in F-40-3b "Sunrise" stopped upon her soul.

In F-9-16 she has been given a crown and title, anticipating the many occasional poems in which she has been made royal, become a "Czar," a "Queen," or an "Empress"—"The Day that I was crowned" (F-29-4, J-356), for example, and "Title divine—is mine!" in which she is both a "Wife" and an "Empress" (J-1072). In F-9-16 she then marvels that such a royal sake has "stooped down" to her, as in "Perhaps you think me stooping" Christ "stooped" (J-833), as in "My Worthiness is all my Doubt" Deity "stoop[s]" (F-37-19, J-751), and as in the *Imitation of Christ* the Disciple repeatedly marvels that Christ has "stooped" down to his unworthy self. In F-9-21 she is not only a "Wife" and a "Czar" but also a "Woman," anticipating "A solemn thing—it was—I said— / A Woman white—to be" (F-14-5, J-271) and "The World—stands—solemner—to me / Since I was wed—to Him," in which she is both "Woman" and "Queen" (J-493). In F-9-21 she then looks back on her "Girl's life," anticipating "I'm ceded—I've stopped being Their's," in which she is baptized, chooses a crown, and is finished with her "childhood" (F-17-7, J-508), as well as "She rose to His Requirement," in which she has "dropt / The Playthings of Her Life / To take the honorable Work / Of Woman, and of Wife" (F-38-12, J-732).

While F-8-11's central trope is of identification, its many resemblances to the betrothal she recollects in F-25-5, then again in F-40-3*b*, confirm the assumption that "At last, to be identified" depicts the event she later recollects. In both poems her transformation is permanent: as in F-40-3*b* sunrise "fastened" her soul in perpetual dawn, so in F-8-11 she will see "the lamps upon thy side" for "The rest of [her] Life." As in the later poem he "bore" her into a realm of timelessness where there were "No Seasons" and "No Night" or "Noon," so in the earlier one she is also past time, "Past Midnight, . . . the Morning Star, [and] Sunrise." As in F-40-3*b* the "Gulf" that had previously separated them has vanished, so in F-8-11 there "*were*" leagues between "our feet, and Day," but now there are not. In both poems she addresses an unidentified other person, and in both her vision is transformed: in F-40-3*b* "He" bore her to a height from which the street of existence looked like an ether street, and here she declares that she now sees, as she had not before, the lamps upon "thy side."

An important difference between the two poems is that F-40-3*b* is a recollection in the past tense, beginning with "It was," whereas F-8-11 is in the present tense: it *is*, "At last, to be identified"; there "*were*" leagues but *now* there are not. The earlier poem's present tense, its two italicized words, and its six exclamation points represent the occasion the protagonist celebrates as having just taken place, an assumption that is strengthened by the poem's variation that appears in F-21, which is nearly identical except that it has no italicized words and only one concluding exclamation point:

> At last—to be identified—
> At last—the Lamps upon your side—
> The rest of life—to see—
>
> Past Midnight—past the Morning Star—
> Past Sunrise—Ah, What Leagues there were—
> Between our feet—and Day!

While this more reflective version, dated 1862, is in the general present, then, the earlier 1860 version is in the immediate present. Her identification is thus represented as having taken place after she had already composed the first seven fascicles, which further explains why in F-40-2 and -4 she recollects that she died and began to compose the fascicles even before she "saw" him, or, as she says in F-8-11, began to "*see*" his eternal lamps.

# THE FORTY FASCICLES AS A SINGLE OEUVRE

Discovering that F-40-2, -3, -3b, and -4 summarize the preceding fascicles' first six occasional poems leads to the discovery that F-40's conversion narrative summarizes many events that have taken place in the preceding fascicles. According to F-40's conversion narrative, after Christ persuaded the meditator to occupy his "House" in poem 6, she renounced the world and began to compose the fascicles. Though in poem 3 she recollects her death to the world as a supremely felicitous occasion when she leaned into "Perfectness," immediately thereafter, as poem 7 reveals, she also began to suffer from the pain of self-denial necessitated by her chosen way of life. Nevertheless, she then experienced a second transcendent day, the union with Christ she recollects in poem 3b. Thereafter, she experienced the many conflicts and sufferings she has in some way resolved or resolves when she utters her meditation: the continuing pain of self-denial (poem 7); the pain of realizing that while she has renounced everything to attain her poetic and spiritual goals, she has no assurance she will attain either (poems 2, 10, and 20); the pain of those dark nights of the soul when she does not feel Christ's presence (poem 15); and the difficulty of maintaining faith (poem 17). Nevertheless, F-40 is an apologia pro vita sua in which she reaffirms the life she has chosen.

Reading the forty fascicles sequentially shows that F-40's conversion narrative is a reprise of events that occurred in the earlier fascicles.[3] Since the forty fascicles begin with the protagonist's vow to die to the world, one retrospectively sees that the dialogue with Jesus she recollects in F-40-6, in which he persuaded her to renounce her old way of life and enter into his "House," his earthly kingdom, is represented as having taken place even before the fascicles begin, very likely during the summer whose passing she commemorates in F-1-1. (He is, after all, present even in the first fascicle, for example, in "On this wondrous sea—Sailing silently," a dialogue between the protagonist and her "Pilot," F-1-20, J-4.) After she died to the world and began to compose the fascicles, she experienced elation, as in F-1-9, "As if I asked a common alms," in which she "stand[s] . . . bewildered" before the stupendous gift she has been given. But though the first seven fascicles are far less turbulent than some of the later ones, she also experienced considerable conflict in these earlier fascicles. In the first fascicle, for example, though she vows to die to the world in its first poem, "The Gentian weaves her fringes," in its fourth poem, "Distrustful of the Gentian," she is just about to "turn away" from her vow when the "fluttering " of the gentian's "fringes / Chid" her "perfidy," a word Dickinson's lexicon defines as the act of violating a vow (J-18; J-20). Though in the first fascicle's fifth poem, she declares, "We lose—because we win," echoing Jesus' words in Matt. 10.39, "he that loseth his life for my sake shall find it," in the same fascicle's final poem she concludes with an apostrophe, "Ah Little Rose—how easy / For such as thee to die!" suggesting that dying to the world is not quite so easy for herself (J-5; J-35).

Similarly, though in the second fascicle's twenty-first poem she reiterates the first fascicle's vow—"I keep my pledge . . . I plight again"—in its twenty-third poem she has a "troubled question" that she flings "on the deep," as Noah dispatched a dove from the ark in the hope that "There may yet be *Land!*" (J-46; J-48). In the third fascicle's sixteenth poem she declares she has never before lost as much, except to the grave, then in a direct address to God as "Burglar! Banker—Father!" laments her present poverty (J-49). In the fourth fascicle's sixth poem a whistler passing beneath her window cheers her heavy heart (J-83); in its seventh poem she cries, "Soul, Wilt thou toss again?" then observes that angels and imps are raffling for her soul (J-139); and in its twelfth poem, the first in which Jesus is specifically named, she tells him, her "Sovereign," that she, too, has not been chosen by those whom she has chosen (J-85). In F-5-25 she observes that "For each ecstatic instant / We must an anguish pay" (J-125); then in F-6-3, that fighting inner battles is far "*gallanter*" than fighting aloud (J-126); and then in F-7-16, that "If pain for peace prepares," she expects " 'Augustan' years" in the future (J-63).

Despite these earlier conflicts, the protagonist experiences the second transcendent day, the union she begins to celebrate in fascicles 8 and 9. Again, she experiences elation, but as she reflects in "I should have been too glad, I see," her new elevated "Circumference" life entails pain as well as joy (F-33-12, J-313). In fascicles 8 through 39 she experiences both. Though she repeatedly celebrates her elevated state, she also suffers from agonizing conflicts. While she does not always reveal the cause of the anguish she describes—as in "I felt a Funeral in my Brain" and " 'Twas like a Maelstrom, with a notch"—in many poems she specifically laments the conflicts she then recollects in F-40. Prominent among these conflicts is the self-denial she recollects in F-40-7. "You're right," she exclaims in F-10-17, " 'the way *is* narrow,' " a response to Jesus' words in Matt. 7.14, "narrow is the way, which leadeth unto life" (J-234). As she discovers, "To put this World down, like a Bundle," as did "the Son of God, . . . Requires Energy—possibly Agony" (F-20-9, J-527). "Renunciation," she reflects, is a virtue, but a "piercing Virtue" (F-37-10, J-745). While her books ease her "Abstinence" (F-24-7, J-

604), she laments the loneliness and rigors of her circumferential life. "It would have starved a Gnat— / To live so small as I," she declares (F-21-5, J-612). In F-22-1 her self-imposed "Prison" has become a friend, though—she adds—at first it was miserable and even now not so sweet (J-652). And she laments the loss of a lover—whether real or longed for—whose face would have put out Jesus' face (F-33-7, J-640).

While she repeatedly assures herself that her deathless poems will "Make Summer" for her readers long after she herself is dead (e.g., F-1-17, J-31; F-34-18, J-675), she does not know if she will ever have readers for her letter to the world that never wrote to her (F-24-14, J-441). And while she repeatedly imagines her entry into heaven (e.g., F-19-17, J-336), she does not yet see how she will be adorned for this "Superior Grace" (F-28-21, J-575). She experiences doubt, as in "I know that He exists," in which she wonders if God might be playing a cruel game and if at death she might therefore be a corpse and nothing more (F-18-4, J-338). She reproaches God for unanswered prayer, as in "I asked no other thing," in which he, a sneering "Merchant," denies her one request (F-32-8, J-621). She also suffers from dark nights of the soul, when she does not feel Jesus' presence even though she is "knocking—everywhere" (e.g., F-18-16, J-502).

Though, as the protagonist observes, her "Sire" has left her with "two Legacies," one of love and the other of pain (F-33-15, J-644), the forty fascicles' overall movement is toward resolution (see note 3). In F-36-2, for example, she imagines her entry into heaven, when she will declare it a "Joy to have merited the Pain" (J-788); then, in an address to "Sir" in F-36-14, she declares, "Where Thou art—that—is Home," whether it be "Cashmere—or Calvary" (J-725). In the same fascicle she twice celebrates the "Liberty" she has acquired as a result of her betrothal, a subject she returns to in F-40: in F-36-6, she declares, "No Prisoner be— / Where Liberty / Himself—abide with Thee," echoing 2 Cor. 3.17, "where the Spirit of the Lord is, there is liberty" (J-720); then in F-36-21, "Let Us play Yesterday," she contrasts her previous girl's life to her present life of freedom, concluding, "God of the Manacle / As of the Free— / Take not my Liberty / Away from Me" (J-728). In F-36's final poem she again addresses "Sir": she will "Alter! [only] When the Hills do" (J-729). In F-37-19 (J-751) she expresses doubts about her own worthiness, as she has done previously (e.g., in F-28-11, J-405, she fears she is "Too scant—by Cubits—to contain / The Sacrament—of Him"): "My Worthiness is all my Doubt," she reflects, and describes herself as the "undivine abode / Of His Elect Content," echoing the series of soul-guest poems in earlier fascicles (e.g., "The Soul that has a

Guest," F-26-4, J-674) and anticipating F-40-3b, where her soul is a place wherein Christ resides.

In F-38-8 the bird/poet rose into the billows of "Circumference," where she is now as at home as she once was on the lowly bough where she was born; then in the same fascicle's thirteenth poem she declares that "this Circumference" feels so vast that she might almost forget the eternal "Circumference" toward which she progresses (J-798; J-802). In F-38's tenth poem she recollects both days of her two-part conversion, the two occasions when she experienced "Eternity in Time," and reflects that this "privilege" is accorded to only a "few" (J-800). Then in its eleventh she observes that she could have committed a "Sin" by becoming "that easy Thing / An independant Man" (J-801)—which she is not, of course, because the second day of her conversion, when "He" and "I" became "us," marked the last day she was a single, solitary "Life" (F-40-3b).

Though some of the thirty-ninth fascicle's poems are melancholy—in its fifth, for example, she experiences a dark night of the soul (J-775), and in its eighth she returns to the subject of loneliness (J-777)—in its third poem she observes that since she has been "Deprived of other Banquet," she has entertained herself, which was at first a "scant nutrition," but has now grown "To so esteemed a size" that " 'Tis sumptuous enough for me" (J-773). In this fascicle's penultimate poem, she reflects that "fading" is enough for her, providing that she "Fades" into "Divinity" (J-682). And in its final poem she reflects that "Happiness" enables one to lift a "Ton," but "Misery" is so incapacitating that it is a struggle to lift even oneself (J-787). Since the forty fascicles show she has lifted a ton—created a work of art that, as she intended, continues to "Make Summer" for readers long after the lady herself lay in "Ceaseless Rosemary" (F-34-18, J-675)—obviously her happiness has exceeded her misery, which is what she declares in F-40.

At the time she utters F-40's meditation, she is so content with her life as Christ's housewife that she challenges him to prove she regrets her choice— the choice she made when she said "yes" on the day of their betrothal, the choice she made when she became a "Woman—white" and dropped her life "Into the mystic well" (F-40-8; F-14-5, J-271). Though in earlier fascicles she lamented her lonely life as poet, in F-40 she celebrates her betrothal even though it has meant the loss of "Our Home," the circuit life she once shared with others (poem 8). There may have been a human lover or lovers in earlier fascicles, but F-40's only lover is Christ, the "Brave Beloved" whom her life and art are intended to glorify (poem 20). In F-40 she does not reproach God, and, in fact, God the Father is conspicuously absent from this final fascicle, which centers upon God the Son. While she still sometimes experiences those dark nights of the soul when Jesus seems to be absent, she acknowledges that even when she does not feel his presence, he is always with her (poems 15 and 19). Nor does she express doubt in F-40. Though in poem 17 she acknowledges that maintaining faith is not always easy, the forty fascicles conclude with five firm declarations of faith.

The narrative thread linking the forty fascicles, then, is the protagonist's account of her poetic and spiritual pilgrimage, an account of her soul's progress from renunciation to illumination to union, and then, after many conflicts, to her contentment with this union. As Thomas à Kempis warns those who follow the way of perfection, some people experience trials at the beginning of their conversions, some toward the end of their course, and others throughout their lives (*Imitation* 41). Reading the forty fascicles sequentially shows that the protagonist experienced some conflict from the beginning, but that her severest trials occur after the union she begins to celebrate in fascicles 8 and 9, and that she does not attain true contentment with their union until F-40.

According to Isaac Walton, Herbert described *The Temple* as "a picture of the many spiritual Conflicts that have passed betwixt God and my Soul, before I could subject mine to the will of Jesus my Master, in whose service I have now found perfect freedom" (Herbert xxxvii). Like Herbert, the forty fascicles' protagonist suffered many conflicts before she attained the boundless freedom she celebrates in F-36-6 and -21 and then again in F-40-5.

# Part II

# The Poems of Analysis:
# Poems 5 Through 16,
# Living the Life of "Circumference"

Having summoned the faculties of sight and memory to create an image of her mind, or soul, the "Place" she intends to contemplate, the meditator next summons the faculty of understanding to contemplate her soul's elevated circumference as Christ's spouse. The parameters of the long section of analysis are signaled by the fifth through eighth poems' "House"-"Home" tropes, which are then echoed in the sixteenth poem's "Door." And while this section is divided into three separate clusters, each with its own key words, its poems are further linked both by their recurring diction of assessment and business—"accounted," "negotiate," "worth," "impute," "Wealth" and "Destitution," "prosperity" and "Reverse," "gain" and "loss," and so forth—and by a common pattern: each cluster's penultimate poem introduces a conflict that is then resolved in its final poem. These twelve poems are linked not only tropically, verbally, and schematically but also by their underlying theme of choice, the meditator's choice to lead what she calls in earlier fascicles the life of "Circumference," rather than the "little Circuit" life. In each of the three clusters she assesses her gains and losses, and though she does not portray her circumferential life as always easy, in each cluster she concludes by reaffirming her chosen way of life.

## POEMS 5 THROUGH 8: THE "HOUSE"-"HOME" CLUSTER

The poems of analysis' theme of choice is introduced in the final stanza of poem 4, which, like the final poem of each of the garland's five clusters, provides the transitional link between its cluster and the next:

> "Which choose I"?
> That—I cannot say—
> "Which choose They"?
> Question Memory!

As the introduction to the poems of analysis' first cluster, whose key words are "House" and "Home," Christ's two questions become, "Which do you choose, the circumferential 'House' or the circuit 'Home'?" then "Which do they—the others—choose?" In this context his two questions are variations of the questions he implicitly asks in this cluster's chief biblical analogue, the parable of the house built upon a rock and the house built upon the sand:

> . . . whosoever heareth these sayings of mine, and doeth them, I will liken him unto a wise man, which built his house upon a rock:
> And the rain descended, and the floods came, and the winds blew, and beat upon that house; and it fell not: for it was founded upon a rock.
> And every one that heareth these sayings of mine, and doeth them not, shall be likened unto a foolish man, which built his house upon the sand:
> And the rain descended, and the floods came, and the winds blew, and beat upon that house; and it fell: and great was the fall of it. (Matt. 7.24–27)

In poems 5 through 8, the meditator directly responds to Jesus' two questions, but for "house upon a rock" she substitutes simply "House," and for "house upon the sand" she substitutes simply "Home," echoing 2 Cor. 5.6, where Paul concludes his discourse on the earthly and heavenly houses by observing that "whilst we are at home in the body," the earthly house, "we are absent from the Lord." In Dickinson's manuscript the fourth poem's transitional final stanza appears on the same page as poem 5. Since her manuscript shows that in some cases she squeezed as many as twenty-two lines on a page (e.g., "Robbed by Death"), while in others she included as few as twelve lines ("Pain—expands the Time"), and since the eighth poem's final transitional stanza also appears on the same page as poem 9, it may be that she wished to draw attention to the transitional role of the fourth poem's final stanza (line counts include stanza breaks and variants; see Appendix B):

> "Which choose I"?
> That—I cannot say—
> "Which choose They"?
> Question Memory!
>
> ———————
>
> A nearness to Tremendousness—
> An Agony procures—
> Affliction ranges Boundlessness—
> Vicinity to Laws
>
> Contentment's quiet Suburb—
> Affliction cannot stay
> In Acres—It's Location    [In Acre—Or Location—]
> Is Illocality—                 [It rents Immensity—]
>
> ———————
>
> "Unto Me"? I do not know you—
> Where may be your House?
>
> "I am Jesus—Late of Judea—
> Now—of Paradise"—
>
> Wagons—have you—to convey me?
> This is far from Thence—
>
> "Arms of Mine—sufficient Phaeton—
> Trust Omnipotence"—

I am spotted—"I am Pardon"—
I am small—"The Least
Is esteemed in Heaven the Chiefest—
Occupy my House"—                                    [House/Breast]

Denial—is the only fact
Perceived by the Denied—
Whose Will—a numb significance—           [Whose Will—a Blank
The Day the Heaven died—                              intelligence]

And all the Earth strove common round—
Without Delight, or Beam—                              [Beam/aim]
What Comfort was it Wisdom—was—
The spoiler of Our Home?

_____

All forgot for recollecting                              [for/through]
Just a paltry One—
All forsook, for just a Stranger's
New Accompanying—

Grace of Wealth, and Grace of Station           [Grace of Rank—
Less accounted than                               and Grace of Fortune]
An unknown Esteem possessing—                [Esteem/content]
Estimate—Who can—

Home effaced—Her faces dwindled—
Nature—altered small—
Sun—if shone—or Storm—if shattered—
Overlooked I all—

Dropped—my fate—a timid Pebble—
In thy bolder Sea—
Prove—me—Sweet—if I regret it—                    [Prove/Ask]
Prove Myself—of Thee—

Although the word "House" actually appears only in poem 6 and the word "Home" only in poems 7 and 8, in each of this cluster's poems the meditator contrasts these two states of being one may choose to "rent" while in the sphere of time. In poem 5, by far the cluster's most elliptical, she contrasts the circumferential house fronting "Boundlessness" with the circuit home in

"Contentment's quiet Suburb." In poem 6 she recollects her debate with Christ, when she, then a circuit dweller, was stubbornly unwilling to re-nounce "This," her circuit home built on sand, to occupy "Thence," his "House" built upon a rock. Then in poem 7 she remembers how she la-mented the loss of her circuit "Home," a loss necessitated by her entry into the house of "Wisdom," both a metonym for Christ, the "wisdom of God" (1 Cor. 1.24), and an allusion to the house upon a rock chosen by the parable's "wise man." Finally, in poem 8 she celebrates their betrothal—which, ac-cording to poem 3b, means her soul has become his place of residence, his house—even though it has meant the effacement of her circuit "Home." As in the parable, her present house upon a rock is impregnable to shattering "Storm."

This cluster's poems, like those of the composition of place, have an envelope structure. In this case two poems concerning her present view of the circumferential "House" vis-à-vis the circuit "Home" bracket two poems concerning the way she once perceived them. In poem 5 she now sees the choice between them as a choice between a safe but limited contentment and a terrifying but limitless freedom. Then in poem 6 (chronologically, the conversion narrative's first poem) she recollects how foolishly unwilling she previously was to give up her safe but limited contentment. Then in poem 7 (the conversion narrative's fourth poem, which chronologically follows the third poem's death and rebirth) she recollects the trauma she experienced immediately after she renounced her circuit home. Finally, in poem 8 she returns to the present to celebrate their betrothal, which has meant the loss of her home but has given her wealth, station, esteem, and, as the variant reveals, a new, inestimably greater "content" than the complacent content-ment of her past circuit home.

In the poems of analysis' first cluster, then, the meditator reaffirms the choice she has made. At the same time, by contrasting the foolish compla-cency of her past circuit self and the placid contentment of the circuit home with the exhilarating freedom, wealth, and esteem of the circumferential house, she presents a strong argument for the latter to the reader she ad-dresses in her letter.

## Poem 5

The fifth poem, which is almost as strange and idiosyncratic as the fourth, is a condensed, witty variation of Jesus' parable of the two houses, though in Emily Dickinson's version the house built upon a rock is a state of freedom, while the home built upon the sand is a state of limitation. Though the words "House" and "Home" do not appear in the poem itself, the reader is asked to deduce them from the poem's diction of real estate and neighbor-hoods and its location in a cluster whose key words are "House" and "Home." And while the meditator describes the circumferential house in some detail, she alludes only briefly to the circuit home, thus asking the reader to deduce her full description from what she says about its opposite:

> A nearness to Tremendousness—
> An Agony procures—
> Affliction ranges Boundlessness—
> Vicinity to Laws
>
> Contentment's quiet Suburb—
> Affliction cannot stay
> In Acres—It's Location
> Is Illocality—

Or, as the variant final three lines read:

> Affliction cannot stay
> In Acre—Or Location—
> It rents Immensity—

The reader's first challenge is to make some sense of the poem's weird syntax. Its first three lines are composed of two clauses, as are its final three lines, and together these six lines form an obscure but coherent poem about "Agony" and "Affliction's" location:

> A nearness to Tremendousness—
> An Agony procures—
> Affliction ranges Boundlessness—
>
> Affliction cannot stay
> In Acres—It's Location
> Is Illocality—
>
> *or*
>
> Affliction cannot stay
> In Acre—Or Location—
> It rents Immensity—

But what, then, is one to do with the fourth and fifth lines' "Vicinity to Laws" and "Contentment's quiet Suburb"? These two phrases appear to have nothing to do with the rest of the poem, except that the former is parallel to "A nearness to Tremendousness," and the latter is parallel to "It's [Affliction's] Location":

> A nearness to Tremendousness
> Vicinity to Laws
>
> Contentment's quiet Suburb
> It's [Affliction's] Location [which is "Illocality"]

Since, according to Dickinson's lexicon—which is of particular import to comprehending this poem—"nearness" is a synonym for "Vicinity," the words are semantically as well as syntactically parallel; but "Tremendousness," a state that excites fear or terror, is the opposite of "Laws," meaning rules. Similarly, "Contentment's quiet Suburb" is syntactically parallel to "[Affliction's] Location" in "Illocality," but "Contentment's" and "Affliction's" are antonyms, as are "Suburb," a place near a city, and "Illocality," no certain place.

These lines' parallelism and synonymous and opposing words lead one to see that poem 5 is, in effect, composed of two parallel poems, one explicit and the other implicit. The "Agony"-"Affliction" poem, which I call 5a, describes the circumferential house built on a rock, while the fourth and fifth lines' phrases are the first and final lines of an implicit poem, which I call 5b, that describes the circuit home built on the sand:

A nearness to Tremendousness—        Vicinity to Laws
An Agony procures—
Affliction ranges Boundlessness—

Affliction cannot stay
In Acres—It's [Affliction's] Location    . . . Contentment's [Location
Is Illocality                            is a] quiet Suburb

          or

Affliction cannot stay
In Acre—Or Location—
It rents Immensity—

It is as though Matthew had omitted the center lines of Jesus' description of the house built on sand and asked the reader to deduce them from his description of the house built on a rock:

>              . . . whosoever heareth these          [he] that heareth these
>          sayings of mine, and doeth            sayings of mine, and doeth
>          them, I will liken him unto a         them not,
>          wise man, which built his house
>          upon a rock:
>              And the rain descended, and
>          the floods came, and the winds
>          blew, and beat upon that house;
>          and it fell not: for it was           and great was the fall of it.
>          founded upon a rock.

From the existing lines' parallelism, synonyms, and antonyms one can deduce at least the essence of the parable's missing lines: he that heareth and doeth not is like an unwise, or foolish, man who built his house, not upon a rock, but upon an opposing substance like Matthew's sand or Luke's "earth" (Luke 6.47–49); when the rains descended, and the floods rose, and the winds blew, and beat upon the house, it fell because it was not founded upon a rock.

Although one can similarly deduce at least the essence of the implicit 5b's intermediary lines from its first and final lines' relation to those of the explicit 5a, one must first come to some understanding of the explicit poem:

>          A nearness to Tremendousness—
>          An Agony procures—
>          Affliction ranges Boundlessness—
>
>          Affliction cannot stay
>          In Acres—It's Location
>          Is Illocality—
>
>                          or
>
>          Affliction cannot stay
>          In Acre—Or Location—
>          It rents Immensity—

One of the explicit poem's most perplexing riddles is its conceptually deviant sentences—that is, its verbs require concrete nouns, but most of its nouns are abstract.[1] In the context of the poem's diction of real estate and neighborhoods—most obviously the implicit poem's "Vicinity" and "Suburb," but also the explicit poem's "Acres," "Location," and "nearness," a synonym for "Vicinity"—"procures" signifies "obtains by purchase," as to "procure titles to estate by purchase," to give an example from Emily Dickinson's lexicon; "ranges" signifies "fronts" (stands in the direction of), as "the front of a house ranges with the line of the street," again Webster's example; "stay" signifies "dwell"; and "rents" signifies "leases." On the other hand, five of the explicit poem's nouns signify abstract states of being. "Tremendousness"—etymologically, that which causes one to tremble"— denotes a state that excites fear or terror. "Agony" and "Affliction" are near-synonyms, the former a state of being in pain or of violent striving and the latter a state of being in pain or of being harassed. Similarly, "Boundlessness" and "Immensity" are near-synonyms, the former a state of limitlessness and the latter, unlimited extension or infinity.

This juxtaposition of verbs that require concrete nouns with nouns that are abstract leads one to see that "Affliction" and its near-synonym "Agony" are metalepses—that is, they are metonymical substitutions for a word that is itself figurative. The poem's diction of real estate, its location in the "House"-"Home" cluster, and its echoes of Christ's house parable show that "Agony" and "Affliction" are metonymical substitutions for "House." The place whose location the meditator describes as near "Tremendousness" and fronting "Boundlessness" is a "[House of] Agony," a "[House of] Affliction." As a place of residence, "House," in turn, is a variation of the implicit 3b's "Place," her soul, which on the day of her betrothal became Christ's place of residence. And since both "Agony" and "Affliction" are metonyms for him, the man of sorrows who suffered both, "[House of] Agony" and "Affliction," in turn, signifies "the soul/house where Christ resides," another variation of the biblical and devotional trope of anima as ecclesia (see, e.g., "habitation of God," Eph. 2.22, and "temple of God," 1 Cor. 3.16).

Thus, in the first stanza the meditator declares that "An Agony"—that is, a soul/house where Christ resides—procures a place near "Tremendousness," that which causes one to tremble in fear and terror. As she then explains, one trembles because "Affliction"—the soul/house where Christ resides—fronts "Boundlessness," a state of unlimitedness. The agony and affliction of the Christian soul, then, is the pain resulting from a terrifying freedom. As Paul wrote to the Corinthians, "where the Spirit of the Lord is, there is liberty" (2 Cor. 3.17), the verse the protagonist echoes in F-36-6: "No Prisoner be— / Where *Liberty* / Himself—abide with Thee" (J-720). In the second stanza she further describes the location of the circumferential house. "Affliction"—the soul/house where Christ resides— "cannot stay / In Acres" because "It's Location / Is Illocality." Both "Acres" and the neologism "Illocality," meaning "no certain place," are allusions to poem *3b*'s betrothal, when Christ bore her high into empty air and the world dropped away like "Counties"—like "Acres" in the poem's second version—from the feet of a balloonist. Since "Illocality" means "no certain place," it also echoes Heb. 13.14, whose faithful have "no continuing city, but . . . seek one to come." The place where Christ bore her and where she now resides, then, is the "no . . . city" of the faithful. As the variant stanza reads, "Affliction"—the soul/house where Christ resides—"cannot stay / In Acre—Or Location [because] It rents Immensity"—unlimited extension, or infinity.

Like "Agony" and "Affliction," "Tremendousness," "Boundlessness," and "Immensity" are metonyms for Christ. The poem's conceit is that when one's soul is Christ's habitation, one's location, or neighborhood, is also Christ— in other words, when one rents a house, one rents a location. As "Agony" and "Affliction," he is the man of sorrows in whose infamy the meditator chose to partake when he paused at her soul's "Door"—that is, when she said "yes" on the day of their betrothal (F-40-2 and -3b). As "Tremendousness"— etymologically, that which causes one to "tremble"—he is the numinous God-man before whom even the devils "tremble" (James 2.19). A soul near Christ/"Tremendousness" is in the position of Paul, who, after his conversion on the road to Damascus, asked—"trembling"—"Lord, what wilt thou have me to do?" (Acts 9.6, the passage she alludes to more specifically in the following poem's debate with Jesus). Such a soul is in the position of the Philippians to whom Paul wrote, "work out your own salvation with fear and trembling [because] it is God which worketh in you" (2.12–13). The soul/ house where Christ resides fronts "Boundlessness," the limitlessness of Christ, who as the "word of God is not bound" (2 Tim. 2.9). Such a soul rents "Immensity"—unlimited extension, or infinity—a fifth metonym for Christ, who throughout F-40 is representative of the infinite sphere, as the meditator is representative of the finite sphere.

The awesome limitlessness of the circumferential soul described in these powerful and elliptical lines is the "glorious liberty of the children of God" (Rom. 8.21): what Herbert called the "perfect freedom" of submitting one's will to Jesus as Master; what Northrop Frye, citing John Milton, for whom the Bible was a "manifesto of human freedom," called the "liberty [that] is the chief thing that the gospel has to bring" (*Great Code* 232). The circumferential soul, then, is the saved soul, the soul who is not guilty of original sin as defined by Frye and others: the human fear of freedom and the human resentment of the discipline and responsibility that freedom brings (*Great Code* 232). As the meditator declares in F-40-20, she has been "Robbed by Liberty"—not *of* liberty, but *by* liberty. The liberty she has gained as a Christian has robbed her of the placid contentment of the circuit life described in the implicit poem 5b.

Judging from the principles of parallelism, synonyms, and antonyms established by "A nearness to Tremendousness"/"Vicinity to Laws" and "Contentment's quiet Suburb"/"[Affliction's] . . . Illocality," the implicit poem's broad outlines are as follows:

| | |
|---|---|
| A nearness to Tremendousness— | Vicinity to Laws |
| An Agony procures [because] | [X procures (because) |
| Affliction ranges Boundlessness— | X ranges Y— |
| | |
| Affliction cannot stay | X can stay |
| In Acres [because] It's | In Acres (because It's)] |
| [Affliction's] Location | Contentment's [Location |
| Is Illocality— | Is a] quiet Suburb— |
| | |
| *or* | *or* |
| Affliction cannot stay | [X can stay |
| In Acre—Or Location [because] | In Acre—Or Location (because) |
| It rents Immensity— | It rents Z—] |

Since the referent for the implicit poem's "Contentment's" is X, then X must be "Contentment," which makes sense because "Contentment" and "Agony"/"Affliction" are antonyms. And since, according to Dickinson's lexicon, "Contentment" literally means a state of being "held within limits," it is also an antonym for both "Boundlessness" (limitlessness) and "Immensity" (unlimited extension), which means that Y and Z must also be "Contentment":

| | |
|---|---|
| A nearness to Tremendousness— | Vicinity to Laws— |
| An Agony procures [because] | [A Contentment procures (because) |
| Affliction ranges Boundlessness— | Contentment ranges Contentment— |

| Affliction cannot stay | Contentment can stay |
|---|---|
| In Acres [because] It's | In Acres (because It's)] |
| [Affliction's] Location | Contentment's [Location |
| Is Illocality— | Is a] quiet Suburb— |

or                             or

| Affliction cannot stay | [Contentment can stay |
|---|---|
| In Acre—Or Location [because] | In Acre—Or Location (because) |
| It rents Immensity— | It rents Contentment] |

While 5*a*'s description of the circumferential life works as a poem, 5*b*'s description of the circuit life, with its seven monotonously repeated "Contentment[s]," definitely does not. But this is apparently the point: neither, according to the meditator, does the circuit life work. Still, when read together, the explicit 5*a* and the implicit 5*b* illuminate each other by showing that choosing Christ is the opposite of choosing contentment. While choosing Christ means choosing a terrifying, limitless freedom, choosing the opposite means electing a safe, limited life of bondage, the life of original sin as defined by Frye. In the fifth poem, then, the meditator describes not only the saved circumferential soul but also the unsaved circuit soul who rejects freedom, the chief thing the gospel has to bring, according to Paul, Herbert, Milton, and Frye—and also according to Dickinson.

Retrospectively one sees that the juxtaposition of the implicit poem's first and final lines, those that actually appear in the text as lines 4 and 5, with the explicit poem's first and final lines, summarizes what the poem is about. When the two first lines are read together, "Tremendousness" and "Laws" are opposed to one another:

A nearness to Tremendousness        Vicinity to Laws

In the context of their parallel phrases and their synonymous first nouns, "Tremendousness" and "Laws" become antonyms. If "Tremendousness" signifies Christ, then "Laws" signifies the absence of Christ; and if "Laws" signifies rules, then Christ signifies the absence of rules. Similarly, when the explicit and implicit poems' final lines are read together, the verbal opposition between "Suburb," a place near a city, and "Illocality," no certain place, sums up and further illuminates the differences between the two locations:

| . . . [Affliction's] Location | . . . Contentment's [Location |
|---|---|
| Is Illocality— | Is a] quiet Suburb |

As previously noted, "Illocality" alludes to the height to which Christ bore her on the day of their betrothal and apparently also to Heb. 13.14, where the faithful have "no continuing city" and seek one to come. But since Dickinson's lexicon defines "Suburb" as a place outside the walls of a city, then "Illocality" is not only Hebrews' "no . . . city" but also, paradoxically, a place within the walls of a city. "Illocality," then, is a metonym for the city of God: in Ps. 46.4 "the holy place of the tabernacles of the most High," and in Dickinson the no place of the souls/houses whose occupant is Christ. When he bore the meditator high into empty air, then, the height she attained was both Hebrews' "no . . . city" of the faithful and the city of God, which became thereafter her soul's "Location" of limitless freedom, the "Liberty" she celebrated in F-36-6 and -21 and will again in F-40-20.

Long before Franklin reassembled the fascicles, Robert Weisbuch rather tentatively proposed several possible interpretations for this obscure, fascinating poem, among them that Emily Dickinson might be justifying her "poetic peculiarities" (*Dickinson's Poetry* 154–55). Reading the poem in the context of its fascicle and its biblical analogues shows that it does, in fact, explain her poetic peculiarities—at least those of the meditator, the fictive author of the forty fascicles—though the explanation she gives is not one that most readers would have expected. Like Milton, she attributes her poetic freedom to her liberty as a Christian, and everything about this strange and wonderful poem demonstrates her poetic freedom from "Laws": her daring treatment of the parable, the weird incantatory impact of the poem's sounds and rhythms, the taut condensation of its conceptually deviant sentences, and most of all the complex riddle of its constituent word game, which invites the reader to reconstruct the implicit poem concealed within.

## Poem 5b as the "House"-"Home" cluster's omitted center

As the implicit poem 3b and the implicit stanza 2b are essential to the reader's comprehension of poem 4 and therefore of the composition of place, so the implicit poem 5b is essential to the reader's comprehension of the fifth poem and therefore of the "House"-"Home" cluster:

"Which choose I"?
That—I cannot say—
"Which choose They"?
Question Memory!

———————————

A nearness to Tremendousness—        Vicinity to Laws—
An Agony procures—                   [A Contentment procures—
Affliction ranges Boundlessness—     Contentment ranges Contentment—

Affliction cannot stay               Contentment can stay
In Acres—It's Location               In Acres—] Contentment's [Location
Is Illocality—                       Is a] quiet Suburb—

        *or*                                          *or*

Affliction cannot stay               [Contentment can stay
In Acre—Or Location—                 In Acre—Or Location—
It rents Immensity—                  It rents Contentment—]

———————————

"Unto Me"? I do not know you—
Where may be your House?

"I am Jesus—Late of Judea—
Now—of Paradise"—

Wagons—have you—to convey me?
This is far from Thence—

"Arms of Mine—sufficient Phaeton—
Trust Omnipotence"—

I am spotted—"I am Pardon"—
I am small—"The Least
Is esteemed in Heaven the Chiefest—
Occupy my House"—                                    [House/Breast]

Denial—is the only fact
Perceived by the Denied—
Whose Will—a numb significance—    [Whose Will—a Blank
The Day the Heaven died—            intelligence]

And all the Earth strove common round—
Without Delight, or Beam—         [Beam/aim]
What Comfort was it Wisdom—was—
The spoiler of Our Home?

---

All forgot for recollecting         [for/through]
Just a paltry One—
All forsook, for just a Stranger's
New Accompanying—

Grace of Wealth, and Grace of Station    [Grace of Rank—
Less accounted than         and Grace of Fortune]
An unknown Esteem possessing—    [Esteem/content]
Estimate—Who can—

Home effaced—Her faces dwindled—
Nature—altered small—
Sun—if shone—or Storm—if shattered—
Overlooked I all—

Dropped—my fate—a timid Pebble—
In thy bolder Sea—
Prove—me—Sweet—if I regret it—    [Prove/Ask]
Prove Myself—of Thee—

Unless the reader reconstructs poem 5b, Jesus' second question in the final lines of poem 4, "Which choose They?" would remain unanswered. The fifth poem would remain an enigma, a series of four clauses forming an independent but opaque poem interrupted by two seemingly unrelated phrases. Moreover, poems 6, 7, and 8 directly allude to 5b as well as to 5a. When in the sixth poem's debate the protagonist declares, "This is far from Thence," the referent for "This" place is 5b's circuit home in contentment's quiet suburb, as the referent for "Thence," that place, is 5a's circumferential house fronting boundlessness. The seventh poem's "spoile[d] . . . Home" similarly alludes to 5b, as does the eighth poem's "effaced . . . Home" and its variant "content." Though in poem *5b* the circuit home is a place of "Content-ment," in poem 8 the meditator has found a new and far superior "content." As in poem 2, her life as Christ's "Housewife" is now what "Contenteth" her.

## Poems 6, 7, and 8

After the complexity of poems 4 and 5, poem 6 is a model of clarity. Whether read within or without its fascicle context, this poem is a debate between the speaker and Jesus in which he has the final word, leaving her not one trochee to respond (see F-40-6 on page 106). In sharp contrast to the fifth poem's brilliance and the sixth poem's clarity and precision, the sev-enth poem shows that Dickinson, like Herbert, did not mind including an inferior poem when it served her narrative purpose (Stewart, *Herbert* 84). This poem's awkward diction and syntax represent the meditator as still shaken by remembering the trauma that followed the third poem's recol-lected death and rebirth. Poem 7's first long, rambling sentence is a series of loosely connected clauses beginning in the general present and shifting midsentence to the meditator's own recollected past:

> Denial—is the only fact [that is]
> Perceived by the Denied [person]
> Whose Will [was] a numb significance—    [Whose Will (was) a Blank
> [On] The Day the Heaven died—                              intelligence]
>
> And all the Earth strove common round—
> Without Delight, or Beam[.]                                    [Beam/aim]

The second sentence's repeated *w*s and *z*s are similarly ungainly as the meditator asks,

> What Comfort was it Wisdom—was [since Wisdom was]
> The spoiler of Our Home?

The "Earth" that "strove common round / Without Delight, or Beam" echoes the parable's flimsy house built on the "earth" in Luke's version. When she renounced the "Heaven" of her circuit home, her soul was sud-denly without a "Beam," its chief timber. Christ's house of wisdom was of no comfort because he himself was the "spoiler of Our Home," echoing his parable of the householder, whose home was "broken up" by a thief (Matt. 24.43), as well as his comparison of himself to a robber who "spoils" one's house by bringing the kingdom of God (Matt. 12.28–29). Very likely "spoiler of Our Home" also alludes to Heb. 10.32–35, where Paul, in concluding his exhortation to the faithful to remain firm, urges them to remember their zeal as it was immediately following their conversions, when they took joyfully the "spoiling" of their goods.[2] While the meditator does as Paul advises, what she recalls is the pain of having her circuit home destroyed, the pain of the self-denial required of all those who choose to dwell in Christ's earthly kingdom.

Though poem 7 represents the meditator as still shaken by remembering all she has renounced, in poem 8 she returns to the present to celebrate what her life has become:

All forgot for recollecting     [for/through]
Just a paltry One—
All forsook, for just a Stranger's
New Accompanying—

Grace of Wealth, and Grace of Station  [Grace of Rank—
Less accounted than      and Grace of Fortune]
An unknown Esteem possessing—   [Esteem/content]
Estimate—Who can—

Home effaced—Her faces dwindled—
Nature—altered small—
Sun—if shone—or Storm—if shattered—
Overlooked I all—

Dropped—my fate—a timid Pebble—
In thy bolder Sea—
Prove—me—Sweet—if I regret it—   [Prove/Ask]
Prove Myself—of Thee—

The "paltry"—that is, the ragged—"One" for whom she has forgotten and forsaken all is Jesus, who, "though he was rich, . . . became poor, that ye through his poverty might be rich" (2 Cor. 8.9). As "forgot" echoes the psalmist, who urges the bride to "forget" her own people and her father's house because the bridegroom is now her Lord (Ps. 45.10–11), so "forsook" alludes not only to Jesus' disciples, who "forsook all" to follow—accompany—him (e.g., Luke 5.11), but also to the marriage vows' "forsaking all others, cleave ye only unto him." Since "to accompany" means not only "to walk with"—as in "Forever at His side to walk" (F-11-13, J-246)—but also "to perform the accompanying part in a musical performance," and since in F-40 Emily Dickinson conflates the meditator's poetic and spiritual life, "paltry One" also signifies her one poetic talent, thus foreshadowing the following cluster, in which her "Flowers"/poems become a central subject.

Because she has renounced all for Christ, who became poor so that his followers might become rich, she *has* become rich. She has acquired both wealth and station, but neither can compare to the inestimable esteem and content she has gained. Since their betrothal she has "Overlooked" all; that is, she has viewed all—including her now "effaced" circuit "Home"—from the circumferential height to which he bore her in the implicit poem *3b*. As in the parable of the two houses, her house upon a rock has become impervious to floods and storms, and as she concludes, she has no regrets. With the image of her fate as a "timid Pebble," she doubly contrasts herself to him, the "bolder Sea." On one level she is "timid," the fifth poem's trembler before his "Tremendousness," and he is "bolder," the twentieth poem's "Brave Beloved" (the variant is "bold Beloved"). But on another level "bolder" is a verbal play on "boulder," as opposed to "Pebble." As in 1 Pet. 2.5–6, she is one of the little "stones" that build up the "spiritual house," while he is the "boulder," the house's "chief corner stone." Although in poem 7 her home built on earth lost its "Beam," its principal timber, here Christ has become the chief "corner stone" of her house built upon a rock.

By contrasting the circumferential life with the circuit life, the meditator begins her assessment of the gains and losses her choice of the former has entailed, and in the process of doing so makes a strong case to the readers of her letter for choosing the circumferential "House." (As she has earlier observed, "The Province of the Saved / Should be the Art— / To save," F-30-8, J-539.) According to her, such a choice means losing the placid contentment and conviviality of the circuit life. It means one can no longer depend upon laws imposed from without, but must rely instead upon self-discipline and self-denial, thus working out one's own course with fear and trembling. Still, she portrays her past life with no little contempt. Before Jesus persuaded her to occupy his house, she was a foolish child, a state she condescendingly recollects in "Let Us play Yesterday" as her girl's life, her "Egg-life" (F-36-21, J-728). By contrast, choosing the circumferential life means gaining maturity, spiritual wealth, self-esteem, a superior kind of contentment, and, most important, liberty, which in her case means poetic liberty as well. As she reveals in the following cluster, her freedom led to the considerable success of her poetic business.


# POEMS 9 THROUGH 11:
# "FLOWERS"/POEMS AND THE PROBLEM OF "NEED"


In this cluster, the meditator focuses upon her need for the absent bridegroom and his brethren, the readers she longs for, and upon his need for her, a poet who, like the psalmist of Psalm 30, sings his praise and tells his truth. As Diagram 2 shows, this center cluster is multiply foregrounded. Its second poem (F-40-10) is the last of the conversion narrative's recollections of events that took place before her meditation begins. One of its two key words, "Flowers," draws attention to its role as the garland's center cluster of "Flowers"/poems. This cluster's meditational focus, the mutual need of the meditator and her bridegroom for each other, is an apt center for the meditation's two-part division according to the spheres of time and eternity because it suggests that the mutual need between Christ and humans links the two spheres. As Diagram 2 also shows, in this center triad she restates and expands upon the poetic purpose she has declared in poems 1 and 2.

As the transitional fourth poem's final stanza appears on the same page as poem 5 in Dickinson's manuscript, so the transitional eighth poem's final stanza appears on the same page as poem 9:


> Dropped—my fate—a timid Pebble—
> In thy bolder Sea—
> Prove—me—Sweet—if I regret it—          [Prove/Ask]
> Prove Myself—of Thee—

    ————————


> I hide myself—within my flower,
> That fading from your Vase—
> You—unsuspecting—feel for me—
> Almost—a loneliness—

    ————————

Had I not This, or This, I said,
Appealing to Myself,
In moment of prosperity—
Inadequate—were Life—

"Thou hast not Me, nor Me"—it said,
In Moment of Reverse—
"And yet Thou art industrious—
No need—hadst Thou—of us"?

My need—was all I had—I said—
The need did not reduce—
Because the food—exterminate—
The hunger—does not cease—

But diligence—is sharper—
Proportioned to the Chance—
To feed upon the Retrograde—
Enfeebles—the Advance—

---

Between My Country—and the Others—
There is a Sea—
But Flowers—negotiate between us—
As Ministry.

As F-40's first and second poems are linked by their recurring *ee* rhyme
and assonance, so the *ee* rhyme and assonance introduced in the eighth
poem's final stanza and extending throughout poems 9, 10, and 11 draw
attention to the continuity between the eighth poem's final stanza and
poems 9 through 11. The meditator's tone of affectionate intimacy, begun in
the eighth poem's final two lines, similarly extends into poem 9 as she
continues to address the bridegroom, but as "You" rather than "Thee," a
reversal of poems 1 and 2, in which she first addresses "You," then "Thee."
Because in this center cluster she focuses upon her flowers/poems, which are
intended to serve the reader as a means of serving Christ, the ninth poem's
"You," like the tenth poem's "Me" and "Me" and the second poem's "Thee,"
signifies both him and the reader, as in the sheep-and-goats parable "I" and
"me" signify both Jesus and his brethren.

Outside its fascicle context, poem 9 is customarily read as one of the little
notes the poet sometimes sent with a gift of flowers to a friend:

I hide myself—within my flower,
That fading from your Vase—
You—unsuspecting—feel for me—
Almost—a loneliness—

When read in this way, she hides herself within her flower so that as her flower fades from the recipient's "Vase," he or she will feel lonely for its sender. This reading fails to explain why "Vase" is foregrounded as the quatrain's only capitalized word, but when "flower" is read as a trope for poem, as it often is in Dickinson (e.g., "My nosegays are for Captives," F-3-8, J-95, and "This is a Blossom of the Brain . . . the Flower of the Soul," J-945), the capitalized "Vase" is explained because then the word's signification changes. In this context, "Vase," literally "vessel," becomes a metonym for "Service," meaning that the meditator, like Paul, considers herself to be Christ's "chosen vessel" whose poems, as in poem 2, are dedicated to his "Service" (Acts 9.15). Reading "flower" as a trope for poem also changes the sentence's syntax. Since flowers and poets fade or die but poems do not, "fading" modifies "myself": within her poems, she hides herself so that as she, being mortal, fades from his poetic service, he and her readers will feel a loneliness for her. Like the psalmist of Psalm 30, whose "prosperity" and reversal are echoed in poem 10, the meditator is reminding him of her mortality and of his need for her to sing his praise and declare his truth to the reader, her poetic purpose according to poems 1 and 2.

While in the ninth poem she hopes her poems will engender a need for herself in him and her readers, in the tenth she recollects a past time when he reminded her of her need for him and them:

Had I not This, or This, I said,
Appealing to Myself,
In moment of prosperity—
Inadequate—were Life—

"Thou hast not Me, nor Me"—it said,
In Moment of Reverse—
"And yet Thou art industrious—
No need—hadst Thou—of us"?

My need—was all I had—I said—
The need did not reduce—
Because the food—exterminate—
The hunger—does not cease—

> But diligence—is sharper—
> Proportioned to the Chance—
> To feed upon the Retrograde—
> Enfeebles—the Advance—

This recollected scene took place at some time after their betrothal when her poetic business had begun to flourish and when in the "moment"—the powerful forward rush—of her poetic prosperity she congratulated herself on her success. At that time, she recalls, "I said . . . Had I not This, or This . . . Life" would be "Inadequate." If one read this poem outside its fascicle context, one could only wonder what the referents for "This" and "This" are. But within the context of its cluster, where it is bracketed by two flower quatrains, the referent for both is the preceding poem's "flower," which is repeated in the eleventh poem's "Flowers." At that time, then, she was looking through her flowers/poems—counting her riches, the eighth poem's "Wealth"—and reflecting that if she did not have "This" poem or "This" poem, her life would not be complete.

But then in a "Moment," an instant, of reverse, her smug self-satisfaction was shattered when "it"—her inner voice, Christ—"said, . . . 'Thou hast not Me [himself], nor Me [his brother, her reader,] . . . And yet Thou art industrious[.] No need—hadst Thou of us'?" It is, of course, true that she does not yet have him, because their union will be complete only in eternity. Nor can she be certain she will ever have him, because that depends on him, the bridegroom with whom she has cast her fate; and his verdict, as in the sheep-and-goats parable and poem 20, is suspended until Judgment Day. It is similarly true that as an unpublished poet she neither has readers for her "Experiment" nor can be certain she will ever have them. "And yet," Christ continued at the time she recollects, "[even though you do not have us,] Thou art industrious," echoing the parable of the talents, whose lord praises the industrious servants who have multiplied their talents. He then asked, "No need—*hadst* Thou of us?" (emphasis added); that is, did she not then—before their recollected dialogue took place—have a "need for us?" Since the poem and its cluster center upon her poetry, his question was, did you not have a need for us to become industrious in the first place? That is, did you not have a need for us when you began your poetic "Experiment"?

In the concluding two stanzas she recollects how she then replied to his question:

My need—was all I had—I said—
The need did not reduce—
Because the food—exterminate—
The hunger—does not cease—

But diligence—is sharper—
Proportioned to the Chance—
To feed upon the Retrograde—
Enfeebles—the Advance—

First she acknowledged that all she had when she began to compose the fascicles, her "Experiment Toward Men," was her need for the men toward whom her experiment was directed, the Gospels' Son of Man—Dickinson's "Emperor of Men" (F-26-4, J-674), the "Man that knew the News" (J-1492)—and his brethren, her readers. And her need for them had not reduced at the time of their dialogue. As she then explained, while her poetry is food for her spirit, her hunger for the bridegroom and for readers "does not cease," a verb phrase whose final spondee causes each of its words to be accented. But then in the final stanza her spirits rallied. Though she did not resume the first stanza's self-satisfaction, she assured him that her "diligence"—the industriousness he admired in stanza 2—is more acute proportioned to the chance that she will one day have both him and readers. As she concluded, she will not think about the "Retrograde," the reverse fact that she does not now have Christ or readers and may never have, because such thoughts would be detrimental to the "Advance" of her poetic/spiritual business. At the time of their recollected dialogue, then, she assured him of her intention to persevere in her goals even though the outcome was uncertain and still is in F-40's fictive present (see Herbert's "Perseverance"). If she never attains either, she will at least have "had / The transport of the Aim" (J-1109, dated 1867).

Christ's recollected reminder introduces this cluster's problem. Moreover, since poem 10 is bracketed and thus foregrounded by the two flower quatrains, and since, as Diagram 2 shows, this center cluster is itself multiply foregrounded, poem 10 introduces the whole fascicle's central problem: though the meditator has "forsook . . . All" to pursue her poetic and spiritual goals, she has no assurance she will attain either. Nevertheless, as poem 10 shows, she continued to persevere in her poetic vocation, and in the eleventh poem, which in Dickinson's manuscript is written on the same page as the tenth poem's final stanza, she firmly restates her poetic intentions:

> Between My Country—and the Others—
> There is a Sea—
> But Flowers—negotiate between us—
> As Ministry.

While bride and bridegroom are separated by the "Sea Between Eternity and Time," and while poet and reader are separated by the "Sea" between one "Consciousness" and another as well as by time and place (F-33-15, J-644), the "Ministry" of her "Flowers"/poems is to "negotiate between us," between him, the sacred Muse, and her, the poet who tells his "News" to the reader. The eleventh poem's alternating catalectic pentameters and dimeters, a departure from the preceding two poems' tetrameters and trimeters, underscore the distance between Christ, herself, and her readers, and her negotiating poems' shortening of this distance.

## THE MEDITATION'S TWO-PART DIVISION

The eleventh poem's period, one of F-40's three strategically placed periods, signals a decided shift in the meditator's focus. While her subject throughout F-40 is her circumferential life and her relationship to Christ, in the poems before the eleventh poem's period, where the first-person-singular pronoun appears in every poem but three, she has focused primarily upon herself and her own past and present life in the sphere of time. Though she has not mentioned her quotidian life (as in earlier fascicles she sometimes alludes to her friend Sue, her sister, her father, unnamed beloved persons, the Amherst hills, the Village, her garden, and so on), she has revealed a great deal about her ars poetica. Poems 1 through 11 begin and end with her declaration of her poetic purpose. Between these two declarations she has revealed that she died to the world—became "Nobody" (F-11-7, J-288)—in order to multiply her one poetic talent by composing the fascicles. She has revealed that she has attained gratifying success in her poetic business and that she longs to have readers for her "Experiment Toward Men." By attributing her poetic freedom to her freedom as a Christian, she has explained her poetic idiosyncracies—and she has done so in one of her most idiosyncratic poems, "A nearness to Tremendousness."

As she has also revealed in the meditation's first half, her progress from the circuit life to the life of circumference that now "Contenteth" her has not been an easy one. She has suffered from the self-denial and renunciation necessitated by her chosen way of life and from not knowing if all her renunciation and labors will result in the poetic and personal immortality she longs for. Still, she has persevered in her poetic and spiritual vocation. In poems 1 through 11 she has posited that one may choose to live the safe, limited circuit life of contentment, or one may choose to live the circumferential life of self-denial, renunciation, and boundless freedom. Having chosen the latter, she reaffirms her choice.

In the meditation's second half—where she uses the first-person-singular pronoun in only three poems and there are no flashbacks, only flashforwards—she centers upon the present and future impact of Christ and the eternal sphere upon herself as one of "Us" who have faith. While she alludes to her poetry, she does not again refer to her need for readers, only to her need, as one of the faithful, for Christ. In poems 12 to 21 she imagines her death, her entry into eternity, and her defense of her life on Judgment Day. She explains why "We," the faithful, possess "Compound Vision," imitate Christ, and believe in his promises. Though she laments those dark nights of the soul when she does not feel his presence, she declares her belief in Jesus' promise to be with his followers until the end of time and "Our" belief in his promise of the immortality of the soul.

Together the meditation's two halves portray the meditator as both a unique poet-pilgrim and a representative of the faithful. As poems 12 through 21 reveal, the faithful she represents are not those for whom faith is a "dull habit" but those for whom it is an "acute fever" (James, *Varieties of Religious Experience* 25).

# POEMS 12 THROUGH 16:
# THE "CIRCUMFERENCE[S]" OF TIME AND ETERNITY

In this final cluster of the poems of analysis, the eleventh poem's "My Country" and Christ's country become the circumference of time, as it is experienced by the faithful, and Christ's eternal circumference. In these five poems she expands upon the preceding cluster's subject, the mutual need between herself and Christ, though she leaves out her need for readers and portrays herself as one of the faithful whose dual goals are those described by Thomas à Kempis in the *Imitation*: to imitate Christ while in the sphere of time and to attain full union with him in the sphere of eternity:

The Admirations—and Contempts—of time—
Show justest—through an Open Tomb—
The Dying—as it were a Hight
Reorganizes Estimate
And what We saw not
We distinguish clear—
And mostly—see not
What We saw before—

'Tis Compound Vision—
Light—enabling Light—
The Finite—furnished
With the Infinite—
Convex—and Concave Witness—
Back—toward Time—
And forward—
Toward the God of Him—


Till Death—is narrow Loving—
The scantest Heart extant
Will hold you till your privilege
Of Finiteness—be spent—

But He whose loss procures you
Such Destitution that
Your Life too abject for itself
Thenceforward imitate—

Until—Resemblance perfect—
Yourself, for His pursuit
Delight of Nature—abdicate—
Exhibit Love—somewhat—

———————

'Tis Sunrise—Little Maid—Hast Thou
No Station in the Day?
'Twas not thy wont, to hinder so—
Retrieve thine industry—

'Tis Noon—My little Maid—
Alas—and art thou sleeping yet?
The Lily—waiting to be Wed—
The Bee—Hast thou forgot?

My little Maid—'Tis Night—Alas
That Night should be to thee
Instead of Morning—Had'st thou broached
Thy little Plan to Die—
Dissuade thee, if I c'd not, Sweet,
I might have aided—thee—


Pain—expands the Time—
Ages coil within                                          [coil/lurk]
The minute Circumference
Of a single Brain—

Pain contracts—the Time—
Occupied with Shot
Gammuts of Eternities                           [Gammuts/Triplets]
Are as they were not—                           [Are/flit—/Show—]

————————————

Fitter to see Him, I may be
For the long Hindrance—Grace—to Me—
With Summers, and with Winters, grow,
Some passing Year—A trait bestow                        [trait/charm]

To make Me fairest of the Earth—
The Waiting—then—will seem so worth
I shall impute with half a pain
The blame that I was chosen—then— ·            [chosen/common]

Time to anticipate His Gaze—                              [Time/Time's]
It's first—Delight—and then—Surprise—                     [It's/the]
The turning o'er and o'er my face
For Evidence it be the Grace—

He left behind One Day—So less
He seek Conviction, That—be This—

I only must not grow so new
That He'll mistake—and ask for me                    [He'll/He—]
Of me—when first unto the Door
I go—to Elsewhere go no more—

I only must not change so fair
He'll sigh—"The Other—She—is Where"? ·        [Other/Real One]
The Love, tho, will array me right                   [array/instruct]
I shall be perfect—in His sight—

If He perceive the other Truth—
Upon an Excellenter Youth—

How sweet I shall not lack in Vain—
But gain—thro' loss—Through Grief—obtain—         [Grief/pain]
The Beauty that reward Him most—                     [most/best]
The Beauty of Demand—at Rest—                    [Demand/Belief]

This cluster's key words, "time" and "eternity," appear either explicitly or implicitly in each of its five poems. In the twelfth, "We"—the twenty-first poem's "Us" who have faith—possess "Compound Vision" enabling "Us" to see both "Back—toward Time" and "forward— / Toward the God of Him," the loving God Jesus describes and personifies. In the thirteenth, time is one's "privilege / Of Finiteness," whereas eternity begins when one "abdicates" time, the "Delight of Nature." In the fourteenth, time passes from "Sunrise" to "Noon" to "Night," but not for the meditator, who imagines herself dead, as having abdicated her life in time. In the fifteenth, because "Time" is both expanded and contracted by pain, the meditator's "Gammuts of Eternities" are destroyed. And in the sixteenth, "Time" will enable her to be fitter for her meeting with the beloved in eternity.

While this cluster's poems are linked by their key words and meditational focus, they are a marvel of formal diversity. The stately twelfth is a definition poem composed of two octaves. The thirteenth is a nuptial poem of three quatrains, whose "Till Death," "hold," and "Thenceforward" wittily echo but reorder the marriage vows' "to have and to hold from this day forward . . . until death us do part." The fourteenth, spoken by Christ, who finds the meditator dead and sadly laments her passing, is a slant Petrarchan sonnet composed of two quatrains and a sestet. Poem 15, which introduces this cluster's conflict, is a lament composed of two grimly succinct quatrains. And the sixteenth, in which she imagines their meeting in eternity, is a slant double-sonnet, each of whose sonnets is composed of three quatrains and a couplet.

# Poem 12

The twelfth poem's definition of "Compound Vision" is F-40's fulcrum. Not only does it introduce the meditation's second half, it also retrospectively explains F-40's first poem and prospectively explains its final poem. In the first the meditator declares that "I"/eye see God and eternity in the finite sphere, then in the twenty-first, that through faith her "Eye"/I sees, though incompletely, the infinite sphere toward which she progresses. As she explains in the pivotal twelfth poem, she sees the eternal in the temporal as well as forward toward the eternal because she, as one of the faithful, possesses "Compound Vision":

> The Admirations—and Contempts—of time—
> Show justest—through an Open Tomb—
> The Dying—as it were a Hight
> Reorganizes Estimate
> And what We saw not
> We distinguish clear—
> And mostly—see not
> What We saw before—
>
> 'Tis Compound Vision—
> Light—enabling Light—
> The Finite—furnished
> With the Infinite—
> Convex—and Concave Witness—
> Back—toward Time—
> And forward—
> Toward the God of Him—

This poem's diction is not only ocular, like the first and twenty-first poems'; it is optical. This is most apparent in the second stanza's "Convex— and Concave," the former a lens correcting farsightedness and the latter a lens correcting nearsightedness. The poem's conceit is that Christ, "the faithful witness and the first begotten of the dead" (Rev. 1.5), is the "Infinite" lens "enabling" the "Finite" eye/I to see "justest," most accurately. With him as the corrective lens, one can see the sphere of time without the usual human hyperopia, and forward toward the sphere of God without the usual human myopia. This eye-lens conceit introduces the first of this emblematic cluster's five circular figures (Diagram 8).

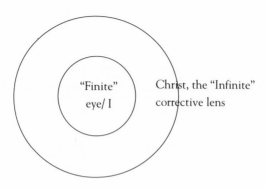

Diagram 8.


The poem's opening sentence elliptically introduces this optical figure:

> The Admirations—and Contempts—of time—
> Show justest [when they are seen] through an Open Tomb.

Since one cannot literally see *through* an open tomb, this sentence, like the fifth poem's "Affliction ranges Boundlessness," is conceptually deviant, showing that "Open Tomb," like the fifth poem's "Affliction," is a metalepsis, a metonymical substitution for a word that is itself figurative. Because one sees through a glass or lens, "Open Tomb" signifies a medium and, in the context of "Convex—and Concave," a lens. This "Open Tomb"/lens is, in turn, Jesus' opened sepulchre, a metonym for him as the "first begotten of the dead," who "abolished death" and "brought life and immortality to light through the gospel" (Rev. 1.5; 2 Tim. 1.10). In this first sentence, then, the meditator observes that one sees "The Admirations—and Contempts—of time" most accurately when one sees them through Christ, the corrective lens.

In the second sentence, she further describes why and how seeing through him corrects the vision of the faithful:

> The Dying—as it were a Hight
> Reorganizes [our] Estimate
> And [therefore] what We saw not          [*no stanza break*]

We distinguish clear—
And mostly—see not
What We saw before [that is, time's "Admirations—and
    Contempts."]

"The Dying" asks the reader to remember 2 Cor. 4, where Paul, like Dickinson's meditator, alludes to those who are blinded by the world, then declares that "We," himself as the epitome of the faithful, always bear "about in the body the dying" of Jesus so that his life "might be made manifest in our body." But "Dying" also echoes Thomas à Kempis's warning to the faithful that they must lead a "dying life," that is, a life dead to the self and lived for Jesus (88)—which is, of course, the meditator's description of her own life in F-40-2 when she reminds him she has died and now lives for him. "The Dying" is thus a second metonym for Christ, whose dying the faithful always bear within, and also a description of the lives led by the faithful, who have died to the world and now live for him.

    This dying life led by the faithful, who always bear within them the dying of Christ, is "as it were a Hight," still another allusion to poem 3b's betrothal, when Christ bore her "high" above the world to the fifth poem's "Illocality," from which she "Overlooked . . . all" in poem 8. "Hight" also introduces this poem's second circular figure, which represents the relation between the circuit and circumferential lives and is essential to comprehending this poem's fourth sentence as well as poems 13 and 15 (Diagram 9).

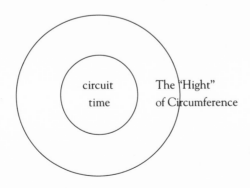

circuit

time

The "Hight"
of Circumference

Diagram 9.

This circumferential "Hight" attained by the soul that has, like the meditator's, been betrothed to Christ "Reorganizes [our] Estimate / And [therefore]
what We saw not [before] / We distinguish clear / And mostly see not / What
we saw before," a visual transformation that echoes Paul's concluding words
in 2 Cor. 4: "we look not at the things which are seen, but at the things
which are not seen: for the things which are seen are temporal; but the
things which are not seen are eternal." Seeing through Christ, then, is
seeing through a lens that magnifies the eternal and diminishes the temporal
so that time's "Admirations—and Contempts" lose their importance.

In the second octave's first line, the meditator then gives a name to "It," the
way of seeing through Christ that she has been describing and will continue to
describe in the poem's following lines: " 'Tis Compound Vision." Interestingly, "Compound Vision" may be an allusion to the poet's own eye problem.
Emily Dickinson spent from late April until Thanksgiving of 1864, the year
she is believed to have made fair copies of F-40's poems, in Boston undergoing
eye treatments. If, as Richard Sewall and Martin Wand propose, her treatments were for "double vision," then she has transformed her own malady into
"Compound Vision," this poem's central trope ("Eyes Be Blind" 400–406).
Whether or not she suffered from double vision, "Compound" calls attention
to this tightly compressed poem's recurring compound constructions:

The Admirations—and Contempts—of time—
Show justest—through an Open Tomb[;]
The Dying—as it were a Hight
Reorganizes [our] Estimate
And [therefore] what We saw not
We distinguish clear—
And mostly—see not
What We saw before[.]

It[, seeing through Christ,] is Compound Vision[, that is, it is]
Light—enabling Light—
The Finite—furnished
With the Infinite[;]
[Omitted subject and verb] Convex—and Concave Witness—
[Omitted words] Back—toward Time—
And forward—
Toward the God of Him [his God, the loving God that Jesus describes
and personifies.]

The poem is composed of two octaves, and each octave is composed of two compounded sentences. The first sentence's subject, "Admirations—and Contempts," is compound. The second sentence's structure is compound-complex, and its second clause's predicate is similarly both compound and complex: "what We saw not We distinguish clear—And mostly—see not What We saw before." The third sentence concludes with a compound predicate, the appositional phrases, "Light—enabling Light" and "The Finite—furnished With the Infinite." The fourth sentence's "Convex—and Concave" are compound adjectives, as "Back toward Time" and "forward Toward . . . God" are compound adverbial phrases. In addition, the poem's conceit is that accurate vision is "Compound" vision, the finite eye empowered by Christ. It introduces two circular figures. And each of its two octaves has two metonyms for him: the first octave's "Open Tomb" and "Dying" and the second octave's "Infinite . . . Light" and "Convex—and Concave Witness." The reader begins to feel as if he or she, too, is seeing double, a feeling that is compounded by the poem's parallel and chiastic structure (Diagram 10).

As Diagram 10 on page 126 shows, the relation between the first octave's two sentences is chiastic, parallel but with a reversal of order. The first sentence begins with "The Admirations—and Contempts—of time" (A) and concludes with "Open Tomb" (B). This order is reversed in the second sentence, which begins with "Dying" (B) and concludes with "What We saw before," that is, "The Admirations—and Contempts—of time." The first octave's two chiastic sentences provide the key enabling one to see that the second octave's two sentences are also chiastic and therefore to deduce at least the essence of the truncated fourth sentence's omitted words. The third sentence's subject and verb are "It [seeing through Christ] is" (A), and its predicate noun is "Compound Vision" (B). This must mean that the fourth sentence's subject and verb are "Compound Vision is" (B), and its predicate noun is "[seeing through Christ, the] Convex—and Concave Witness" (A), an epithet that echoes not only Revelation's "faithful witness" (1.5), but also Dickinson's "Our Lord—indeed—made Compound Witness" (F-30-19, J-553).

The second octave's first "Light" is the poem's third metonym for Christ, who is "light" throughout the New Testament, as in John 8.12, where he himself said, "I am the light of the world: he that followeth me shall not walk in darkness, but shall have the light of life." The second "Light"—enabled by Christ, the infinite "Light"—is the finite "eye," as in the Sermon on the Mount, when Jesus first advises his hearers to "Lay not up for yourself

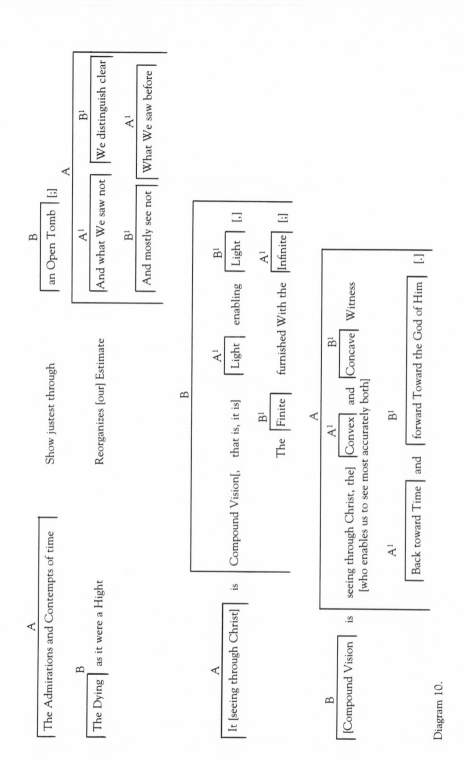

Diagram 10.

treasures upon the earth, where moth and rust doth corrupt"—in other words, "Reorganize [your] Estimate" of the "Admirations and Contempts of time"—then tells them that the "eye" is the "light of the body" and that if one's eye is sound, then one's whole body is full of light (Matt. 6.19–22). Since Christ is the infinite light enabling the finite light, or eye, the following lines are a chiastic reversal in which the "Finite" light, or eye, is "furnished / With the Infinite" light of Christ:

'Tis Compound Vision [, that is, it is

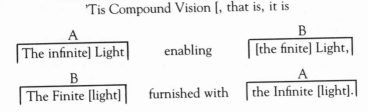

But these lines also retrospectively explain the first octave's "what We saw not / We [now] distinguish clear": with Christ, the "Infinite . . . Light," as lens, the "terrestrial eye" (J-1448) sees "The Finite [world] furnished with the Infinite," as in poem 1 the poetic "I"/eye sees eternity and meets only God while traversing the street of existence.

The fourth sentence, this elliptical poem's most opaque, is doubly foregrounded. Not only is "Convex—and Concave Witness" the poem's only catalectic tetrameter line, the four lines' parallelism also interrupts the poem's recurring chiasms:

A         B

⌐Convex⌐   and   ⌐Concave⌐   Witness

A         B

⌐Back toward Time⌐   and   ⌐forward Toward the God of Him⌐

These lines are parallel rather than chiastic because a "Convex" lens corrects farsightedness, the inability to see accurately what is close by, in this case the sphere of "Time," whereas a "Concave" lens corrects nearsightedness, the inability to see accurately what is at a distance, in this case forward toward the sphere of God. "Back—toward Time— / And forward— / Toward the God of Him" alludes to the first octave's circumferential "Hight" and further explains this poem's second circular figure (see Diagram 9) showing the relation between circuit time and the "Hight" of circumference (Diagram

11). By ascending into circumference, the faithful have left the world be-hind and moved closer to the eternal sphere. From this "Hight" they see most accurately both back toward "Time," which they see furnished with the infinite, and forward toward "the God of Him," the loving God that Jesus, the "Convex—and Concave Witness," describes and personifies.

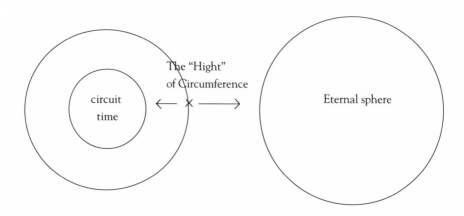

Diagram 11.

Between poems 12 and 13 Emily Dickinson did not draw the line custom-arily separating one poem from the next. Because poem 12 is a long poem, she may have omitted the line because she did not have room for it. Or she may have done so to draw attention to the close relation between the two poems. Both center upon the faithful soul's need for Christ. In poem 12 she needs him as the lens enabling her to see time and eternity with twenty-twenty vision. And as the meditator explains in poem 13, it is the "Destitution"—the need—engendered by the faithful soul's betrothal to him that causes her to "imitate" him.

## Poem 13

The thirteenth poem's metonym for Christ, by far F-40's longest, is a convo-luted series of clauses and phrases consisting of twenty-seven words begin-ning with the second stanza's "He" and concluding with the third stanza's "abdicate":

Till Death—is narrow Loving—
The scantest Heart extant
Will hold you till your privilege
Of Finiteness—be spent—

But *He whose loss procures you*
*Such Destitution that*
*Your Life too abject for itself*
*Thenceforward imitate—*

*Until—Resemblance perfect—*
*Yourself, for His pursuit*
*Delight of Nature—abdicate—*
Exhibit Love—somewhat—
                              (emphasis added)

This nuptial poem begins as a comparison between ordinary human marriage and spiritual betrothal to Christ. In its first stanza, echoing the marriage vows' "to have and to hold . . . until death us do part," the meditator observes that loving "Till Death" is only a narrow kind of loving because even the most parsimonious heart will "hold" you until your "privilege of Finiteness"—your life in time—is spent. "But," as she continues, when your (one's) bridegroom is Christ, as hers is, he elicits a far superior form of love in his bride, the soul (here, as in the Bible, feminine, whether a man's or a woman's).

The subject of the second of this poem's two sentences is "He," and its uninflected verb is "Exhibit," meaning that he has, does, and will exhibit a superior form of love by eliciting the transforming eternal love in one's soul she describes in the intervening "whose" clause. When its ellipses are filled in and its punctuation and syntax regularized, this long, complicated "whose" clause reads as follows:

(He) whose loss procures you Such Destitution that [as a result] Your Life [becomes] too abject for itself [and thus you] Thenceforward imitate [his life

and you continue to do so] Until [your] Resemblance [to him is] perfect[, that is, until] Yourself for his pursuit abdicate Delight of Nature—

The former stanza reminds one of the great Christian mystics who, after the glorious but brief moments of their betrothal to Christ, experience great destitution, a longing for him and a sense of their own littleness and unworthiness by comparison with his ineffable greatness (e.g., Underhill, *Mysticism* 337–57; Teresa of Avila, *Interior Castle* 85–119). As a result of her longing and her perception of her own unworthiness, the bride-soul "Thenceforward"—from the day of their betrothal forward—imitates his life, an explanation that retrospectively illuminates the many Dickinson poems in which the protagonist portrays Christ as the model of perfection whom she imitates (see, e.g., my discussion on page 45). As she continues in the latter stanza, the bride's imitation of the bridegroom continues until her resemblance to him is perfect, a goal never to be attained in this life but, she hopes, in the next. When she follows him into eternity, abdicates "Delight of Nature," her wish is, as she says in poem 16, to be so "perfect— in His sight" that he won't even recognize her as the imperfect bride "He left behind One Day," the day of their betrothal.

Through this transforming eternal love he inspires in his bride, Jesus exhibits a love far superior to ordinary married love. But why, then, is it only "Love—somewhat," that is, love to a certain extent? Retrospectively it dawns on the reader that the poem is a comparison of married love, which lasts only till death and is "narrow" (defined by Dickinson's lexicon as a limited circle), with the far greater love of the faithful soul for Christ, which is love "somewhat" (defined by Webster as a certain degree of a circle's circumference), and of both forms of human love with the infinite circumference of divine love. Her double comparison, then, is a witty variation of the twelfth poem's second circular figure (see Diagram 11) showing the relation between circuit, circumference, and the eternal sphere or circumference (Diagram 12). As she has reflected in F-35-19, "The Love a Life can show Below / Is but a filament, I know, / Of that diviner thing," Christ's infinite love for humans (J-673).

## Poem 14

In the fourteenth poem the meditator's mind shifts to an imagined future time when the bridegroom finds her dead and sees that she has, in fact, imitated him until she abdicated "Delight of Nature." As he worked the works of the God that sent him while it was day because "night cometh, when no man can work," so she has diligently labored at her poetic work until night came for herself (John 9.4):

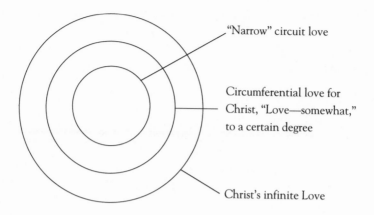

"Narrow" circuit love

Circumferential love for
Christ, "Love—somewhat,"
to a certain degree

Christ's infinite Love

Diagram 12.

> 'Tis Sunrise—Little Maid—Hast Thou
> No Station in the Day?
> 'Twas not thy wont, to hinder so—
> Retrieve thine industry—
>
> 'Tis Noon—My little Maid—
> Alas—and art thou sleeping yet?
> The Lily—waiting to be Wed—
> The Bee—Hast thou forgot?
>
> My little Maid—'Tis Night—Alas
> That Night should be to thee
> Instead of Morning—Had'st thou broached
> Thy little Plan to Die—
> Dissuade thee, if I c'd not, Sweet,
> I might have aided—thee—

This dramatic monologue's setting is a conflation of John's "night . . . when no man can work," Matthew's parable of the trusty servant who is found by his master to have been industriously laboring at his task during the master's absence, and the parable of the talents, whose lord, having similarly been absent, returns to ask what his servants have done with the talents he has entrusted to them. Because this poem's faithful servant, the master's "Little Maid," was during her lifetime a poet who customarily labored from sunrise to nightfall to perfect her one poetic talent—wedding the "Lily" to the "Bee," transforming the experiential world into literature by means of her poetic power—she is, of course, the meditator. Obviously her labors have been successful because her master, who assumes at first she is only sleeping, repeatedly urges her to resume her work, then in line 9, where he realizes she is dead, sadly laments her passing. In poem 9, "I hide myself— within my flower," she longed to engender in him a loneliness and need for her through her poetry, and here she imagines that after her death he does, in fact, miss her poetry and therefore herself.

This poem's speaker typifies F-40's Jesus. He is an asker of questions, he takes the initiative by speaking first, and his lines are straightforward, a model of clarity. While his diction and syntax are simple and direct, he is also figurative. As in the sixth poem's dialogue he refers to himself metonymically as "Omnipotence" and "Pardon," so here he refers periphrastically to the meditator's poetic vocation as wedding the "Lily" to the "Bee." His monologue echoes but varies his scriptural words: as in the parable of the talents and poem 10, he compliments his faithful servant's industry. He is gentle, but persistent. As he refuses to take no for an answer in the sixth poem's debate, so here he persists in his questions until he finds out why his little maid is not at her usual station. Moreover, he cares deeply for the meditator. As in their debate he is determined to persuade her to give up her foolish circuit life, so here he grieves for the dead little maid whose life has been dedicated to his service.

As poem 14 reveals, he is himself a poet, whose monologue is a slant Petrarchan sonnet composed of two quatrains and a sestet. More specifically, his monologue is a Miltonic sonnet whose turn occurs in the ninth line's "Alas." Before this turn he speaks as her kindly but exacting master, attempting to awaken his apparently sleeping maid so that she can resume her poetic labors. But after this turn, when he suddenly realizes she is dead, he speaks as her lover/bridegroom, lamenting her death. He thus reveals himself to be both her master and bridegroom, as he is throughout F-40.

But why, the literal-minded reader asks, if the master/bridegroom is Jesus—her soul's permanent occupant, her inner voice, the omnipotent sun/Son who is now of Paradise—did he not know from the beginning that she was dead? The sixteenth poem's slant double-sonnet poses a similarly puzzling question: why does he not immediately recognize her when she enters the door of eternity? The explanation lies in the two poems' chief biblical sources, the parable of the talents and the parable of the ten virgins, which are no more realistically accurate than Dickinson's two sonnets. One might similarly ask why the talents parable's lord entrusts such vast sums of money to his servants and why, if this lord is God, he does not know until his return from the far country what they have done with their talents. One might also ask why in the ten-virgins parable the wedding takes place at midnight. In the sonnets, as in the parables, the reader is apparently meant to see they are not realistically accurate and then search for their figurative meanings.

The poems' sonnet form provides a clue to their figurative meanings. Together poems 14 and 16 form a sonnet sequence, and as such they explore the relationship between the two lovers, their love and longing for one another. They therefore need be no more realistic than the parables they echo. Another clue to their figurative meanings is in the poems' relation to the preceding fascicles' series of poems in which the protagonist also imagines what her death and entry into eternity might be like. In "I heard a Fly buzz—when I died," for example, she imagines herself as recollecting her own death scene (F-26-3, J-465). In "The face I carry with me—last— / When I go out of Time," she imagines her entry into eternity, when an angel will present her with a crown and display her to an "admiring sky" as one who, like the saved in Rev. 22.4, "bore her Master's name" (F-19-17, J-336). This series of cognate poems is fanciful and no more realistically accurate than the two sonnets that culminate the series, because no one knows what one's own death will be like, or what eternity will be like. As in 1 Cor. 2.9, the twenty-first poem's chief biblical source, "Eye hath not seen, nor ear heard, neither have entered into the heart of man, the things which God hath prepared for them that love him."

As the conclusion of the poems of analysis, in which the meditator summons the faculty of understanding, poems 14 and 16 represent what one can know of death and eternity through reason and imagination. As the concluding poems of faith show, these subjects are ultimately matters for faith. While in the poems of faith her chief meditational focus becomes death and eternity, she does not imagine their details as she does in the two sonnets and in the series of poems they culminate. Rather, she summons the faculty of will to declare her belief in the immortality of the soul and eternity's "New Horizons" because Christ, who is himself the "truth," has said so.

## Poem 15

Christ's loving lament for the dead poet in the sonnet's sestet is followed by her own grim lament in poem 15. Unlike any other F-40 poem, number 15 includes neither words spoken by Jesus nor any metonym or pronoun for him. His absence from the text is one of several clues leading the reader to see that the cause of the pain whose effects she contemplates are the dark nights of the soul described by the psalmist as when God's face is turned away and by Thomas à Kempis as when Jesus is absent and "everything is difficult" (e.g., Ps. 30.7; *Imitation* 76):

> Pain—expands the Time—
> Ages coil within                                    [coil/lurk]
> The minute Circumference
> Of a single Brain—
>
> Pain contracts—the Time—
> Occupied with Shot
> Gammuts of Eternities                    [Gammuts/Triplets]
> Are as they were not—                   [Are/flit—/Show—]

Another clue leading the reader to see her lament concerns Jesus' absence is that this poem's meditation on "Pain" is a diminished reversal of the twelfth poem's meditation on "Compound Vision." Each poem is composed of two stanzas, and each stanza is composed of two sentences. The word "time" appears in each of the poems' two stanzas, but in the twelfth poem's first stanza "time" is uncapitalized, whereas in the fifteenth's first stanza "Time" is capitalized, drawing attention to the opposition between the two. In poem 12 seeing through Christ puts the "Admirations—and Contempts—of time" in perspective because he is a lens magnifying the eternal and diminishing the import of the temporal. But in poem 15 the pain of his absence expands "Time" so that all one sees is the temporal, the "Ages" coiled within one's own "single Brain." Seeing through Christ, then, is "Compound Vision," seeing with the eye/I corrected by the infinite lens; but seeing without him is "single" vision, seeing with an I/eye that, unaided by him, can only focus inward. The fifteenth poem's first stanza thus reverses the twelfth poem's first circular figure (see Diagram 8): in the fifteenth poem's first stanza, the twelfth poem's two concentric circles become a single circle (Diagram 13).

The first stanza's witty conceit is that the "Circumference / Of a single Brain" is a watch or clock with a spring coiled within, echoing F-26-13, "When Bells stop ringing—Church—begins," where the circumference of the brain is a watch or clock whose "Cogs" will eventually stop (J-633). The variant "lurk" draws attention to the menacing aspects of this coiled "Ages"/

Diagram 13.

spring. As a serpent coils waiting to strike, so "Ages" coil within the brain. And when Jesus is absent, this coiled "Ages"/spring is released, causing the clock/brain to strike time, the I/eye to see only the temporal.

As this first stanza reverses the twelfth poem's first circular figure, so its second stanza reverses the twelfth poem's second figure (see Diagram 11). There seeing through Christ is like a "Hight" enabling one to see both back toward time and forward toward the eternal sphere. But here the pain of his absence contracts the time, reduces one from the circumferential "Hight" back to the little circuit sphere (Diagram 14).

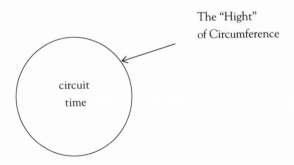

Diagram 14.

As "Shot" and the variant "Triplets" show, the second stanza's conceit is that the bird/poet who has been shot cannot sing:

Pain contracts—the Time—
[When the bird/poet is] Occupied with Shot
Gammuts of Eternities                    [Gammuts/Triplets]
Are as they were not—                    [Are/flit—/Show—]

This stanza's situation and emblem similarly reverse an earlier "Circumference" poem:

She staked her Feathers—Gained an Arc—
Debated—Rose again—
This time—beyond the estimate
Of Envy, or of Men—

And now, among Circumference—
Her steady Boat be seen—
At home—among the Billows—As
The Bough where she was born—
                                   (F-38-8, J-798)

Though in the earlier poem the bird/poet has soared from the circuit sphere, "The Bough where she was born," into the circumferential height, in F-40-15's second stanza she cannot ascend because of the searing pain of the "Shot" within.

Her "Gammuts of Eternities" thus vanish. Since the "gamut" is the musical scale, the whole range of notes used by musicians, "Gammuts" are the bird/poet's notes, her song, a musical signification underscored by the variant "Triplets." The explanation for the plural "Eternities" lies once more in poem 12. There she sees only the eternal; that is, she sees the eternal toward which she progresses, as well as the eternity time becomes for one who has died to circuit time. But here, because her compound vision has been destroyed, her poetic notes—her "Gammuts"—for singing about these two "Eternities" are also destroyed. Like Herbert's speaker in "Denial," who urges the absent Jesus to return and "mend my rhyme," Dickinson's meditator is unable to write poetry when she does not feel his presence.

Since this is a fine poem, she is not suddenly in the middle of her meditation experiencing a dark night of the soul but remembering such occasions in the past and dreading those in the future. The dark night of the soul is, after all, a part of the religious life, according to both the psalmist and Thomas à

Kempis, who warns the faithful, "At times, God will withdraw from you" (*Imitation* 85). As Thomas also observes, being without Jesus is "hell most grievous" (77). Since her lament for his absence follows her imagined death and precedes her imagined entry into eternity, it seems likely that the poem implicitly describes what hell would be like: being without Jesus throughout eternity. As she has said in F-39-21, her wish is to "Fade . . . unto Divinity" (J-682).

The second stanza's onomatopoetic "Shot"-"not," this cluster's first true rhyme, both underscores the piercing impact of those dark nights of the soul and anticipates the following poem's pattern of fourteen rhymed couplets.

## Poem 16

After the preceding poem's dark lament, the meditator bolsters her spirits by imagining the future meeting she longs for with the bridegroom in eternity. Then there will be no more dark nights of the soul and none of the other conflicts she has remembered and lamented in the poems of analysis: the pain of self-denial, the uncertainty whether she will attain full union with the bridegroom, the destitution and longing for him engendered by their betrothal. This wistful poem of hope and love is the fifth F-40 poem in which Jesus speaks and, if one counts the implicit 3b, the fifth poem in which she describes her union with Jesus as a betrothal (poems 2, 3b, 8, 13, and 16). Poem 16 is also the conclusion of the poems of analysis; the culmination of the series of poems, extending throughout the fascicles, in which the protagonist imagines her entry into eternity; and, as a slant double-sonnet, the conclusion of the sonnet sequence begun in poem 14:

[first sonnet]

Fitter to see Him, I may be
For the long Hindrance—Grace—to Me—
With Summers, and with Winters, grow,
Some passing Year—A trait bestow                          [trait/charm]

To make Me fairest of the Earth—
The Waiting—then—will seem so worth
I shall impute with half a pain
The blame that I was chosen—then—                         [chosen/common]

Time to anticipate His Gaze                                [Time/Time's]
It's first—Delight—and then—Surprise—                     [It's/the]
The turning o'er and o'er my face
For Evidence it be the Grace—

He left behind One Day—So less
He seek Conviction, That—be This—

[second sonnet]

I only must not grow so new
That He'll mistake—and ask for me                          [He'll/He]
Of me—when first unto the Door
I go—to Elsewhere go no more—

I only must not change so fair
He'll sigh—"The Other—She—is Where"?                       [Other/Real One]
The Love, tho, will array me right                          [array/instruct]
I shall be perfect—in His sight—

If He perceive the other Truth—
Upon an Excellenter Youth—

How sweet I shall not lack in Vain—
But gain—thro' loss—Through Grief—obtain—                  [Grief/pain]
The Beauty that reward Him most—                            [most/best]
The Beauty of Demand—at Rest—                               [Demand/Belief]

Though the fourteenth poem's slant sonnet is Miltonic, the first of this poem's slant double-sonnets is Shakespearean, three quatrains and a couplet whose turn occurs with the thirteenth line's "So." Its second sonnet is an intriguing fusion of the Shakespearean and the Petrarchan. Like the Shakespearean sonnet, it is composed of three quatrains and a couplet, but its couplet and turn—"If He perceive the other Truth / Upon an Excellenter Youth"—come before, rather than after, its third quatrain. This makes the second sonnet Petrarchan as well: two quatrains followed by a sestet composed of a couplet and a quatrain. Emily Dickinson further departs from the sonnet's conventions with her tetrameter lines arranged in a pattern of fourteen rhymed couplets, all but five of them true rhymes.

That she slants the sonnet form to suit herself is hardly surprising—especially since the poems of analysis begin with the fifth poem's declaration of the meditator's freedom from poetic "Laws." What *is* surprising is that

Emily Dickinson is writing sonnets and couplets at all. As the fourteenth and sixteenth poems show, she was perfectly capable of writing a Miltonic, Shakespearean, or Petrarchan sonnet when she chose to, which she appears to have done here because the poems are about the two lovers' mutual love and longing for one another. As poem 16 shows, she was equally capable of writing rhymed couplets when she chose to. Since the rhymed couplet is Shakespeare's customary ending for an act or scene, and since it calls to mind the Age of Reason, she may have chosen the rhymed couplet as an appropriate conclusion to the poems of analysis, in which the meditator summons the faculty of understanding.

The first sonnet's first two quatrains focus upon the "long Hindrance" of years between the meditation's fictive present and the ultimate union of the meditator and Christ in eternity. During this time, she hopes she may become "Fitter to see Him"—more prepared like the parable's prepared virgins who entered the "door" of the bridal chamber, this poem's "Door / I go—to Elsewhere go no more." With the passing years, she hopes that the grace bestowed upon her may grow and, some year, may bestow upon her a trait to make her the "fairest of the Earth," echoing Canticles' bride, whom the bridegroom and others repeatedly address as "thou fairest among women" (Song of Sol. 1.8, 5.9, 6.1). If so, then the long years of waiting for their full union will seem so worth it that she will count as only half a pain the blame that she was "chosen"—the variant is "common," echoing 1 Cor. 1.26, whose "called" are rarely the noble, but instead those who are common. That she was "chosen" echoes several earlier occasional poems. In "The Day that I was crowned," the "Grace" that she was "chose" surpassed the crown she was given (F-29-4, J-356). Similarly, in "The World—stands—solemner—to me— / Since I was wed—to Him," she marvels that "munificence . . . chose" her even though she was common, "So unadorned—a Queen" (J-493). The difference is that here she sees having been chosen oxymoronically as both a grace and a blame because of the pain it has entailed, the seventh poem's self-denial, the tenth poem's uncertainty, the thirteenth poem's "Destitution," and the fifteenth poem's dark night of the soul. As in F-33-15, her master has left her two legacies, one of love and the other of pain (J-644).

As she continues in the first sonnet's third quatrain, the long hindrance of intervening years will also give her time to anticipate his gaze when they finally meet in eternity, a scene she then vividly imagines with tropes of sacred parody, as in the Song of Songs. His face will reflect first his "Delight" at seeing such a perfected soul, then his "Surprise" when she tells him who she is, whereupon he will turn her face over and over for evidence that she is, in fact, the imperfect bride he left behind "One Day," the day of their betrothal depicted in the implicit poem *3b*. (That the bridegroom is delighted to see her even before he recognizes her underscores that this is no human lover waiting in heaven for her and her alone.) "So," the first sonnet's turn begins, to avert the possibility that he may find it hard to believe that "That" imperfect bride has become "This" perfected one, she will do as she extravagantly resolves in the first two stanzas of the second sonnet. She will be sure not to become so much the "new man" (Col. 3.10) she began to become when she "leaned into Perfectness." Otherwise, he might mistake her for someone else—as Mary Magdalene mistook him for the gardener on Easter morning (John 20.15)—and ask her perfected self what has become of her previously imperfect self. She must not become so "fair," again like Canticles' bride, that he will disappointedly sigh, "The Other" one—where is she? The meditator concludes her imagined scene by assuring herself that the love between them will array her correctly—not like Matthew's wedding guest but like Revelation's bride of the lamb. She will be "perfect in His sight," again echoing Canticles, whose bridegroom tells his bride, "Thou art all fair, my love; there is no spot in thee" (Song of Sol. 4.7).

The second sonnet's final couplet and quatrain, its sestet, are not only its resolution, as in the Petrarchan sonnet, but also the resolution of the entire poem. If he does perceive "the other Truth"—that is, beauty, as in "I died for Beauty," where "Truth" and "Beauty" are one and the same—upon an "Excellenter Youth," the first stanza's "Fitter" youth, the parable's more prepared virgin, then she will not have lacked in vain. Through loss and grief—the variant is "pain," again those losses and griefs she has recollected and lamented in the poems of analysis and throughout the fascicles—she will have obtained the "Beauty that reward Him most," which is "The Beauty of Demand at Rest." These final lines are reminiscent of Rev. 21.4, "God shall wipe away all tears from their eyes . . . neither shall there be any more *pain*" (emphasis added), and also of Christ's words to the Disciple in the *Imitation:* "Consider the results of your work, . . . its approaching end, and its boundless reward. Then it will not make you unhappy, but powerfully strengthen your resolution; . . . in Heaven . . . you will enjoy good things without fear of loss. . . . There you will receive glory in return for insults suffered here; a robe of honour instead of *grief*" (161, emphasis added). Whether or not Emily Dickinson had these lines in mind when she wrote poem 16, they describe what the meditator does in this double-sonnet. She strengthens her resolve by imagining what she hopes will be the results of her work and its deprivations and what she hopes will be her boundless reward—as well as what will "reward Him—most": receiving into heaven a soul who has imitated his perfection while in the sphere of time and whose "Demand"—need—for him is now finally "at Rest."

As a dramatization of her meeting with Christ in eternity, poem 16 resembles "Love (3)," The Temple's final poem, in which Herbert's speaker, too, meets Christ in eternity. But Herbert's setting is heaven, whereas Dickinson's is the fictive present in which the meditator imagines herself in heaven. Though Herbert, too, is imagining heaven, he portrays his speaker as already there, while Dickinson portrays hers as hoping to be there at some future time.

After expressing her hope and love in poem 16, the meditator declares her faith in the following cluster.

# Part III

## The Poems of Faith:
## Poems 17 Through 21,
## "He who in Himself believes"

Both the composition of place and the poems of analysis conclude with the meditator's death and rebirth into a higher sphere. The composition of place concludes with her recollected death to the circuit life and rebirth into "Perfectness," a spiritual and poetic transformation that led to her even greater transformation on the day she was betrothed to Christ and began to lead the fully expanded circumferential life. The poems of analysis conclude with her imagined death to the finite sphere and rebirth into the eternal sphere, when she hopes she will attain her goals, perfection and full union with the bridegroom. In the poems of faith, her chief meditational focus becomes the literal death and rebirth she imagined in the fourteenth and sixteenth poems' sonnet sequence. Here she summons the faculty of will and submits it to Christ by declaring her belief in his truthfulness and therefore in his promises that death is not final, that he will be with his followers always, that there will be a Judgment, and that there is an eternal life:

He who in Himself believes—
Fraud cannot presume—                    [Fraud/Lie]
Faith is Constancy's Result—
And assumes—from Home—                   [assumes/infers]

Cannot perish, though it fail
Every second time—
But defaced Vicariously—                  [But/When—/if—]
For Some Other Shame—                     [For Another Shame—]

---

Color—Caste—Denomination—
These—are Time's Affair—
Death's diviner Classifying
Does not know they are—

As in sleep—All Hue forgotten—
Tenets—put behind—
Death's large—Democratic fingers
Rub away the Brand—

If Circassian—He is careless—
If He put away
Chrysalis of Blonde—or Umber—
Equal Butterfly—

They emerge from His Obscuring—
What Death—knows so well—
Our minuter intuitions—
Deem unplausible                          [unplausible/incredible]

I make His Crescent fill or lack—
His Nature is at Full
Or Quarter—as I signify—
His Tides—do I control—

He holds superior in the Sky
Or gropes, at my Command
Behind inferior Clouds—or round
A Mist's slow Colonnade—

But since We hold a Mutual Disc—
And front a Mutual Day—
Which is the Despot, neither knows—
Nor Whose—the Tyranny—

---

Robbed by Death—but that was easy—
To the failing Eye        [failing/Dying—/clouding]
I could hold the latest Glowing—
Robbed by Liberty

For Her Jugular Defences—
This, too, I endured—
Hint of Glory—it afforded—
For the Brave Beloved—             [Brave/bold]

Fraud of Distance—Fraud of Danger,
Fraud of Death—to bear—
It is Bounty—to Suspense's
Vague Calamity—

Staking our entire Possession      [entire/divine—]
On a Hair's result—
Then—Seesawing—coolly—on it—
Trying if it split                [As to estimate]


Unfulfilled to Observation—
Incomplete—to Eye—
But to Faith—a Revolution
In Locality—

Unto Us—the Suns extinguish—
To our Opposite—
New Horizons—they embellish—   [embellish/Replenish]
Fronting Us—with Night.    [Turning Us—their Night.]

    This final cluster's poems are linked both verbally and metrically as well as thematically. Their key word, "Faith," which appears in poems 17 and 21, is implicit in the other three. As the poems of the composition of place are further linked by the meditator's recurring diction of sight and memory and the poems of analysis by her recurring diction of business and assessment, so the poems of faith are further linked by her recurring diction of cognition— "believes," "presume," "assumes," "infers," "intuitions," and "know," which occurs three times. All the poems of faith are in hymn meter, alternating tetrameters and trimeters, and all but poem 19 are trochaic, metrically underscoring the strength of her faith. Stanzaically they are neatly arranged in a pattern of 2-4-3-4-2, that is, the seventeenth and twenty-first are composed of two stanzas, the eighteenth and twentieth of four, and the nineteenth of three.

In the seventeenth she declares her belief in Jesus' truthfulness by reflecting that one who believes in him who is himself the "truth" cannot presume he is ca pable of "Fraud." Though in poem 17 she acknowledges that faith requires perseverance, in the following poems she declares her firm belief in his promises. In the eighteenth she declares her faith in his promise that death is not final, even though "Our minuter intuitions"—the faculties of sight and understanding she has summoned in F-40's preceding poems—may deem this "unplausible." In the nineteenth she declares her belief in his promise, in the book of Matthew's final sentence, to be with his followers always, "even unto the end of the world"—or, as the meditator expresses it, until doomsday, the "Mutual Day" they front. In the twentieth she demonstrates her belief in the Judgment by rehearsing how she will plead her case on that final day. And though she acknowledges that she cannot be certain she herself will be among the saved sheep, in poem 21 she declares her faith in eternity's "New Horizons."

The subjects and ordering of F-40's concluding six poems are thus strikingly similar to the subjects and ordering of the concluding six poems of The Temple's "Church." In Herbert's "A Wreath" Jesus is "farre above deceit," as in Dickinson's seventeenth poem he is incapable of "Fraud," a synonym for "deceit." In both works these tributes to his veracity are followed by four poems about four of the five last things, which are reflected in Herbert's titles—"Death," "Dooms-day," "Judgement," and "Heaven"—with both poets omitting hell, customarily the fourth "last thing." In The Temple these five poems are followed by "Love (3)," a dramatization of the speaker's meeting with Jesus in heaven, while in F-40 these five poems are preceded by poem 16, also a dramatization of the speaker's meeting with Jesus in heaven. This means that the concluding six poems of the two works are as follows:

| The Temple's "Church" | F-40 |
| --- | --- |
|  | 1. Dramatization of the meditator's entry into eternity and meeting with Jesus (poem 16) |

1. Jesus as "farre above deceit" ("A Wreath")
2. "Death"
3. "Dooms-day"
4. What the speaker will say at the "Judgement"
5. "Heaven"
6. Dramatization of the speaker's entry into eternity and meeting with Jesus ("Love [3]")

2. Jesus as incapable of "Fraud" (poem 17)
3. Death (poem 18)
4. Doomsday, the "Mutual Day" they "front" (poem 19)
5. What the speaker will say at the Judgment (poem 20)
6. Heaven, eternity's "New Horizons" (poem 21)

While none of these poems resembles its Herbertian counterpart to the extent that Dickinson's dialogue between the meditator and Christ (F-40-6) resembles Herbert's "Dialogue," there are some interesting similarities between them.

## POEM 17

The seventeenth poem's first sentence—"He who in Himself believes . . . cannot presume . . . Fraud," or "Lie," as the variant reads—echoes Heb. 6.18: it is "impossible for God to lie." Her conceit is that since Jesus is himself the "truth," and since "no lie is of the truth" (1 John 2.21), it is logically impossible for one who believes in him to presume his promises to be lies:

> He who in Himself believes—
> Fraud cannot presume—                [Fraud/Lie]
> Faith is Constancy's Result—
> And assumes—from Home—              [assumes/infers]

As she then observes, "Faith" is the result of "Constancy," his immutable veracity, which, according to both Dickinson's lexicon and concordance, is the basis for the "saving faith" she declares in this final cluster (Cruden, *Complete Concordance* 199). But "constancy" also signifies lasting affection as well as persevering resolution. Faith, then, is assumed because of Jesus' veracity, but it is also the result of the loving perseverance of the human

believer who assumes "from Home," here not the circuit home of poems 5
through 8 but more generally the sphere of time.

The second stanza is at first puzzling because its first sentence's subject is
missing, and its second sentence's subject and auxiliary verb are both missing:

> [X] Cannot perish, though it fail
> Every second time—
> But [Y is] defaced Vicariously—          [But/When—/if—]
> For Some Other Shame

Since "Faith" is the subject of the preceding sentence, of the poem, and of its
cluster, this sentence's subject, too, must be "Faith." But since the faith of
some people does in some cases perish, fail entirely, and since the poem is
about the faith of one who believes in Jesus' veracity—which, of course,
includes the meditator—the sentence reads,

> [The faith of one who believes in Jesus' veracity] Cannot perish,
> [even] though it fail Every second time.

A faith firmly grounded in his truthfulness, then, cannot fail entirely even
though it may often fall short.

This second stanza, like the poem's first sentence, echoes the sixth chapter of Hebrews. In verses 4 through 6 Paul warns the faithful that if they "fall
away," it is impossible to renew them again unto repentance because by
falling away they crucify Jesus afresh and "put him to an open *shame*" (emphasis added). In Dickinson's version, she causes the meditator to make a
distinction between "perish," fail entirely, and "fail," fall short. While the
faith of one who believes in Jesus' veracity may sometimes fall short, it
cannot perish. But, she adds, when it does fall short, Christ is "defaced
Vicariously," that is, he is put to an open shame "For Some Other Shame,"
the shame of the believer's lapse in faith. A decompressed version of the
poem's four sentences thus reads as follows:

> He who in Himself believes cannot presume Fraud.
> Faith is Constancy's Result and assumes from Home.
> [The faith of one who believes in Jesus' veracity] Cannot
>     perish, [even] though it [may] fail Every second time.
> But [when one's faith fails, Jesus is] defaced Vicariously
> For Some Other['s, the wayward believer's,] Shame.

The poem, then, is a declaration of faith based upon Jesus' truthfulness, but also an acknowledgment of the difficulty of maintaining faith, a difficulty that retrospectively explains the preceding poem's variant for "Demand," which is "Belief":

> How sweet I shall not lack in Vain—
> But gain—thro' loss—Through Grief—obtain—
> The Beauty that reward Him most—
> The Beauty of Belief—at Rest—
>
> (poem 16, final stanza)

Once in the eternity she aspires to, she will no longer have to work at belief, which, as she observes in poem 17, requires perseverance and sometimes falters. Though the protagonist does not express doubt anywhere in F-40, she sometimes did in the preceding fascicles before she attained this final fascicle's plateau of joy and confidence. But then, experiencing doubt is not a rare phenomenon among believers. As Christ reassures the Disciple in the *Imitation*'s concluding paragraphs, "Often it is very profitable that the servant of God should experience such doubts, since the Devil does not tempt unbelievers and sinners who are already his own; but he tempts and vexes the faithful and devout in every way he can." According to Thomas à Kempis, then, experiencing doubt is as much a part of the believer's life as are those dark nights of the soul when Jesus seems to be absent.

# POEM 18

After declaring her faith in Jesus' veracity and presumably admitting penitently that her own faith sometimes falters, the meditator declares her belief in his promise of immortality:

> Color—Caste—Denomination—
> These—are Time's Affair—
> Death's diviner Classifying
> Does not know they are—

As in sleep—All Hue forgotten—
Tenets—put behind—
Death's large—Democratic fingers
Rub away the Brand—

If Circassian—He is careless—
If He put away
Chrysalis of Blonde—or Umber—
Equal Butterfly—

They emerge from His Obscuring—
What Death—knows so well—
Our minuter intuitions—
Deem unplausible                    [unplausible/incredible]

This poem bears some interesting resemblances to Herbert's "Death":

Death, thou wast once an uncouth hideous thing,
                    Nothing but bones,
          The sad effect of sadder grones:
Thy mouth was open, but thou couldst not sing.

For we consider'd thee as at some six
                    Or ten yeares hence,
          After the losse of life and sense,
Flesh being turn'd to dust, and bones to sticks.

We lookt on this side of thee, shooting short;
                    Where we did finde
          The shells of fledge souls left behinde,
Dry dust, which shed no tears, but may extort.

But since our Saviours death did put some bloud
                    Into thy face;
          Thou art grown fair and full of grace,
Much in request, much sought for as a good.

For we do now behold thee gay and glad,
                    As at dooms-day;
          When souls shall wear their new aray,
And all thy bones with beautie shall be clad.

Therefore we can go die as sleep, and trust
Half that we have
Unto an honest faithful grave;
Making our pillows either down, or dust.

Both poems focus upon a personified "Death." As Herbert contrasts how "we" once viewed Death with how "we" now perceive him "since our Saviours death," so Dickinson contrasts what "Our minuter intuitions" tell us about Death with how he is viewed through faith. Herbert's transformed Death is now fair, full of grace, gay, and glad, while Dickinson's is a democrat for whom time's classifying according to color, caste, and denomination does not exist, a kindly sexton who himself knows his obscuring is only temporary. Moreover, Herbert's image of the "shells of fledge souls left behind" is a version of Dickinson's traditional image of the "Butterfly"-soul escaped from its "Chrysalis."

Emily Dickinson appears to have had in mind Gal. 3.28, "There is neither Jew nor Greek, there is neither bond nor free, there is neither male nor female: for ye are all one in Christ Jesus." But the poem's emphasis on the unimportance of color suggests that she also had in mind the Civil War then raging, and more specifically the question of race. In the first stanza "Color" is time's affair and of no importance to Death; in the second "Hue" is forgotten because Death rubs away the brand; and in the third Death does not care whether the chrysalis is "Blonde" or "Umber." In an otherwise relatively straightforward poem, the third stanza's syntax is ambiguous. Apparently "He is careless" applies to both the preceding and the following phrases, so that a paraphrase would read, "Death does not care if the Chrysalis he puts away is Circassian or if it is Blonde or Umber; all will emerge from his obscuring as Equal Butterflies." Since the Circassians are an Asian Muslim people, it appears that "Circassian" is a synecdoche for all peoples from faraway places who may espouse different religious faiths, the first line's "Denomination[s]." Such a reading is strengthened by the meaning of "Circassian" in the only other Dickinson poem in which the word appears, the seventh fascicle's eighteenth poem, one of several F-7 poems that focus upon the resurrection both of humans and of nature in the spring (J-64). This earlier poem, a salute to spring, begins, "Some Rainbow— coming from the Fair! / Some Vision of the world Cashmere— / I confidently see!" Then, after cataloging the butterflies, bees, robins, and flowers that have suddenly appeared, the protagonist concludes, "Whose Multitudes are these? / The children of whose turbaned seas— / Or what Circassian Land?" Since in the earlier poem "Circassian," like "Cashmere," signifies exotic, strange, and wonderful, it makes sense to suppose that in the later poem, too, "Circassian" signifies exotic—that is, foreign—though in the context of the later poem's democratic emphasis "Circassian" takes on the added signification of religious tolerance. As in Heb. 2.9, Jesus "taste[d] death for every man."

The final stanza's "emerge from His Obscuring," to reappear after being eclipsed, introduces the following poem's astronomical imagery.

# POEM 19

In poem 19 the meditator declares her faith in Jesus' promise to his followers in the book of Matthew's final sentence, "I am with you alway even unto the end of the world." By doing so she resolves the conflict introduced in poem 15, the pain of those dark nights of the soul. In poem 16 she imagined heaven, where *all* her griefs will have ended; but here she directly addresses the pain of his periodic absences by declaring that she knows he is always with her and by acknowledging that when she does not feel his presence, the fault lies with herself.

This poem's emblematic conceit is that he, the moon, and she, the earth, are held together by bonds of faith and love as strong as the gravitational pull between the moon and earth, an astronomical version of the circular figures introduced in the preceding cluster (Diagram 15).

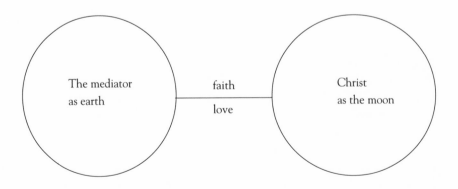

Diagram 15.

I make His Crescent fill or lack—
His Nature is at Full
Or Quarter—as I signify—
His Tides—do I control—

He holds superior in the Sky
Or gropes, at my Command
Behind inferior Clouds—or round
A Mist's slow Colonnade—

But since We hold a Mutual Disc—
And front a Mutual Day—
Which is the Despot, neither knows—
Nor Whose—the Tyranny—

The earth-moon system—sometimes called a "double planet"—is a delightfully apt figure for the meditator's union with Christ. Though we ordinarily say the moon revolves about the earth, it is more accurate to say that together the earth and moon revolve about their common center of mass, because it is the center of this earth-moon system, rather than the center of the earth, that describes an elliptical orbit around the sun (*New Columbia Encyclopedia*, 4th ed., s.v. "moon"). The problem is that the moon is not always fully visible from the earth. When seen from the earth the moon appears to have phases, the first stanza's trope. And sometimes the moon is obscured by the earth's atmosphere, the second stanza's trope.

In the first stanza, "I"—the meditator as earth—"make His Crescent fill or lack[;] His Nature is at Full / Or Quarter—as I signify," which is, of course, true of the moon and earth. Although the moon is always present, reflecting the sun's light, when viewed from the earth the moon's disc appears to be sometimes a crescent, sometimes full, sometimes quarter, and at new moon we cannot see the moon's disc at all. So great is her power over the moon that she even controls "His Tides," that is, the earth's oceans' tides. Because the moon's gravitational pull is chiefly responsible for the tides of the terrestrial oceans, the "Tides" are his. But because she controls the moon, she also controls his influence upon the earth's tides. Very likely a pun on "Tides" and "tidings" is intended: he is the sacred Muse whose "News," or tidings, she tells, and when her Muse seems to fail, it is really her fault because she controls the moon that controls his "Tides"/tidings. Similarly, in the second stanza it is the earth's atmosphere that interferes with her perception of the moon's perpetual reflection of the sun's light. At her command, he gropes like a blind man behind the earth's clouds or like a prisoner behind columns of mist, though it is not, of course, he who is blinded or imprisoned, but rather she herself who is blinded and imprisoned by the earth's clouds and mist.

Having boasted of her awesome power in the first two stanzas, she concludes that so interdependent are they that neither of them really knows which is the "Despot," he—the "Despot . . . of Down" (J-1334)—or she, because they hold a "Mutual Disc," the reciprocal face the moon and earth present to one other, with "Disc" singular because "Themself are One" (F-21-9, J-449). They are a double planet, though she is only terrestrial, while he is the celestial moon brightly shining in the darkness, a witty variation of the usual sun/Son pun. And so they will remain, "even unto the end of the world," the "Mutual Day" they front, doomsday and the day of Judgment she anticipates in poem 20.

# DICKINSON'S AND HERBERT'S DEPICTIONS OF DOOMSDAY

Except for its allusion to doomsday as the "Mutual Day" they front, Dickinson's poem 19 bears no resemblance to Herbert's "Dooms-day." But there are some striking resemblances between his dramatization of the occasion and hers in the thirtieth fascicle's first poem:

No Crowd that has occurred
Exhibit—I suppose
That General Attendance
That Resurrection—does—

Circumference be full—
The long restricted Grave      [restricted/subjected]
Assert her Vital Privilege—      [Assert His Primogeniture]
The Dust—connect—and live—      [connect/adjust]

On Atoms—features place—
All Multitudes that were
Efface in the Comparison
As Suns—dissolve a star—      [dissolve/annul]

Solemnity—prevail—
It's Individual Doom
Possess each separate Consciousness—
August—Absorbed—Numb—                    [August—Resistless—dumb]

What Duplicate—exist—
What Parallel can be—                                    [Parallel/scenery]
Of the Significance of This—                  [Significance/stupendousness]
To Universe—and Me?

 . . . . . . . . . .


                    *Dooms-day*
                        Come away,
                    Make no delay.
            Summon all the dust to rise,
            Till it stirre, and rubbe the eyes:
            While this member jogs the other,
            Each one whispering, *Live you brother?*


                        Come away,
                    Make this the day.
            Dust, alas, no musick feels,
            But thy trumpet: then it kneels,
            As peculiar notes and strains
            Cure Tarantulas raging pains.


                        Come away,
                    O make no stay!
            Let the graves make their confession,
            Lest at length they plead possession:
            Fleshes stubbornnesse may have
            Read that lesson to the grave.


                        Come away,
                    Thy flock doth stray.
            Some to windes their bodie lend,
            And in them may drown a friend:
            Some in noisome vapours grow
            To a plague and publick wo.

Come away,
Help our decay.
Man is out of order hurl'd,
Parcel'd out to all the world.
Lord, thy broken consort raise,
And the musick shall be praise.

Both poets "reinvent" received notions of the general resurrection, as Helen Vendler writes of Herbert's "Dooms-day" (*Poetry of George Herbert* 31, 55). Both depart from the customary severe view, perhaps most gruesomely depicted in Michael Wigglesworth's "Day of Doom," with their fantasy and wit, what William Empson calls Herbert's "saintly impertinence" (*Seven Types of Ambiguity* 238). As Herbert's newly awakened dead jog one another in amazement, so Dickinson's protagonist wryly observes that no doubt the general resurrection will be well attended, then puns that "Circumference" will then be "full"—that is, the "Circumference" of time will be completed and the "Circumference" of eternity full of the assembled crowd. In both poems a personified grave gives up the dead—though Dickinson's will do so gladly, but Herbert's may do so reluctantly—whereupon Herbert's "dust" will rise and Dickinson's "Dust" will connect and live. As Herbert's newly resurrected have eyes to "rubbe," so Dickinson's have faces with "features."

Dickinson's speaker then observes (which Herbert's does not) that the world's multitudes will be effaced in the way the comparatively minor light of a star is obscured by the overpowering brilliance of the "Suns," an observation that anticipates her wish to "Fade" into "Divinity" (F-39-21, J-682) and also F-40's final poem, where upon entry into eternity the superior splendor of the "Suns"—God the sun and Jesus the sun/Son—will "extinguish . . . Us." Both poems conclude with a return to the present as both speakers focus upon themselves as well as upon their fellow creatures. Herbert's speaker directly addresses the Lord, asking him to raise his "consort," both himself as Jesus' companion and all his fellows, the human company of musicians who will then sing his praises, and Dickinson's concludes with a rhetorical question: what parallel could there possibly be to the stupendous significance of the scene she has just imagined—both to the "Universe," her fellow creatures, and to herself? The answer is, of course, that there is nothing of comparable significance. As in "A Solemn thing within the Soul / To feel itself get ripe," "Harvest"—Judgment Day (Matt. 13.30)—is the single goal of some lives, including her own (F-22-12, J-483). As she declares in poem

20, she has staked all on a single goal: the hope of being among the saved sheep at the Judgment.


# POEM 20


F-40's penultimate poem, like its second, concerns Judgment Day. Though the word "Judgment" appears in neither poem, it is obviously the subject of the second because there the meditator paraphrases Jesus' prediction of the Judgment in the sheep-and-goats parable. That this final day is also the twentieth poem's imagined setting is less obvious, but the text provides several telling clues. One is its echoes of poem 2: there the meditator declares her intention to "endure" in her service to the bridegroom, and here she boasts that she *has* "endured" in her service to the "Brave Beloved." Other clues lie in the poem's legal diction and the past tense of its first two stanzas' verbs, which lead one to see that in this dramatic monologue she is imagining how she will sum up and defend her life in time after it is over:

> Robbed by Death—but that was easy—
> To the failing Eye          [failing/Dying—/clouding]
> I could hold the latest Glowing—
> Robbed by Liberty
>
> For Her Jugular Defences—
> This, too, I endured—
> Hint of Glory—it afforded—
> For the Brave Beloved—                    [Brave/bold]
>
> Fraud of Distance—Fraud of Danger,
> Fraud of Death—to bear—
> It is Bounty—to Suspense's
> Vague Calamity—
>
> Staking our entire Possession        [entire/divine—]
> On a Hair's result—
> Then—Seesawing—coolly—on it—
> Trying if it split—                        [As to estimate]

Rather than wail, tear her hair, and plead for mercy, like those about to be judged in Wigglesworth's "Day of Doom," the meditator is high-spirited and confident as she begins her imagined defense by boasting of all she has endured in her service to the "Brave Beloved." Since in the sheep-and-goats parable it is Jesus who will separate the sheep from the goats, he is here the judge she addresses. But since he has also promised to be with his followers "even unto the end of the world," doomsday, he will also be her advocate (1 John 2.1), the "Brave Beloved" she has devoted her life and art to serving. Apparently she has decided that the best defense is an offense, because she describes herself as having been robbed and defrauded, though, as her lines show, she does not regret the life she has chosen.

She begins her defense by declaring she has been robbed by her own death to the world, robbed, as in poem 5, of her limited, complacent life in "Contentment's quiet Suburb." But, she continues, that was "easy," echoing Jesus' words in Matt. 11.28–30, as she did in the sixth poem's debate and will again in this poem's second stanza: "Come unto me, all ye that labour and are heavy laden, and I will give you rest. Take my yoke upon you, . . . For my yoke is easy." The dying life she began to lead when she took his yoke upon herself has been easy because, as she then explains, it has resulted in her poems. "Glowing," defined in Dickinson's lexicon as "white heat," echoes "Dare you see a soul at the 'White Heat'?" in which she describes her poetic process as her transformation of "Ore" into "designated Light" (F-20-6, J-365). Bearing his yoke has been easy because to her dying eye she could hold the latest "Glowing," her most recent undying poem.

Her defense continues as follows: she has been robbed by liberty—not *of* liberty but *by* liberty—again, as in poem 5, robbed *of* the safe limitations of the circuit dwellers' "Laws" *by* the terrifying limitless liberty she has gained with her betrothal to Christ. While she does not say it was easy, this, too, she endured because it allowed her to glorify the beloved, who is himself boldly unafraid of freedom. Though the essential meaning of her second robbery is clear, its first sentence, which begins in the first stanza's last line, is at first puzzling:

> [I was] Robbed by Liberty
> For Her Jugular Defences.

Liberty's "Jugular Defences" is the first of this poem's two far-fetched conceits. According to Dickinson's lexicon, "jugular" is derived from "jugum," meaning "yoke," and is therefore another allusion to Jesus' yoke in Matt. 11.

The sentence reads, "I was robbed by liberty for her yoke's defences." Discovering what it is that liberty's yoke defends one against depends upon the reader's remembering another biblical "yoke" passage, Gal. 5.1: "Stand fast"—endure—"in the liberty wherewith Christ hath made us free, and be not entangled again with the yoke of bondage." By wearing the yoke of liberty, then, she has been defended from the yoke of bondage, the fifth poem's "Laws."

In the following two stanzas, a single long sentence, the meditator, like a skilled lawyer, sums up and elaborates upon the points she has just made, then presents her final point, and then rests her case:

> Fraud of Distance—Fraud of Danger,
> Fraud of Death—to bear—
> It is Bounty [when compared] to Suspense's
> Vague Calamity [which means]
>
> Staking our entire Possession                          [entire/divine—]
> On a Hair's result [and]
> Then—Seesawing—coolly—on it—
> Trying if it split—                                    [As to estimate]

In the first two stanzas she testifies that she was robbed by her death to the world and by the liberty she therefore acquired, but here she testifies that she was defrauded by her death, which has meant living the dangerous life of liberty at a distance from all she had renounced—banished "from native Eyes— / In sight of Native Air" (F-27-4, J-561). But, she imagines herself telling the almighty judge, "It," her death and all it entailed, is bounty when compared to the uncertain misery of not knowing the outcome of her pilgrimage through time. She cannot, of course, know, because salvation cannot be earned by even the most exemplary life, it depends upon faith and ultimately upon God's grace. As she puns, his sentence is suspended until the Judgment, and the "Suspense" mangles her like a "Gnat" (J-1331).

Because one cannot know the outcome of one's pilgrimage, leading the kind of life she has chosen means staking "our" entire divine possession—one's privilege of finiteness and one's soul—on a "Hair's result," then seesawing coolly on this hair, testing it to see if it will split or remain intact. Again, the essential meaning of these lines is quite clear. Since one cannot strike a bargain with Jesus, agreeing to lead a life in his service in exchange for the guarantee of eternal life, leading the Christian life entails risk. It could be that despite one's life of service, the almighty judge will find one's faith to be insufficient or decide for his own divine reasons to withhold union with himself.

While the lines' essential meaning is clear, the hair conceit is puzzling until the reader realizes that "Hair," like the preceding poem's gravitational pull between the moon and earth, is a metonym for "faith," this cluster's key word and meditational focus. Though this conceit is almost as far-fetched as liberty's "Jugular Defences," it resembles several other Dickinson poems in which she represents faith—etymologically, according to Dickinson's lexicon, a rope or cable—as a slender but tough and resilient filament or force connecting the faithful soul to God. In J-915, for example, which is also dated 1864 but not included in a fascicle, faith is an invisible suspension bridge that is as strong as though its foundation were of steel:

> Faith—is the Pierless bridge
> Supporting what We see
> Unto the scene that We do not—
> Too slender for the eye [and yet]
>
> It bears the soul as bold
> As [though] it were rocked in Steel

Similarly, in a late poem dated 1878, "our Faith" treads on a bridge that is "brittle," but also trustworthy because God himself built it, then sent his "Son" to test it, and his Son "pronounced it firm" (J-1433). While that poem's bridge is "brittle," in F-18-5 Jesus "strained" her faith—as one might strain a rope or the string of a musical instrument (Webster's examples)—and found it, not brittle, but "supple" (J-497).

Although Emily Dickinson must surely be the first to depict faith as a "Hair"—which, as she comments in a letter dated late 1885 to Sue, "is very fine, but . . . never dissolves" (L-1024)—she is by no means the first to portray faith as a filament linking Christ to humans. Her tropes of faith as an invisible suspension bridge, a rope or string, gravity, and a hair, like Herbert's "silk twist let down from heav'n to me," are reminiscent of the traditional emblem of the soul making her way across a labyrinth by holding one end of a thread, while Divine Love stands on a high tower holding the other end of the thread ("The Pearl"; Lewalski, *Protestant Poetics* 192) (Fig. 5). Presumably Emily Dickinson was familiar with this emblem, because it appears in Quarles's *Emblems, Divine and Moral*, a book, now at Houghton Library, that was in the Dickinson libraries.

Fig. 5.

Her conceit in "Robbed by Death," then, is that since one cannot know the outcome of one's quest, one wagers or pledges one's life and soul on a hair's—faith's—"result," then seesaws on this hair of faith, testing it to see if it will split. As this final cluster's only true rhyme, "it"-"split" underscores the crucial import of her experiment. Still, she is seesawing "coolly"— calmly and deliberately, rather than anxiously and fearfully—because she has confidence in the hair's "result," defined in Dickinson's lexicon as both "resilience" and "consequence." She has confidence that her own faith will remain resilient and supple because her faith has withstood trials before, as evidenced by the preceding fascicles. She also has confidence in her faith's "consequence," that the bond of faith and love between her and the bridegroom will remain intact through eternity—though that decision, of course, lies with him in whom she has cast her fate.

In this final cluster, the meditator declares a "saving faith" as it is defined in Emily Dickinson's lexicon and concordance. The meditator begins with the foundation of saving faith, her belief in Christ's immutable veracity, then submits her affection and intellect—her "minuter intuitions"—as well as her will to him by declaring her belief in his promises. By means of her poems, her "Glowing[s]," she has demonstrated a faith that "worketh by love" for him and her fellow creatures, rather than an idle, inactive faith (Gal. 5.6). And in poem 20 she accepts that her final salvation depends not on herself but on him.

Poem 20 bears some interesting resemblances to Herbert's "Judgement":

> Almightie Judge, how shall poore wretches brook
>     Thy dreadfull look,
> Able a heart of iron to appall,
>     When thou shalt call
> For ev'ry mans peculiar book?
>
> What others mean to do, I know not well;
>     Yet I heare tell,
> That some will turn thee to some leaves therein
>     So void of sinne,
> That they in merit shall excell.
>
> But I resolve, when thou shall call for mine,
>     That to decline,
> And thrust a Testament into thy hand:
>     Let that be scann'd.
> There thou shall find my faults are thine.

Both Herbert's and Dickinson's speakers imagine what they will say to the almighty judge on Judgment Day, but the tone of each is no more grim and solemn than in their depictions of doomsday. What each plans to say is different, though in some ways not so different as it appears initially. Herbert's resolves that when the almighty judge asks for his book of life, he will cheekily thrust a Testament into his hand and tell him, "There thou shall find my faults are thine." By doing so, he will decline the doctrine of merit and trust to Paul's doctrine of Christ's having taken human sins upon himself, thereby acknowledging that his salvation depends upon Christ and not upon himself (Hutchinson, commentary on *The Temple*, in *Works of George Herbert* 542–43). Dickinson's meditator, on the other hand, plans to begin by describing rather fully her life of service. But after doing so she will acknowledge that a life of service does not guarantee ultimate salvation, that it depends on faith and ultimately upon him.

Both rehearsals for Judgment are followed by poems about heaven, and though these poems are unlike one another except for their subject, both are declarations of the speaker's faith in eternal life.

# POEM 21

As the twentieth poem returns to the subject of the second poem, so the twenty-first returns to the subject of the first poem: what the twelfth poem's "Compound Vision" enables the meditator to see:

> Unfulfilled to Observation—
> Incomplete—to Eye—
> But to Faith—a Revolution
> In Locality—
>
> Unto Us—the Suns extinguish—
> To our Opposite—
> New Horizons—they embellish—        [embellish/Replenish]
> Fronting Us—with Night.        [Turning Us—their Night.]

As she begins F-40's meditation by declaring that "I"/eye see only the immanent God while traversing the finite sphere, so she concludes her meditation by declaring that through faith her "Eye"/I sees, though incompletely, the infinite sphere of the transcendent God toward which she progresses. As she begins F-40's meditation by describing herself as a poet-pilgrim who "traverses" the "Street" of "Existence," so she concludes her meditation by declaring her belief that eternity will be a "Revolution in

Locality" from the street of existence she now traverses to the "New Horizons" of eternity. In F-40's first poem she receives bulletins from Immortality all "Day," and in its final poem the faithful will at last be fronted with "Night," here, as in the first fascicle's eleventh poem, the unknown afterlife, the "dark" her "faith . . . adores" (J-7).

This final poem is F-40's fifth in which circular tropes emblematically represent the relation between the finite and infinite circumferences, echoing the seventeenth-century poets and writers whose favorite emblem for both man and God is a circle (Nicolson, *Breaking the Circle*). In poem 12, "The Admirations—and Contempts—of time," Christ, the "Convex—and Concave Witness," is the infinite lens that empowers the terrestrial eye of the faithful, giving them the compound vision that enables them to see most accurately both back toward the sphere of time and forward toward the sphere of God. In poem 13, "Till Death—is narrow Loving," the meditator contrasts "narrow" circuit love with circumferential love, which is "Love—somewhat," love to a certain degree, and both forms of human love with the infinite circumference of divine love. In poem 15, "Pain—expands the Time," she counters the twelfth poem's circular emblems by describing those dark nights of the soul when, without Christ as lens, the solitary I/eye sees only itself and is reduced again to the limited circuit sphere. In poem 19, "I make his Crescent fill or lack," she in turn counters the fifteenth poem's circular emblems by declaring that even when she does not feel his presence, he is always with her, and that their mutual love and faith bind them together as the moon and earth are bound together by their gravitational pull. As she concludes in poem 21, the finite "Eye"/I empowered by Christ, the infinite lens, sees, though incompletely, the eternal circumference's "New Horizons" (Diagram 16).

Though in poem 16 she imagines in the language of sacred parody what her entry into eternity might be like, here she anticipates the conjunction of the finite and infinite circumferences—the "Junction" where "Love that was—and Love too best to be— / Meet" (F-32-9, J-622)—with the images of light and circularity that are also often favored by devotional poets (e.g., Herbert's "The Glance" and Henry Vaughan's "The World"). By doing so, she implicitly acknowledges that eternity is a riddle whose answer will be given only then, that "Eye hath not seen, nor ear heard, neither have entered into the heart of man, the things which God hath prepared for them that love him" (1 Cor. 2.9). Appropriately, the poem is itself a riddle in which the word "eternity" does not appear, though it is obviously the focus of her meditation.

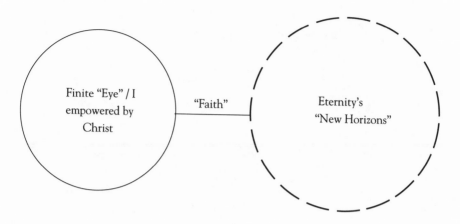

Diagram 16.

While eternity is unfulfilled to observation and incomplete to eye, it is "to Faith"—that is, "Unto Us" who have faith—a revolution in "Locality" from "Illocality" (the "no continuing city" of the faithful to which Christ bore her on the day of her betrothal) to his heavenly city, his heavenly kingdom. Then the "Suns"—God the sun and Jesus the sun/Son—will extinguish "Us" to "our Opposite." As in 1 Cor. 15.51, "we shall all be changed," and as in Dickinson's imagined doomsday, "we" will be obscured by the superior splendor of the suns. By embellishing eternity's new horizons, the "Suns" will front "Us" with night, or as the variant reads, they will turn "Us" their night, the unknown afterlife that has puzzled the faithful throughout their pilgrimage in time. In eternity the riddle will at last be solved.

The fortieth fascicle's third and final period firmly concludes the meditator's declaration of faith in the eternal "Circumference," as well as her five declarations of faith, her F-40 meditation, and her "Experiment Toward Men."

# Conclusion.
# The Forty Fascicles' "Experiment"

When the meditator declared in F-40's opening sentence, "The Only News I know / Is Bulletins all Day / From Immortality," she declared what the reader subsequently discovers is her meditation's dual purpose: to contemplate what she now knows through sight and memory, understanding, and faith, and to contemplate the merits of Christ and his past, present, and future relation to herself. With "I" she thus introduced F-40's setting, the "Circumference" of her own mind, as with "I" and "Immortality" she introduced this final fascicle's two dramatis personae, herself and Christ, her inner voice, her better self. F-40, then, is both highly traditional and intensely modern. It is not only a meditation but also a variation of the dramatic monologue, a favorite nineteenth-century form that was prefigured in the seventeenth-century's dramatic lyric and remains a favorite in the twentieth, as well as a variation of the interior monologue, anticipating another favorite twentieth-century form.

F-40 portrays a drama enacted in the meditator's mind—the "Only Theatre recorded" that its "Owner cannot shut" (F-37-4, J-741)—though that poem's lovers are Romeo and Juliet, while F-40's are Christ and herself. Retrospectively one sees that while in F-40 she has revealed her own character and portrayed his with remarkable fullness, he is a static character and in a sense so is she. Though she views him and his relation to herself from multiple perspectives, his character does not change—which is hardly surprising, since Deity is unchanging. And though she recollects her own past conflicts and comes to terms with them in F-40, her character does not really change either: she is as much a triumphantly assured Christian poet-pilgrim in her meditation's first poem, when she declares the "Only News" she knows and tells is her bulletins from Christ, as she is in its final poem, when she declares her faith in eternity's "New Horizons."

F-40's most fluid "character" is the reader who has been pulled into this uncanny text and forced to enact the role of sleuth. What changes most is the "Circumference" of the reader's mind. Though the text is no doubt richer than any reading of it, including this one, the reader has progressed from ignorance to enlightenment, from seeing F-40 as a random collection of singularly cryptic poems in Emily Dickinson's late style to seeing F-40 as an architectural tour de force, a three-part meditation, a letter addressed to the reader, a garland of praise, and a conversion narrative, as well as the triumphant conclusion of the protagonist's account of her poetic and spiritual pilgrimage from renunciation to illumination to union and finally, after many conflicts, to contentment with this union. The protagonist's pilgrimage thus ends happily, and so does the reader's arduous but exhilarating journey of discovery through F-40: the forty fascicles' protagonist has reached a plateau of joy and confidence, and the reader's "Ear" has proved to be "Not too dull" to hear at least a good part of what the protagonist, in its first poem, declares she knows, and tells.

Retrospectively one sees that F-40's Jesus is the Jesus of the Bible and Christian tradition, though Emily Dickinson varies and embellishes her biblical and traditional sources. Retrospectively one also sees that she has drawn upon a vast number of biblical passages to create F-40's portrait of him. In its first poem he is "Immortality," echoing his own proclamation, "I am the resurrection" (John 11.25), as well as Paul's description of him as he who "abolished death" and "brought life and immortality to light through the gospel" (2 Tim. 1.10). As the sender of the meditator's bulletins, he is the Logos, the mediator between God and humankind. As the bringer of the only news she knows and tells in F-40, he is the sacred Muse. Then in poem 2 he is the master/bridegroom whom she serves and whom she addresses as "Sweet," as well as the "Stranger" the world did not know (John 1.10), the crucified Savior, the judge who on the final day will separate the saved sheep from the damned goats (Matt. 25.31–46), and, as king of the "Life" that means "Love," the bringer of the new dispensation, who proclaimed that the first great commandment is to love God and that the second is like it, to love one's neighbor as oneself (Matt. 22.36–39). In poem 3 he is both "Perfectness," he who was made perfect (Heb. 5.9), and the soul's cultivator (Mark 4.29; Rev. 14.15), the sower of the "secret seed" that came to fruition on the day of her death at summer's close and the wielder of the "Flail." In poem 3b he is the quiet but persistent suitor who stands knocking at the door of the soul (Rev. 3.20), then, when the meditator heard his voice and said "yes," the powerful bridegroom who bore her high above the world (Rev. 21.10) and as "Sunrise" became her soul's permanent illuminator (Rev. 21.23). Because on that day her soul became his place of residence (Eph. 2.22) and he therefore became her inner voice, her better self, he interrupts the fourth poem's meditation to ask two questions, the first of his five speeches in F-40.

In poem 5 he is "Agony" and "Affliction," the man of sorrows; "Tremendousness," the numinous God-man before whom even the devils tremble (James 2.19); "Boundlessness," he who as the word of God is not bound (2 Tim. 2.9); and "Immensity," or infinity, the representative of the infinite sphere, as he is throughout F-40. As the bringer of the "glorious"—but terrifying—"liberty of the children of God" (Rom. 8.21), he is the spiritual and poetic liberator of the meditator's soul. In the sixth poem's recollected dialogue, he himself says he is both human and divine, "Late of Judea" and "Now—of Paradise"; "Omnipotence," the all-powerful God; and "Pardon," the Redeemer who died to gain forgiveness for all (Isa. 59.20, 60.16). Moreover, as his lines reveal, he is kind but persistent, an accomplished debater who is quick with the rejoinder and adroit with the pun. In poem 7 he is both "Wisdom" (1 Cor. 1.24) and the "spoiler of Our Home," the thief of Matthew's parable, who "broke up" the householder's home by bringing the kingdom of God (Matt. 24.43, 12.28–29). In poem 8 he is both the "paltry" or ragged "One" who was rich but became poor so that his followers might become rich (2 Cor. 8.9) and the "bo[u]lder," the chief corner stone (1 Pet. 2.6), of the house built upon a rock (Matt. 7.24).

In poem 9 he is the Lord of Psalm 30, whom the meditator, echoing the psalmist, reminds of his need for her to sing his praise and tell his truth. In poem 10 he is again her inner voice, reminding her that she is not as rich as she supposes (Rev. 3.17), because she does not have "Me, nor Me," neither him nor the readers she intends her "Experiment" to serve as a means of serving him. Still, like the lord of the parable of the talents, he praises her industry because she has not, like the parable's slothful servant, buried her one talent

(Matt. 25.24–26). In poem 11 he is again the second and eighth poems' "Stranger," one from another country, the sphere of eternity, and again, as in poems 1 and 2, both the source of her poems and the one whom they are ultimately intended to serve. In poem 12, as Revelation's "faithful witness and the first begotten of the dead" (1.5), he is the infinite lens who empowers the finite eye of the faithful, giving them "Compound Vision." In poem 13 he is again the bridegroom who elicits such an all-consuming love in the soul who is betrothed to him that after the day of their betrothal the bride is so devastated by his absence that she "Thenceforward" imitates his life (e.g., Teresa of Avila, *Interior Castle* 85–119). As poem 14 then reveals, the master/ bridegroom/Muse is himself a poet, whose monologue is a slant Miltonic sonnet. Though he is absent from the fifteenth poem's lament, in poem 16 he is the bridegroom of the parable of the ten virgins and of Canticles, who, as in poems 6 and 14, is so lovingly concerned for each of his followers that if he does not immediately recognize the meditator's (she hopes) perfected self when she at last enters the door of eternity, he will anxiously ask where she is.

In poem 17 and throughout the poems of faith he is "truth" (John 14.6) and therefore incapable of "Fraud." In poem 18 he has tasted death for "every man" (Heb. 2.9), regardless of "Color" or "Denomination." In poem 19 he is the moon, brightly shining in the darkness, whether or not the meditator feels his presence (Rev. 21.23). In the twentieth poem's rehearsal for Judgment Day, he is, as he predicted in the sheep-and-goats parable, the judge to whom she will present her defense, but he is also her advocate (1 John 2.1), the "Brave Beloved" to whom her life and art have been dedicated. And in poem 21 the "Suns," God the sun (Ps. 84.11) and Jesus the sun/Son (Mal. 4.2), will embellish eternity's "New Horizons."

Having discovered that comprehending the cryptic fortieth fascicle depends upon recollecting the preceding fascicles, one also sees the other fascicles from a newly enlightened perspective. Deciphering F-40 first and then returning to the earlier fascicles to study them is like reading the concluding chapter of a detective story and then, knowing its outcome, reading the story from the beginning. Retrospectively one sees that the fortieth fascicle directly alludes to the first fascicle. While in F-40 the protagonist is a wife who has attained success in her pilgrimage, in F-1 she is a "maiden" (J-33) who is setting out on her pilgrimage with an enthusiasm that is underscored by the first fascicle's thirty-one exclamation points. While the word "Day" appears throughout F-40, in F-1 she celebrates "this morning," "this Summer's day," and "Today." Although in F-40 there are few natural images, F-1, like F-40-3 ("Midsummer, was it, when they died"), is "full"—that is, F-1 is filled with summer's creatures and especially with flowers, most of them in shades of purple or red like the "Anemone," the "Orchis," the violet, and the "Gentian," which appears two times, as well as the "Rose" (whose color is not specified), which appears five times. Moreover, the parable of the talents is central to F-1, as it is to F-40. In both fascicles death and rebirth are recurring themes, and so are gain and loss. Both include two poems anticipating heaven. Both include a second character whom the protagonist refers to and addresses. Both include dialogues with Jesus, though there are five in F-40 and only one in F-1 (J-4). In the first fascicle, as in the fortieth, the protagonist's poetic intention is to serve both her readers and her master: as in F-40-14 she is her master's "Maid," so in F-1-4 and -18 she is his "hand," that is, his servant (J-20, J-32). Most important, having discovered that the final fascicle is a three-part meditation, one discovers when one returns to study F-1 that it, too, is a three-part meditation. Its first four poems form its composition of place. Poems 5 through 16 form its poems of analysis. And poems 17 through 22 form its concluding colloquy (Ignatius, Spiritual Exercises 56). Though a detailed analysis of the first fascicle will require a long chapter in another book, the following summarizes its broad outlines.

In the first fascicle's first four poems, the protagonist/meditator summons the powers of sight and memory to create her meditation's setting:

> The Gentian weaves her fringes—
> The Maple's loom is red—
> My departing blossoms
>    Obviate parade.
>
> A brief, but patient illness—
> An hour to prepare,
> And one below, this morning
> Is where the angels are—
> It was a short procession,
> The Bobolink was there—
> An aged Bee addressed us—
> And then we knelt in prayer—
> We trust that she was willing—
> We ask that we may be.
> Summer—Sister—Seraph!
> Let us go with thee!

In the name of the Bee—
And of the Butterfly—
And of the Breeze—Amen!

Frequently the woods are pink—
Frequently, are brown.
Frequently the hills undress
Behind my native town—
Oft a head is crested
I was wont to see—
And as oft a cranny
Where it used to be—
And the Earth—they tell me—
On it's Axis turned!
Wonderful rotation—
By but *twelve* performed!

A sepal, petal, and a thorn
Upon a common summer's morn—
A flask of Dew—A Bee or two—
A Breeze—a'caper in the trees—
And I'm a Rose!

Distrustful of the Gentian—
And just to turn away,
The fluttering of her fringes
Chid my perfidy—
Weary for my ———
I will singing go—
I shall not feel the sleet—then—
I shall not fear the snow.

Flees so the phantom meadow
Before the breathless Bee—
So bubble brooks in deserts
On Ears that dying lie—
Burn so the Evening Spires
To Eyes that Closing go—
Hangs so a distant Heaven—
To a hand below.

In the first poem she describes the season as the close of summer, when the "Gentian" blooms; next she recollects the funeral she and summer's creatures held for summer's passing; and finally she vows to die as the summer has done. This first poem, which is in itself a three-part meditation, introduces many of the first fascicle's recurring themes, tropes, and key words. Its three-part meditational structure and concluding three-line benediction—invoking the "Bee," "Butterfly," and "Breeze" (Father, Son, and Holy Ghost)—introduce this fascicle's recurring threeness: as fiveness appears throughout F-40, so threeness appears throughout F-1. That the summer has died and "this morning / Is where the angels are" introduces the first fascicle's recurring theme of death and rebirth, its recurring allusions to summer and angels, and its emphasis upon "today" and "this Summer's day." Similarly, the first poem's funeral, "prayer," vow, and benediction are echoed in this fascicle's subsequent sacramental and liturgical diction, the sixth poem's "chancel" and the twenty-first poem's "ordained" (J-22; J-34).

Having portrayed the setting as the close of summer in poem 1, the protagonist/meditator then recollects in poem 2 the varying seasonal appearances of the hills behind her "native town." This poem's first three parallel lines ("Frequently the woods are pink— / Frequently, are brown. / Frequently . . . undress") repeat the first poem's triplicity, as its description of the death and rebirth of the seasons repeat the first poem's death and rebirth of both summer and herself. Having portrayed the panoramic vista of the hills, she then in poem 3 focuses upon a single "Rose." This poem, whose setting is a "summer's morn," echoing the first poem's "Summer" and "morning," is a description of what it takes to make both a rose, meaning the flower, and a poem about a rose. The poem thus blurs the distinction between flower and poem, as do several of the following F-1 poems. Moreover, since the poem is spoken by the rose, and since "I" signifies the protagonist/meditator throughout F-1, this poem also blurs the distinction between flower, poem, and herself, anticipating F-40-9, "I hide myself within my flower," as well as the first fascicle's final two poems, in which she again blurs the distinction between flower, poem, and herself.

In poem 4 she recollects a time after the first poem's vow, though the season is still either the close of summer or autumn because the "Gentian" is still blooming (the fringed gentian, harbinger of the season's end, begins to bloom in August, L-207n, and continues to bloom until "just before the Snows," F-24-15, J-442). On this recollected occasion she was "just" about to "turn away" from her vow when the "fluttering" of the gentian's "fringes / Chid" her "perfidy," defined in Dickinson's lexicon as the act of violating a vow. (In a late poem, "The Gentian has a parched Corolla," J-1424, dated 1877, the fringed gentian is an emblem of "Fidelity.") This fourth poem also introduces a second character identified only as "————." But there are several clues enabling the reader to infer this second character's identity. One is that the line in which "————" appears reveals that the missing name or title is a trochee: "Wéarȳ fór m̃y —́ ˘—." Another is that in this poem's final line the protagonist is a "hand below," a pun on her hand writing these poems and on herself as —́ ˘—'s hand/servant, a pun that will occur again in this fascicle's eighteenth poem, "When Roses cease to bloom, Sir." The "—́ ˘—" for whom she labors and is "Weary" is therefore her "mástĕr," defined by Dickinson's lexicon as one who has servants.

That the fourth poem repeats the first poem's "Gentian" provides one of several indications that poem 4 concludes this meditation's composition of place. Another is the abrupt shift from the first four poems' lush visual images from nature to the fifth poem's spare diction of losing and winning:

> We lose—because we win—
> Gamblers—recollecting which
> Toss their dice again!

As the first of the first fascicle's twelve poems of analysis, poem 5, a tercet reiterating this fascicle's triplicity, states the fifth through sixteenth poems' subject for contemplation: losing and winning, loss and gain, death and rebirth. Poem 5 also draws attention to the first fascicle's chief biblical analogues. One is Matt. 10.39, "he that loseth his life for my sake shall find it." Another is John's parable of the corn of wheat that must die in order to bear fruit, which concludes, "He that loveth his life shall lose it," but "he that hateth his life in this world shall keep it until life eternal." But most important to F-1, as to F-40, is the parable of the talents, in which the fearful, slothful servant hid his talent in a hole in the earth, while the two industrious servants multiplied their talents by putting them out to exchangers, that is, by taking a risk, by being "Gamblers" (J. Hillis Miller, *Tropes, Parables, Performatives* 142). In F-1 the protagonist has thus chosen to "lose" her former way of life, to die to the world, in order to "find" her life and "keep it until life eternal"; she has chosen to multiply her talents even though she realizes that doing so entails risks, being a "Gambler," as in F-40-20, "Robbed by Death," she is "Staking" her entire possession.

Retrospectively one sees that the fourth poem's "hand"/servant, who is "Weary" from laboring for her master, is a typological variation of the parable of the talents' industrious "servants" who multiplied their lord's talents. As one also sees, poem 6 echoes all three of the parables implicit in poem 5:

> All these my banners be.
> I sow my pageantry
> In May—
> It rises train by train—
> Then sleeps in state again—
> My chancel—all the plain
>      Today.
>
> To lose—if one can find again—
> To miss—if one shall meet—
> The Burglar cannot rob—then—
> The Broker cannot cheat.
> So build the hillocks gaily
> Thou little spade of mine
> Leaving nooks for Daisy
> And for Columbine—
> You and I the secret
> Of the Crocus know—
> Let us chant it softly—
> "*There* is no more snow!"
>
> To him who keeps an Orchis' heart—
> The swamps are pink with June.

This poem, like F-1-3, blurs the distinction between flowers and poems. In the first of its three stanzas, the protagonist might simply be a gardener who is proudly surveying her "banners"/flowers. By reflecting that she sows her "pageantry" in May, that it "rises" in summer, then "sleeps" again in winter, she reiterates this fascicle's theme of death and rebirth. And by declaring the plain is today her "chancel" (that part of the church where the altar is placed), she adds a sacramental and liturgical dimension to her gardening, recalling the sacramental and liturgical diction of this fascicle's first poem and anticipating its penultimate poem's "ordained." The second stanza's first two lines allude to the death and rebirth of her flowers, which she loses and misses in fall and winter, then finds and meets again in spring and summer. But, as the third and fourth lines reveal, what she ultimately hopes to find and meet again is something far more permanent than flowers, something that "The Burglar cannot rob," echoing Jesus' words in the Sermon on the Mount: "lay up for yourselves treasures in heaven, where . . . thieves do not . . . steal" (Matt. 6.20). This poem's subject, then, is not simply flowers but the permanent treasures she is laying up for herself in heaven, her flowers/poems. Retrospectively one sees that the second stanza's first line, "To lose—if one can find again," paraphrases Matt. 10.39, "he that loseth his life for my sake shall find it," and that in this poem the protagonist *has* lost her former way of life and found a new life as a gardener, a sower of the word (Mark 4.14). Retrospectively one also sees that it is her master whom she misses and hopes to meet in the "eternal life" of John's corn parable. The second stanza concludes with her apostrophe to her "spade," recalling the parable of the talents' servant who "digged" a hole in the earth and hid his talent in it. Unlike the parable's "slothful" servant, she industriously uses her spade to make her garden of flowers/poems flourish.

In poem 7, "I had a guinea golden / I lost it in the sand" (J-23), her lament for a "missing friend" who is now "In country far from here" echoes the sixth poem's "To miss—if one shall meet" again, as well as the talents parable, whose lord, after presenting his servants with talents, departed to a "far country." Poems 8 through 11 form a unit in which two poems about rebirth are bracketed by two poems anticipating heaven, the ultimate rebirth. In poem 8, "There is a morn by men unseen" (J-24), she imagines heaven as a "remoter green" where "maids . . . Keep their Seraphic May." In poem 9, "As if I asked a common alms" (J-323), she celebrates her own rebirth. In poem 10, "She slept beneath a tree" (J-25), a red flower blooms, is reborn in spring. Then in poem 11, "The feet of people walking home" (J-7), she again anticipates heaven. Though in F-40-5 through -8 "Home" is the protagonist's renounced past life in "Contentment's quiet Suburb," in F-1-11 "home" is heaven. Another of this poem's tropes for the unknown afterlife is "Night," as it is in F-40's final poem, "Unfulfilled to Expectation," but here she further describes this unknown afterlife as both "Larceny" and "legacy": the loss of one's temporal life and the gain of one's eternal life, another variation of the poems of analysis' theme of loss and gain. Still another of F-1-11's tropes for heaven is the "shore" reached by "Bargemen," anticipating the nautical imagery of F-1's sixteenth and twentieth poems, "Adrift! A little boat adrift!" and "On this wondrous Sea—Sailing silently."

The first fascicle's twelfth poem, like the fortieth fascicle's twelfth poem, defining "Compound Vision," is its fascicle's fulcrum:

It's all I have to bring today—
This, and my heart beside—
This, and my heart, and all the fields—
And all the meadows wide—
Be sure you count—sh'd I forget
Some one the sum could tell—
This, and my heart, and all the Bees
Which in the Clover dwell.

Here the meditator/protagonist interrupts her analysis of gain and loss, death and rebirth, to address her master directly. By doing so, she reveals more about the vow she made in F-1-1 and also introduces the subject she returns to in this meditation's concluding six poems: her poetic intentions. This poem's "bring" and "count" draw attention to its chief biblical source, once more the parable of the talents, whose lord, after giving talents to his servants and departing into a far country, returns and "reckoneth"— Webster's synonym for "counts"—with his servants. Moreover, the servant who was given five talents "brought" five more talents to his master. In poem 12, then, the servant/meditator addresses her master, first telling him that "It's"—that is, this gathering of poems is—"all I have to bring today," one of this fascicle's several slant allusions to its own gathering of poems. She then asks him to be sure to "count"—"reckon"—indicating that her intention/ vow is to bring him more gatherings of flowers/poems in the future.

Poem 12 is not only pivotal to F-1, it also introduces a series of "bring" poems that occur throughout the fascicles, but primarily in the earlier ones. In the second fascicle's tenth poem, "If I should cease to bring a Rose," for example, only her own death could possibly prevent her from bringing her master a "Rose"/poem (J-56). In the same fascicle's twenty-first poem, "I keep my pledge," she tells him that because "Death did not notice me . . . I bring my Rose, . . . I plight again" (J-46). Similarly in the tenth fascicle's final poem, she addresses her master, "I've nothing else—to bring, You know / So I keep bringing These" (J-224). In F-1, then, the forty fascicles' protagonist vows to multiply her talents and to "bring" her "Rose"/poems to her master, then in the following fascicles reaffirms her vow and does, in fact, bring him many more "Rose"/poems.

After the twelfth poem's interruption of the poems of analysis, the following four poems return to the subject of loss and gain, death and rebirth. Poem 13, "Morns like these—we parted" (J-27), is an elegy for an unnamed woman or girl. In poem 14, "So has a Daisy vanished" (J-28), the protagonist reflects upon the death of the preceding poem's female, concluding with an apostrophe to her: "Are ye then with God?" Then in poem 15, "If those I loved were lost" (J-29), she reassures herself that this dead person and the others she has lost to death are not permanently lost. The poems of analysis conclude with "Adrift! A little boat adrift!" (J-30), still another variation of these poems' theme of gain and loss, in which the "little boat" is a metonym for the meditator herself. While "Sailors"—the eleventh poem's "Barge-men," the men of this world—believe she has gone down, been lost, "an-gels" know the boat/protagonist has "redecked it's sails— / And shot—exultant on!"

Poems 17 through 22, all direct addresses, form this meditation's colloquy:

> Summer for thee, grant I may be
> When Summer days are flown!
> Thy music still, when Whippowil
> And Oriole—are done!
>
> For thee to bloom, I'll skip the tomb
> And row my blossoms o'er!
> Pray gather me—
> Anemone—
> Thy flower—forevermore!

---

> When Roses cease to bloom, Sir,
> And Violets are done—
> When Bumblebees in solemn flight
> Have passed beyond the Sun—
> The hand that paused to gather
> Upon this Summer's day
> Will idle lie—in Auburn—
> Then take my flowers—pray!

---

> Oh if remembering were forgetting—
> Then I remember not!
> And if forgetting—recollecting—
> How near I had forgot!

And if to miss—were merry—
And to mourn were gay,
How very blithe the maiden
Who gathered these today!

---

On this wondrous sea—Sailing silently—
Ho! Pilot! Ho!
Knowest thou the shore
Where no breakers roar—
Where the storm is oer—

In the silent West
Many—the Sails at rest—
The Anchors fast.
Thither I pilot thee—
Land! Ho! Eternity!
Ashore at last!

---

Garlands for Queens, may be—
Laurels—for rare degree
Of soul or sword.
Ah—but remembering me—
Ah—but remembering thee—
Nature in chivalry—
Nature in charity—
Nature in equity—
The Rose ordained!

---

Nobody knows this little Rose—
It might a pilgrim be
Did I not take it from the ways
And lift it up to thee.
Only a Bee will miss it—
Only a Butterfly,
Hastening from far journey—
On it's breast to lie—          [no stanza break]

Only a Bird will wonder—
Only a Breeze will sigh—
Ah Little Rose—how easy
For such as thee to die!

In poems 17 and 18, the meditator declares that her flowers/poems are intended for both her readers and her master. Whereas in F-40-2, "Wert Thou but ill," she declares in a single poem they are her intended audience, in F-1-17 and -18 she does so in two poems that are paired by their similar form and repeated words. Both 17 and 18 are composed of eight lines (though poem 17's "Anemone" appears on a separate line), and both include some version of the words "Summer," "day," "flower," "pray," "bloom," and, most important, "gather," a key word that appears again in poem 19, another poem of eight lines. Because in poem 17 her poems are "blossoms" and she, too, is a "flower," she again blurs the distinction between herself and her poems, as she does in F-1-3. This poem's "gather" appears to be a pun: with "Pray gather me," she asks that the reader "pluck" her flowers/poems but also that the reader "gather"/ infer her meanings (cf. J-1723, in which "gathered" signifies inferred). Then in poem 18, in which she asks that "Sir," her master, take her "flowers"/poems, the meaning of "gather" becomes "to assemble, to collect a number of separate things into one aggregate body" (all definitions are from Dickinson's lexicon). The eighteenth poem's "hand that paused to gather / Upon this Summer's day" is thus, as in F-1-4, both herself as her master's "hand"/servant and her "hand" that is gathering/assembling this first fascicle's poems. Similarly, in poem 19, in which she assures her master that she remembers her vow but that she misses him (as in F-1-6 and -7), she is "the maiden / Who gathered [assembled] these [flowers/poems] today!"

After directly referring to her gatherings of poems in these three poems, she returns in poem 20 to the eternal life she hopes to gain. In this dialogue with her "Pilot," echoing Heb. 2.10, in which Jesus is "the captain of . . . salvation," she asks if he knows "the shore / Where no breakers roar— / Where the storm is oer." Her "Pilot" replies that the peaceful shore she seeks is only in the "silent West" and that he is piloting her "Thither," to "Eternity." That this poem is a variation of a poem Emily Dickinson sent to Susan Dickinson in a letter dated 1853 (L-105) shows that the poet had written at least one of F-1's poems long before she copied, gathered, and bound them in 1858. It seems likely that she had written others, too, before 1858. Poem 7, "I had a guinea golden," for example, which is of little or no poetic interest, appears to be a poem from her earlier years.

After the twentieth poem's dialogue with her "Pilot," in poem 21 the protagonist/meditator first looks to her future, which may bring "Garlands for Queens," that is, garlands fit for queens. Since, according to Dickinson's lexicon, a garland is both a "wreath" of "intermixed flowers" and "a collection of little printed pieces," the "Garlands" she anticipates are future gatherings of flowers/poems, foreshadowing her reference to the fascicles as "nosegays" in F-3-8 (J-95) as well as F-40's garland of praise. After envisioning future "Garlands" and also "Laurels," future honors, she turns to the past in the following six lines to remember "me" and "thee." The "thee" she remembers is "Nature in chivalry— / Nature in charity— / Nature in equity," a variation of the triune Deity she invoked in the first poem's "Bee," "Butterfly," and "Breeze," the "names" her "buds commemorate" in F-2-10, "If I should cease to bring a Rose" (J-56). This chivalrous, charitable, equitable Deity has "ordained . . . The Rose," both her poems and herself, retrospectively explaining the first poem's vow and the sixth poem's "chancel" and echoing Jesus' words to his disciples in John 15.16: "I have chosen you, and ordained you, that ye should go and bring forth fruit, and that your fruit should remain" (a passage also echoed in the fourth fascicle's twelfth poem, " 'They have not chosen me,' he said," another dialogue with Jesus, J-85).

The first fascicle's final poem, like its pivotal twelfth, is a "bring" poem. As in poem 12 she brings her poems, her heart, and all the meadows wide to "You," so here she lifts up her "Rose . . . to thee," echoing Psalm 25, "Unto thee, O Lord, do I lift up my soul." In this final poem, then, she lifts up her heart, as well as the "Rose"/flower she has immortalized in her "Rose"/poem. Since in the final eight lines the "Rose" will be missed only by a "Bee," "Butterfly," "Bird," and "Breeze"—a literal and expanded version of the first poem's figurative "Bee," "Butterfly," and "Breeze"—and since this "Rose" will die, it is not in these final lines a "Rose"/poem but literally a flower that the protagonist/meditator addresses in the poem's final lines, just as she addressed Summer in F-1-1:

> Ah Little Rose—how easy
> For such as thee to die!

As she followed the example of the "Summer" with her vow to die in poem 1, and as she followed the example of the faithful "Gentian" that "Chid" her "perfidy" in poem 4, so here she hopes to follow the example of the "Rose"/ flower, which finds it easy to die.

As the following thirty-nine fascicles reveal, she does not find it easy to die to the world. As they also reveal, the first fascicle's meditation, whose first poem is itself a meditation, introduces the principle underlying each of the following fascicles. Though all forty are not formal three-part meditations, all are meditative gatherings of poems focusing upon a single theme or, more often, upon several interwoven themes. And though these forty meditative gatherings do not form a narrative in the sense that *The Odyssey* is a narrative poem, the forty fascicles are linked by a narrative thread: the inner drama of the meditator/protagonist's variegated progression from the first fascicle's vow to the fortieth fascicle's plateau of joy and confidence.

The ninth fascicle, for example, focuses upon the conflicts surrounding her decision to forsake "All"—as she declares she has done in F-40-8, "All forgot . . . All forsook"—in order to devote her life completely to the Word, that is, to Christ and her poetic vocation. Although in F-9's sixteenth poem she has acquired a "title" and "Crown" and in its twenty-first poem declares, "I'm 'Wife'!" (J-195; J-199), this fascicle also includes many poems of anguish and suffering. Its first poem begins with indecision:

> What shall I do—it whimpers so—
> This little Hound within the Heart—
> All day and night—with bark and start—
> And yet—it will not go?
>
> Would you untie it—were you me—
> Would it stop whining, if to Thee
> I sent it—even now?
>
> It should not tease you—by your chair—
> Or on the mat—or if it dare—
> To climb your dizzy knee.
>
> Or sometimes—at your side to run—
> When you were willing—
> May it come—
> Tell Carlo—He'll tell me!

This poem's trope of the "Hound" whimpering to get to its master and its question, "May it come[?]" recall Psalm 42: "As the hart panteth after the water brooks, so panteth my soul after thee, O God . . . when shall I come?" This poem of longing and indecision is followed by many in which the protagonist is portrayed as lonely, forgotten, and forsaken by her friends. In poem 3, "Make me a picture of the sun," for example, she is alone in her room and cold, while "Others" are warm (J-188). In poem 5, "What is— 'Paradise,' " she hopes that heaven won't be as "lonesome" as New England (J-215). In poem 12, "Poor little Heart," "they" have not only forgotten and forsaken her, "they" have broken her heart (J-192). In two poems, "I shall know why—when Time is over" and "He forgot—and I—remembered," she compares her sufferings to Peter's denial of Christ (F-9-13, J-193; F-9-25, J-203). And two anguished poems are about "Dollie," a nickname for Susan Dickinson. In poem 7, "You love me—you are sure," she begs Dollie not to "sting" her again (J-156). Then in poem 18, "Dying! Dying in the night," she imagines her own death scene, in which her chief concern is that a faithless Dollie will fail to arrive (J-158).

F-9 also includes two poems about wrestling until dawn, recalling Jacob's wrestling with God "until the breaking of the day," a story Emily Dickinson re-creates in F-7-1, "A little East of Jordan" (J-59). In the ninth fascicle's tenth poem, "He was weak and I was strong—then," the protagonist "strove" (Webster's synonym for "wrestled") with "him" until "Day knocked" (J-190). In its twenty-third poem, "Two swimmers wrestled on the spar— / Until the morning sun" rose, when one wrestler emerged victorious, while the other wrestler drowned (J-201). Variations on this theme of wrestling until dawn appear in two other F-9 poems about storms that are followed by the morning sun: "On this long storm the Rainbow rose / On this late Morn—the Sun" and "An awful Tempest mashed the air," which concludes, "The morning lit . . . And peace—was Paradise" (F-9-14, J-194; F-9-20, J-198). As these wrestling and storm poems end with morning, so the tempestuous ninth fascicle ends in resolution. In its penultimate poem, "The Flower must not blame the Bee," she turns the tables on those who have forgotten and forsaken her, declaring that "Mistress"—the twenty-first poem's "Wife"—is " 'not at home' . . . To people—any more!" (J-206). And in its final poem, "Some—keep the Sabbath—going to church," she is now content to be alone in her garden with the "Bobolink" as her chorister and "God" as her preacher (J-324).

The ninth fascicle's two poems about "Dollie," Sue Dickinson, draw attention to the question addressed in this book's introduction: how close is the forty fascicles' protagonist to Emily Dickinson herself? Is the protagonist's pilgrimage merely a fiction, or is it a mythic account of Emily Dickinson's own spiritual and poetic pilgrimage? Although I have always been among those who have steadfastly maintained that, as the poet wrote to Higginson, her poems' speaker is not herself but a "supposed person," the striking parallels between the fascicles' protagonist and her creator argue that the poet reveals a great deal about herself in the fascicles, that, as she wrote to Elizabeth Holland, "a Book is only the Heart's Portrait—every Page a Pulse." The protagonist, like her creator, lives in Amherst; has a sister and a friend, Sue; has red hair and hazel eyes; and has rejected the church of her contemporaries, choosing instead to keep the Sabbath alone in her garden. More important, she is represented as the forty fascicles' author. She, like Emily Dickinson, died to the world. She, too, is an unpublished poet who has been freed from poetic "Laws." Her business, too, is loving, singing, and "Circumference."

Whether or not the poet possessed her protagonist's firm faith in Jesus and his promises, Emily Dickinson continued to write poems to and about him long after she had completed the fascicles. In "Recollect the Face of Me," for example, an 1874 variation of the thief's request to be saved (J-1305; Luke 23.42), the speaker concludes, "We commend ourselves to thee / Paragon of Chivalry," another of Dickinson's many epithets for Christ, echoing the knightly tropes in the series of poems in which her soul is host to the divine guest (e.g., "The Soul should always stand ajar," J-1055). In "All that I do / Is in review / To his enamored Mind" (J-1496), dated 1880, wherever she turns "omnipresence" lies in wait to make her his "Bride," echoing the forty fascicles' recurring metonyms for Christ and their recurring nuptial poems, as well as the two stanzas Emily Dickinson copied from "Mattens" in which Herbert similarly portrays God as the heart's persistent wooer (see Figs. 1–4). In "The Savior must have been / A docile Gentleman"—still another epithet for him—dated 1881, Jesus has "leveled" the way for his "little Fellowmen," as in F-35-13 he is the "Tender Pioneer" who "hath traversed first" so that "No New Mile remaineth— / Far as Paradise" (J-1487; J-698).

Similarly, whether or not Emily Dickinson, like her protagonist, experienced a transcendent day in which she "saw" and was betrothed to Christ, her speaker recalls a singularly transcendent day in poems dated as late as 1883. In "To be forgot by thee" she was "Raised from oblivion / A single [royal—/signal—/hallowed] time" (J-1560). And in "The farthest Thunder that I heard / Was nearer than the Sky"—whose tropes echo the earlier occasional poem, "Struck, was I, nor yet by Lightning" (J-925, dated 1864)—the "Lightning" that preceded the thunder that still "rumbles" in her mind (as her soul was permanently "notched" in "Joy to have merited the Pain," F-36-2, J-788) "Struck no one but myself." "But," she adds, "I would not exchange the Bolt / For all the rest of Life—" (J-1581).

In view of the remarkable resemblances between the forty fascicles' protagonist and her creator, presumably Emily Dickinson, too, longed for readers for her "Experiment Toward Men," at least at the time she composed its poems. Why, then, did she not seek to publish the forty fascicles? One probable reason is that she saw that her magnum opus was too far ahead of its time. If so, she was no doubt correct. F-40, which provides the key to comprehending the fascicles' long lyric cycle, is as complex and convoluted as *The Waste Land*. Its riddling poems are as idiosyncratic and enigmatic as *Ulysses*. A nineteenth-century America that preferred Longfellow to Whitman would hardly have applauded the forty fascicles' "Experiment." It seems likely, too, that she continued to believe, as she wrote to Higginson, "If fame belonged to me, I could not escape her" (L-265). Still, she did not quite leave the fate of her poems to providence. By willing all her earthly possessions to Lavinia, she, in effect, whether intentionally or not, left the fate of her poems to her devoted sister, as Herbert left the fate of his poems to Nicholas Farrar. And as Farrar was the savior of Herbert's poems, so Lavinia Dickinson proved to be the savior of Emily Dickinson's poems. If the poet, like her fascicles' protagonist, wished to serve readers as a means of serving Christ, she accomplished her goal only through the good offices of her energetic, determined sister.

Though Emily Dickinson's thoughts about publication must remain conjectural, reading F-40 in the larger context of the preceding fascicles and of the entire canon shows that her données, her forms, and many of her most arresting tropes place her within the tradition of Christian devotion. The Bible pervades her mind and art, as it does the mind and art of all Christian devotional poets and writers. And the Bible was not, as many have supposed, merely a source of imagery for her. Rather, the Bible is essential to her structure and meaning, the very sum and substance of her art. By drawing upon biblical texts to depict events in the life of her protagonist, she treats the Bible typologically and revitalizes and contemporizes biblical texts. Many of her tropes are her own variations of biblical tropes. Her riddling poems are parabolic. Her metonyms, kennings, dynamic parallelism, chiasms, and envelope structures, as well as her use of key words to link related poems, are favorite figures of biblical writers. Moreover, F-40's recurring pentology echoes the pentology of the Bible—for example, the five books of Moses, the five parts to the Psalms, Matthew's five great discourses of Christ, and the five parables concluding his fifth eschatological discourse. Very likely, too, she composed forty fascicles rather than, say, thirty-nine or forty-one because forty is a biblical number. The Israelites wandered in the desert for forty years; Moses remained on Mount Sinai for forty days; the rain of Noah's flood lasted for forty days and forty nights; and, most important, Jesus retreated into the wilderness for forty days—a retreat that is often a symbol of the soul's retirement to solitude for prayer and meditation (Martz, *Poetry of Meditation* 89).

For Emily Dickinson, as for George Herbert and other Christian devotional poets, nature is a second Scripture that provides "God's introductions" (F-38-4, J-797). Her imagery, like theirs, is often sacramental, as in her poems equating poetry with the eucharist and in those occasional poems in which her protagonist celebrates her elevated state with tropes of ordination, baptism, and betrothal. Her predominating forms are also those of Christian devotion: the meditation, the letter, the garland of praise, the conversion narrative. Her concerns, like those of other devotional poets, are often eschatological, death for her a Christian experience, a means of transit from the "Circumference" of time to Christ's eternal "Circumference." Most tellingly, throughout the Dickinson canon, as in *The Temple*, *The Imitation of Christ*, and other devotional writings, Jesus Christ is a major figure, whose portrait she stunningly and lovingly draws in F-40.

Why, then, have readers not always regarded Emily Dickinson as a Christian devotional poet? One important reason is that because the Bible has become peripheral to many twentieth-century readers, we have missed her oblique biblical allusions and their importance to interpreting her poems. Another is that before Franklin reassembled the fascicles, thus presenting us with the challenge of reading *all* their poems, we were free to choose only those with the most meaning for ourselves. Frequently those chosen have been Dickinson's more secular poems, which have an appeal for the often secular tastes of twentieth-century readers. We have been particularly drawn to those poems depicting her protagonist's lapses of faith and reproaches to God, while we have slighted many of those in which her faith remains firm. The eighteenth fascicle's fourth poem, for example, which begins, "I know that He exists," but concludes with her wondering if God may be playing a cruel game and if, therefore, at death she will remain a corpse and nothing more, is widely known and commented upon. Yet the same fascicle's following poem, "He strained my faith," in which Jesus tried her faith and found it "supple" and she identifies herself as his "little 'John,' " is far less well known. By privileging some poems while slighting others, we have, in effect, created a bowdlerized Dickinson canon.

Moreover, for almost one hundred years we have been reading the poems outside their fascicle context. As Ferdinand de Saussure's famous chessman does not have the same signification when it is viewed outside the context of its chessboard and the game of chess, so a single Dickinson poem does not have the same signification when it is read outside the context of the fascicles. When read as a single isolated poem, for example, "Midsummer, was it, when They died" appears to be a peculiar elegy for "Two" people for whom the speaker, for some unexplained reason, feels no regret. When read outside F-40's concluding poems of faith, "He who in Himself believes" could be an obscure poem about having faith in oneself. Until one sees that the fascicles are the account of a long spiritual and poetic pilgrimage, the first fascicle's first poem, "The Gentian weaves her fringes," appears to be only a mock-elegy for the passing of summer. But even within their fascicle context Emily Dickinson's poems do not immediately reveal the Christian nature of her mind and art, because she, who believed riddles to be "healthful" (L-362), tells "all the Truth" but tells it "slant" so that the truth she tells dazzles "gradually." She is like her "Fox," who finds it "Good to hide, and hear 'em hunt," but even "Better, to be found." Her linguistic obscurities, metonymic evasions, and oblique biblical allusions conceal what she tells. But she "fits" her readers with signals that enable their "dull . . . Ears" to begin to hear what her meditator declares in F-40's first poem she knows and tells—and then to hear both the forty fascicles and the Dickinson canon in a new and different way.

# Appendix A:
# Transcript of the Fortieth Fascicle

Capitalization, punctuation, and line lengths are according to Johnson, *Poems*, except for the sixth poem's " 'Unto Me'?" where I have followed Dickinson's manuscript as it appears in Franklin's *Manuscript Books*, 981. As I state in the Textual Note, here and throughout this book I have placed variant readings in brackets on the same line as the preferred readings because F-40's variants are sometimes of crucial import to comprehending its poems.

[Poem 1]

The Only News I know
Is Bulletins all Day
From Immortality.

The Only Shows I see—
Tomorrow and Today—
Perchance Eternity—                    [Three—with Eternity—
                                       /And some Eternity]
The Only One I meet
Is God—The Only Street—
Existence—This traversed               [traversed/traverst]

If Other News there be—
Or Admirabler Show—
I'll tell it You—                      [I'll Signify—/I'll testify—]

------------

[Poem 2]

Wert Thou but ill—that I might show thee
How long a Day I could endure
Though thine attention stop not on me
Nor the least signal, Me assure—                     [Me/Mine]

Wert Thou but Stranger in ungracious country—
And Mine—the Door
Thou paused at, for a passing bounty—           [passing/doubtful]
No More—

Accused—wert Thou—and Myself—Tribunal—
Convicted—Sentenced—Ermine—not to Me
Half the Condition, thy Reverse—to follow—            [Condition/
Just to partake—the infamy—                           distinction]

The Tenant of the Narrow Cottage, wert Thou—
Permit to be
The Housewife in thy low attendance
Contenteth Me—

No Service hast Thou, I would not achieve it—      [achieve/attempt]
To die—or live—
The first—Sweet, proved I, ere I saw thee—      [proved I/That was]
For Life—be Love—          [be Love—/is—Love—/means—Love—]

---

[Poem 3]

Midsummer, was it, when They died—
A full, and perfect time—
The Summer closed upon itself
In Consummated Bloom—

The Corn, her furthest kernel filled
Before the coming Flail—
When These—leaned into Perfectness—      [When These Two—
Through Haze of Burial—                              leaned in—Perfectness—]

---

[Poem 4]

The first Day that I was a Life
I recollect it—How still—
The last Day that I was a Life
I recollect it—as well—

'Twas stiller—though the first
Was still—
'Twas empty—but the first
Was full—

This—was my finallest Occasion—
But then
My tenderer Experiment
Toward Men—

"Which choose I"?
That—I cannot say—
"Which choose They"?
Question Memory!

---

[Poem 5]

A nearness to Tremendousness—
An Agony procures—
Affliction ranges Boundlessness—
Vicinity to Laws

Contentment's quiet Suburb—
Affliction cannot stay
In Acres—It's Location                    [In Acre—Or Location—]
Is Illocality—                            [It rents Immensity—]

---

[Poem 6]

"Unto Me"? I do not know you—
Where may be your House?

"I am Jesus—Late of Judea—
Now—of Paradise"—

Wagons—have you—to convey me?
This is far from Thence—

"Arms of Mine—sufficient Phaeton—
Trust Omnipotence"—

I am spotted—"I am Pardon"—
I am small—"The Least
Is esteemed in Heaven the Chiefest—
Occupy my House"—                         [House/Breast]

[Poem 7]

Denial—is the only fact
Perceived by the Denied—
Whose Will—a numb significance—          [Whose Will—a Blank
The Day the Heaven died—                              intelligence]

And all the Earth strove common round—
Without Delight, or Beam—                          [Beam/aim]
What Comfort was it Wisdom—was—
The spoiler of Our Home?

———————

[Poem 8]

All forgot for recollecting                          [for/through]
Just a paltry One—
All forsook, for just a Stranger's
New Accompanying—

Grace of Wealth, and Grace of Station          [Grace of Rank—
Less accounted than                              and Grace of Fortune]
An unknown Esteem possessing—                  [Esteem/content]
Estimate—Who can—

Home effaced—Her faces dwindled—
Nature—altered small—
Sun—if shone—or Storm—if shattered—
Overlooked I all—

Dropped—my fate—a timid Pebble—
In thy bolder Sea—
Prove—me—Sweet—if I regret it—                  [Prove/Ask]
Prove Myself—of Thee—

———————

[Poem 9]

I hide myself—within my flower,
That fading from your Vase—
You—unsuspecting—feel for me—
Almost—a loneliness—

————————

[Poem 10]

Had I not This, or This, I said,
Appealing to Myself,
In moment of prosperity—
Inadequate—were Life—

"Thou hast not Me, nor Me"—it said,
In Moment of Reverse—
"And yet Thou art industrious—
No need—hadst Thou—of us"?

My need—was all I had—I said—
The need did not reduce—
Because the food—exterminate—
The hunger—does not cease—

But diligence—is sharper—
Proportioned to the Chance—
To feed upon the Retrograde—
Enfeebles—the Advance—

————————

[Poem 11]

Between My Country—and the Others—
There is a Sea—
But Flowers—negotiate between us—
As Ministry.

————————

[Poem 12]

The Admirations—and Contempts—of time—
Show justest—through an Open Tomb—
The Dying—as it were a Hight
Reorganizes Estimate
And what We saw not
We distinguish clear—
And mostly—see not
What We saw before—

'Tis Compound Vision—
Light—enabling Light—
The Finite—furnished
With the Infinite—
Convex—and Concave Witness—
Back—toward Time—
And forward—
Toward the God of Him—

[Poem 13]

Till Death—is narrow Loving—
The scantest Heart extant
Will hold you till your privilege
Of Finiteness—be spent—

But He whose loss procures you
Such Destitution that
Your Life too abject for itself
Thenceforward imitate—

Until—Resemblance perfect—
Yourself, for His pursuit
Delight of Nature—abdicate—
Exhibit Love—somewhat—

[Poem 14]


'Tis Sunrise—Little Maid—Hast Thou
No Station in the Day?
'Twas not thy wont, to hinder so—
Retrieve thine industry—

'Tis Noon—My little Maid—
Alas—and art thou sleeping yet?
The Lily—waiting to be Wed—
The Bee—Hast thou forgot?

My little Maid—'Tis Night—Alas
That Night should be to thee
Instead of Morning—Had'st thou broached
Thy little Plan to Die—
Dissuade thee, if I c'd not, Sweet,
I might have aided—thee—



[Poem 15]


Pain—expands the Time—
Ages coil within                                    [coil/lurk]
The minute Circumference
Of a single Brain—

Pain contracts—the Time—
Occupied with Shot
Gammuts of Eternities                    [Gammuts/Triplets]
Are as they were not—                    [Are/flit—/Show—]

[Poem 16]

Fitter to see Him, I may be
For the long Hindrance—Grace—to Me—
With Summers, and with Winters, grow,
Some passing Year—A trait bestow                    [trait/charm]

To make Me fairest of the Earth—
The Waiting—then—will seem so worth
I shall impute with half a pain
The blame that I was chosen—then—              [chosen/common]

Time to anticipate His Gaze—                         [Time/Time's]
It's first—Delight—and then—Surprise—                  [It's/the]
The turning o'er and o'er my face
For Evidence it be the Grace—

He left behind One Day—So less
He seek Conviction, That—be This—

I only must not grow so new
That He'll mistake—and ask for me                     [He'll/He—]
Of me—when first unto the Door
I go—to Elsewhere go no more—

I only must not change so fair
He'll sigh—"The Other—She—is Where"?        [Other/Real One]
The Love, tho, will array me right                 [array/instruct]
I shall be perfect—in His sight—

If He perceive the other Truth—
Upon an Excellenter Youth—

How sweet I shall not lack in Vain—
But gain—thro' loss—Through Grief—obtain—            [Grief/pain]
The Beauty that reward Him most—                      [most/best]
The Beauty of Demand—at Rest—                   [Demand/Belief]

[Poem 17]

He who in Himself believes—
Fraud cannot presume—                                    [Fraud/Lie]
Faith is Constancy's Result—
And assumes—from Home—                                   [assumes/infers]

Cannot perish, though it fail
Every second time—
But defaced Vicariously—                                 [But/When—/if—]
For Some Other Shame—                                    [For Another Shame—]

---

[Poem 18]

Color—Caste—Denomination—
These—are Time's Affair—
Death's diviner Classifying
Does not know they are—

As in sleep—All Hue forgotten—
Tenets—put behind—
Death's large—Democratic fingers
Rub away the Brand—

If Circassian—He is careless—
If He put away
Chrysalis of Blonde—or Umber—
Equal Butterfly—

They emerge from His Obscuring—
What Death—knows so well—
Our minuter intuitions—
Deem unplausible                                          [unplausible/incredible]

[Poem 19]

I make His Crescent fill or lack—
His Nature is at Full
Or Quarter—as I signify—
His Tides—do I control—

He holds superior in the Sky
Or gropes, at my Command
Behind inferior Clouds—or round
A Mist's slow Colonnade—

But since We hold a Mutual Disc—
And front a Mutual Day—
Which is the Despot, neither knows—
Nor Whose—the Tyranny—

———————

[Poem 20]

Robbed by Death—but that was easy—
To the failing Eye                              [failing/Dying—/clouding]
I could hold the latest Glowing—
Robbed by Liberty

For Her Jugular Defences—
This, too, I endured—
Hint of Glory—it afforded—
For the Brave Beloved—                          [Brave/bold]

Fraud of Distance—Fraud of Danger,
Fraud of Death—to bear—
It is Bounty—to Suspense's
Vague Calamity—

Staking our entire Possession                   [entire/divine—]
On a Hair's result—
Then—Seesawing—coolly—on it—
Trying if it split—                             [As to estimate]

[Poem 21]

Unfulfilled to Observation—
Incomplete—to Eye—
But to Faith—a Revolution
In Locality—

Unto Us—the Suns extinguish—
To our Opposite—
New Horizons—they embellish—                    [embellish/Replenish]
Fronting Us—with Night.                    [Turning Us—their Night.]

# Appendix B:
# Facsimile of the Fortieth Fascicle

The numbers, zeros, and "No's" on some pages were not written by Emily Dickinson, but by her early editors. Franklin does not specify who underlined Emily Dickinson's cross in the first poem's ninth line and the corresponding alternate reading "traverst." But he speculates that Martha Dickinson Bianchi cancelled the sixteenth poem's alternates "He" and "instruct" (Franklin, *Manuscript Books*, pp. xvi–xviii, 1386).

The Only news I know
Is Bulletins all Day
From Immortality.

The Only shows I see –
Tomorrow and Today –
+ Perchance Eternity –

The Only One I meet
Is God – The Only Street –
Existence – This + traversed

If Other news there be –
Or Admirabler show –
+ I'll tell it You –

+ three – withi Eternity –
And some Eternity –
+ traverst    + signify – Testify.

[Poem 1]

Wert thou but ill . that
I might show thee
How and I could
Endure
Though their attention
stops not on me
Nor the least signal .
+ Me assure -

Wert thou but strange
in ungracious Country .
And mine . the door
Thou paused at . on a
+ passing bound ; -
No more .

Accused . wert thou .
And Myself . Tribunal .
Convicted . Sentenced -
Ermine . not to Me

Half the Condition, the
Reverse - to others -
Just to partakes - the
Incomes -

The Tenant of the Manor
Cottage, were that -
Permit to be
The Housemaid on the
For attendance
Contenteth, me -

No Service hast thou,
I would not achieve it -
To Die - Or Live -
The first - Smit - would
I, On I saw thee -
For light - Or Love -

+ Mine + bountiful + Distinction
+ Attempt + That was + light
is - Means -

[Poem 2, conclusion]

My

Midsummer, was it, when
They died.
A full, and perfect -
time -
The Summer closed
upon itself
In Consummated Bloom.

The Corn, her furthest Kernel
filled
Before the Coming + flail -
When these + Leaned
into Perfectness -
Through Haze of Burial -

+ These Two - Leaned in -

[Poem 3]

The first day that
I was a life
I recollect it - How
still -
The last day that
I was a life
I recollect it - as well-

'Twas stiller - though
the first
Was still -
'Twas empty - but
the first
Was full -

This - was my finalest
Occasion -
But then
My tenderer Experiment -
toward Men -

[Poem 4, first three stanzas]

209

"Which Choose ?"
"That - I Cannot say -"
"Which Choose This"?
Question Memory!

---

A nearness to Tremendousness -
An Agony procures -
Affliction ranges Boundlessness -
Vicinity to Care -

Contentment's quiet Suburb -
Affliction x Cannot stay
In Acre - Its Location
Is Illocality -

x In Acre. Or Location -
Or Yere Immensity .

[Poem 4, final stanza; Poem 5]

210

"Unto Me?" I do not
know You —
Where may be Your House?

"I am Jesus — Late
of Judea —
Now — of Paradise" —

Wagons — have You — to
convey Me?
"This is far from Thence —

"Arms of Mine — sufficient
Phaeton —
Trust Omnipotence" —

I am spotted — "I am
Pardon" —
I am small — "the Least
Is esteemed in Heaven the Chiefest —
Occupy my Stall" — Guest.

[Poem 6]

Denial - is the only
fact -
Perceived by the Denied -
Whose Will - a
numb significance -
The Day the Heaven
died -

And all the Earth
strove common round -
Without Delight - or Beam -
What Comfort was it
Wisdom - was -
The spoiler of Our Home?

+ Blank intelligence + Grim -

[Poem 7]

212

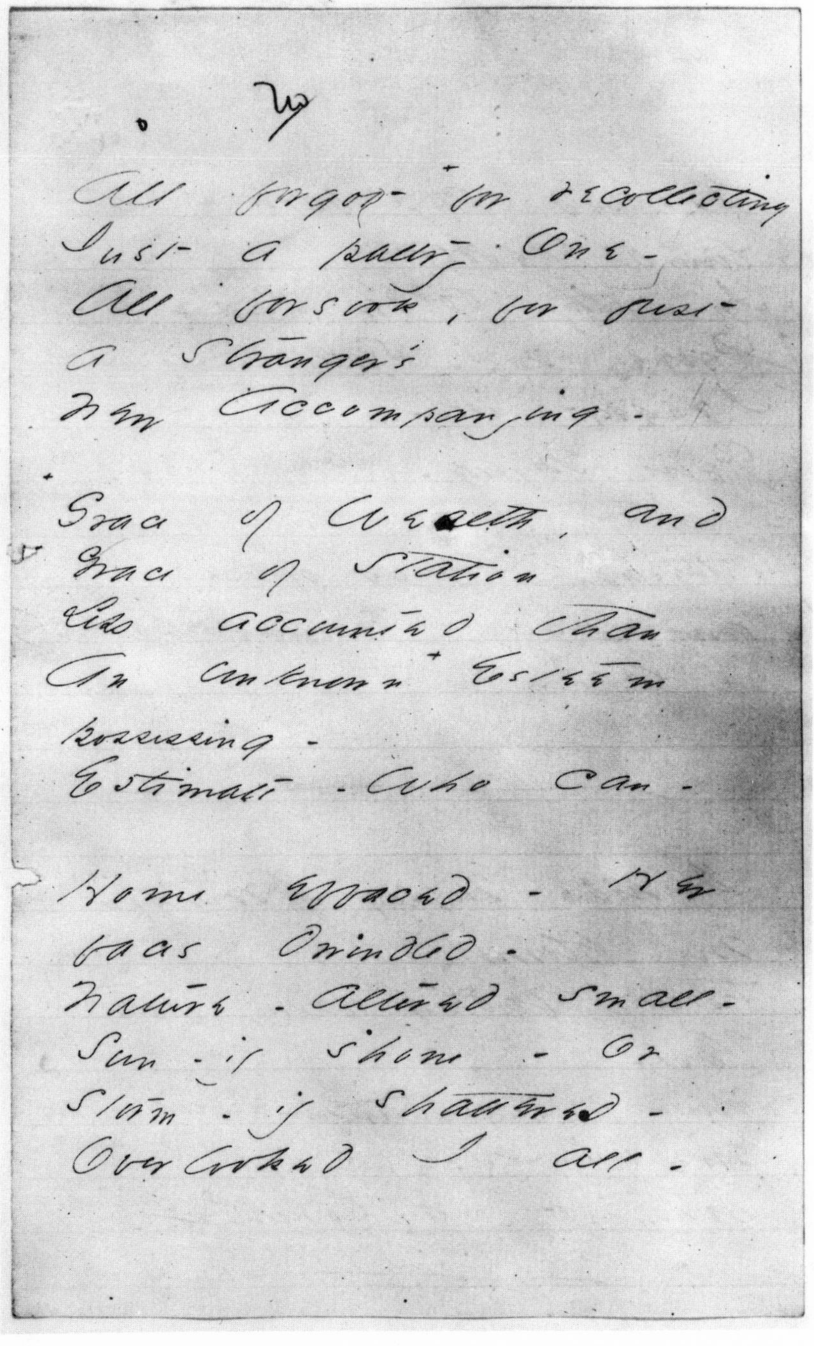

[Poem 8, first three stanzas]

Dropped . my vase — a
timid Prayer —
In the Golden Sea —
+ Prove . me . Small — I
resign it — .
Poor myself — of thee —

+ through . Grace of Rank —
and . Grace of Fortune + Content
+ Ask .

———————————

I hide myself — within
my flower —
That fading from your
Vase —
You — unsuspecting — feel for
me —
Almost — a loneliness —

———————————

[Poem 8, final stanza; Poem 9]

214

Had I not this, or
this, I said,
Appealing to myself,
In moment of prosperity.
Inadequate — were life —

"These had not me,
nor me it said,
In moment of Reverse.
"And yet that are
industrious.
No need — hadst thou — of his.

My need — was all I had,
I said.
The need did not
reduce.
Because the bird — exterminate.
The hunger — does not cease.

[Poem 10, first three stanzas]

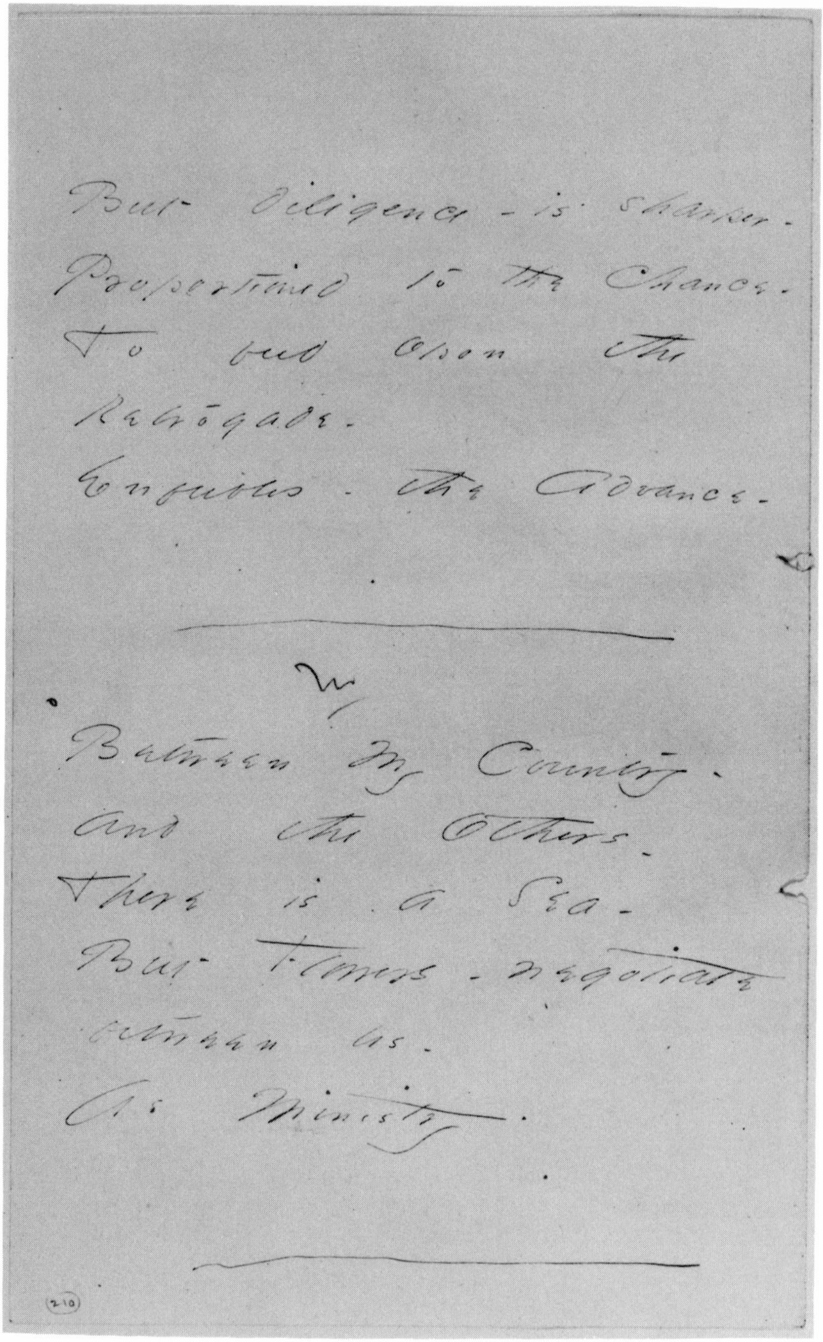

But - Diligence - is sharper -
Proportioned to the Chance -
To feed upon the
Retrograde -
Enfeebles - the Advance -

Between My Country -
And the Others -
There is a Sea -
But Flowers - negotiate
between us -
As Ministry.

[Poem 10, final stanza; Poem 11]

The Admiration's – and
Contempts – of time –
Show justest – through
An Open Tomb –
The Dying – as it were
a Hight
Reorganizes Estimate
"And what We saw
not –
We distinguish Clear –
And mostly – see not
What We saw before –

"'Tis Compound Vision –
Light – enabling Light –
The Finite – furnished
With the Infinite –
Convex – and Concave Witness –
Back – toward Time –
And forward –
Toward the God of Him –

[Poem 12]

217

Till Death - is narrow
Loving -
The scantest Heart extant
Will hold us till our
privilege
Of Finiteness - be spent -

But He whose loss
procures us
Such Destitution that
Our Life too abject for
itself
Thenceforward imitates -

Until - Resemblance perfect -
Yourself, for His pursuit
Delight of Nature - abdicate -
Exhibit Love - somewhat -

[Poem 13]

218

'Tis Sunrise – Little Maid –
Hast thou
No Station in the Day?
'Twas not thy wont, to
hinder so –
Retrieve thine industry –

'Tis Noon – My little Maid –
Alas – and art thou sleeping
yet?
The Lily – waiting to be Wed –
The Bee – Hast thou forgot?

My little Maid – 'Tis Night –
Alas
That Night should be to thee
Instead of Morning – Hadst
thou broached
Thy little Plan to Die –
Dissuade thee, if I could not, Sweet,
I might have aided – Thee –

[Poem 14]

No

Pain - expands the Time -
Ages + Coil within
the minute Circumference
Of a single Brain -

Pain contracts - the Time -
Occupied with Shot -
+ Gammuts of Eternities
+ Are as they were not -

+ Ague + Triplets + His -
- Shot -

[Poem 15]

Fitter to see Him, I
may be
For the long Hindrance –
Grace – to Me –
With Summers, and
with Winters, grow,
Some passing Year – A
Trait bestow

To make Me fairest
of the Earth –
The Waiting – then – will
seem so worth
I shall impute with
half a pain
The blame that I was
Chosen – then –

Time to anticipate His Gaze –
It's first – Delight – and
then – Surprise –

[Poem 16, continued on the following verso and recto]

The Turning o'er and o'er
My face
For Evidence it be the
Grace.

He left behind One Day,
So less
He Less Conviction, that
be this.

I only must not grow
so near
that he'll mistake and
Ask for me
Of me when first unto
the door
I go. to lose when go
no more.

I only must not change
so fair

[Poem 16, the second of three pages]

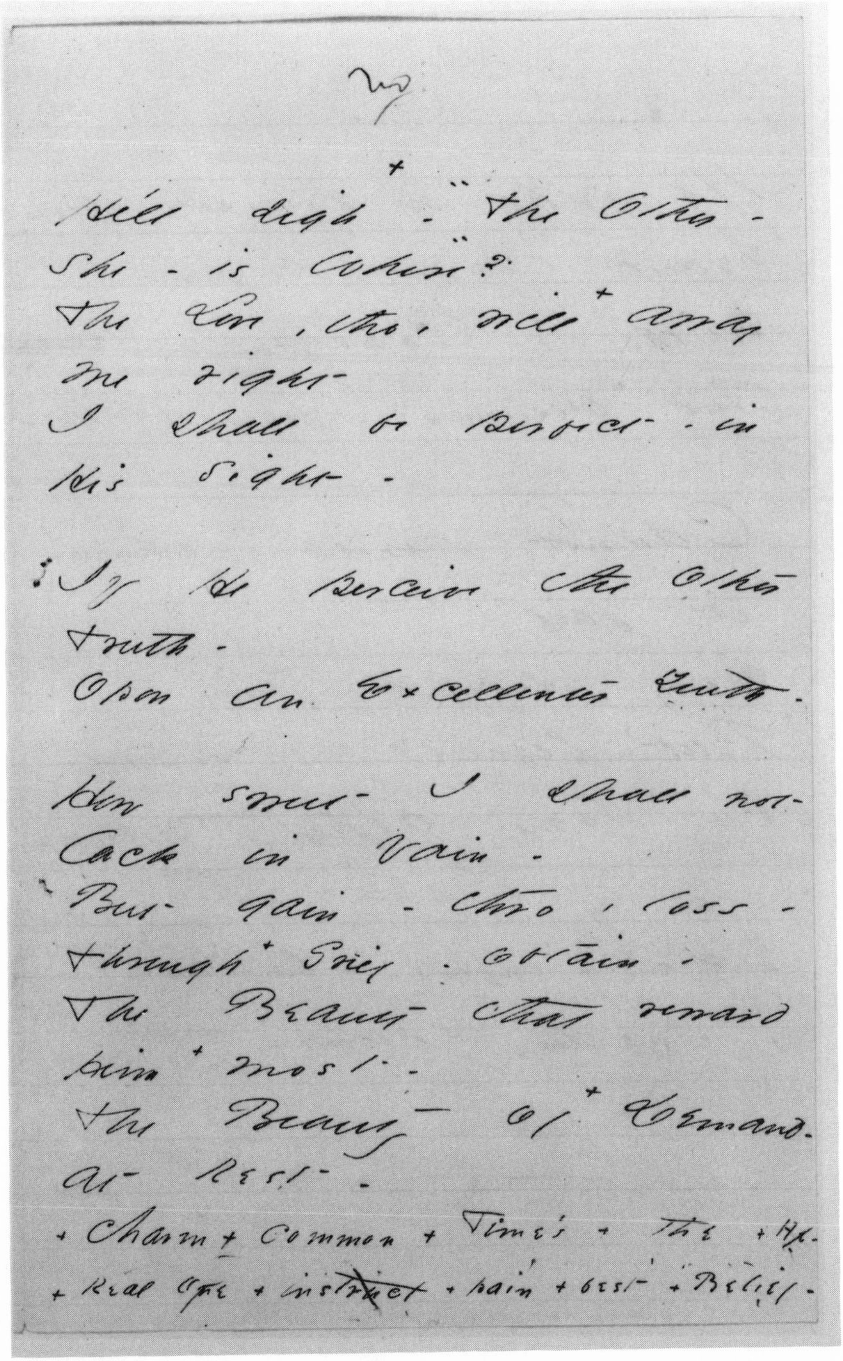

[Poem 16, conclusion]

He who in Himself believes -
Fraud Cannot presume -
Faith is Constancy's Result
And assumes - from Home -

Cannot perish ; though
it fail
Every second time -
But Defaced Vicarious.
For some other Shame.

+ Lie + lingers + when - +
+ Another Sham -

Color - Caste - Denomination
these - are Time's Affair -
Death's Diviner Classifying
does not know they are -

As in Sleep - all Hue
forgotten -
Tenets - put - behind -
Death's large - Democratic
fingers
Rub away the Brand -

If Circassian - He is Careless -
If He put away
Chrysalis of Blonde - or Umber -
Equal Butterfly -

They emerge from His Obscuring -
What Death - knows so well -
Our minuter intuitions -
Deem + unplausible + incredible -

[Poem 18]

225

No

I make His Crescent fill
or lack –
His Nature is at Full
Or Quarter – As I signify –
His Tides – do I Control –

He holds superior in the Sky
Or gropes at my Command
Behind inferior Clouds –
Or round
A Mist's slow Colonnade –

But since We hold a
mutual Disc –
And front a mutual Day –
Which is the Despot,
neither knows –
Nor Whose – the Tyranny –

Robbed of Death - but that
was Easy -
To the failing Eye
I could hold the latest Glowing -
Robbed by Liberty -

For Her Jugular Defences -
This, too, I Endured -
Shame of Glory - it awarded -
For the Brave Beloved -

Fraud of Distance - Fraud of Danger,
Fraud of Death - to bear -
It is Bounty - to Suspense's
Vague Calamity -

Staking Our entire Possession
On a Hair's result -
Then - Seesawing - coolly - on it -
Trying if it split -
Or Going - climbing - bold - divine -
As to Estimate

Unfulfilled 10 Observation.
Incomplete . 10 Eye.
But 10 Faith . a Revelation
In Locality .

Unto us . the Suns
Extinguish .
To our Opposite .
New Horrors . they
+ Embellish .
+ Fronting us . with Night .

+ Replenish . Fronting us .
This Night .

[Poem 21]

# Notes

## Introduction: The Fortieth Fascicle and the Poetry of Meditation

1. See Ralph W. Franklin, ed., *The Manuscript Books of Emily Dickinson*, 2 vols. (Cambridge: Belknap Press of Harvard University Press, 1981), for a full description of the booklets and their history. Emily Dickinson's will, now in the Dickinson Collection at Houghton Library, is reprinted in Jay Leyda, *The Years and Hours of Emily Dickinson* (New Haven: Yale University Press, 1960; reprint, Hamden, Conn.: Archon Books, 1970), 2:236–37.

2. See Dorothy Huff Oberhaus, "In Defense of Sue," *Dickinson Studies*, no. 48 (Bonus 1983):1–25, for an account of Emily Dickinson's lifelong personal and literary friendship with Susan Dickinson.

3. Ralph W. Franklin, *The Editing of Emily Dickinson: A Reconsideration* (Madison: University of Wisconsin Press, 1967), 147 n. 4.

4. Franklin, *Manuscript Books*, xiii.

5. According to Franklin, *The Manuscript Books of Emily Dickinson* "restores the original forty fascicles arranged chronologically" (xi); that is, it establishes not only "the internal sequence for each of the forty bound fascicles" (xiii) but also the forty fascicles' chronology, the order in which the poet, who did not number the fascicles, copied and assembled them. Since Franklin adds that his ordering in *Manuscript Books* is "open to refinement" (xv), it may be that he will include refinements in his forthcoming variorum.

6. Franklin is among those who believe that Dickinson assembled the fascicles chronologically as a means of ordering her poems. See, e.g., his "Emily Dickinson Fascicles," *Studies in Bibliography* 36 (1983): 1–20. Ruth Miller, in "The Fascicles," the final chapter of *The Poetry of Emily Dickinson* (Middletown, Conn.: Wesleyan University Press, 1968), was the first to propose that the fascicles are artistic gatherings. M. L. Rosenthal and Sally Gall, in "American Originals II: Emily Dickinson's Fascicles," in *The Modern Poetic Sequence: The Genius of Modern Poetry* (New York: Oxford University Press, 1983), argue that fascicles 15 and 16 are interdependent poetic sequences and predict that a close study of all the fascicles will reveal that they are too. William H. Shurr, in *The Marriage of Emily Dickinson: A Study of the Fascicles* (Lexington: University Press of Kentucky, 1983), the first book-length study of the fascicles, argues that the fascicles are love letters to the Reverend Charles W. Wadsworth.

7. Sharon Cameron, in *Choosing Not Choosing: Dickinson's Fascicles* (Chicago: University of Chicago Press, 1992), writes that "in the ten years since the publication of *The Manuscript Books of Emily Dickinson* there has been no useful commentary, virtually no commentary at all, on how the gathering of poems into fascicles influences our understanding of how to read Dickinson's verse." According to her publisher, Cameron's book is "the first book-length consideration of the poems in their manuscript context," which it is if one discounts William Shurr's 1983 book, as Cameron and her publisher appear to have done.

8. See, e.g., David Porter, *Dickinson: The Modern Idiom* (Cambridge: Harvard University Press,

1981); Suzanne Juhasz, ed., *Feminist Critics Read Emily Dickinson* (Bloomington: Indiana University Press, 1983); Cristanne Miller, *Emily Dickinson: A Poet's Grammar* (Cambridge: Harvard University Press, 1987); and Barton Levi St. Armand, *Emily Dickinson and Her Culture: The Soul's Society* (New York: Cambridge University Press, 1984).

9. For discussions of Emily Dickinson as a meditative or metaphysical poet, see Louis L. Martz, *The Poem of the Mind: Essays on Poetry, English and American* (New York: Oxford University Press, 1966), 90–104; Judith Banzer Farr, "Compound Manner: Emily Dickinson and the Metaphysical Poets," *American Literature* 32 (1961): 417–33; Dorothy Huff Oberhaus, " 'Engine against th' Almightie': Emily Dickinson and Prayer," *ESQ: A Journal of the American Renaissance* 32 (1986): 153–72; idem, "A Reading of Emily Dickinson," in *"Like Season'd Timber": New Essays on George Herbert*, ed. Edmund Miller and Robert Di Yanni (New York: Peter Lang, 1987), 345–68; and Richard B. Sewall's discussion of Emily Dickinson and *The Imitation of Christ* in *The Life of Emily Dickinson* (New York: Farrar, Straus & Giroux, 1974), 2:688–94. See also Jack L. Capps, *Emily Dickinson's Reading: 1836–1886* (Cambridge: Harvard University Press, 1966), for a detailed account of Dickinson's literary and biblical allusions.

10. *Bolts of Melody: New Poems of Emily Dickinson*, ed. Mabel Loomis Todd and Millicent Todd Bingham (New York: Harper, 1945), first and second printings, 125; *New Yorker*, June 16, 1945, 15–16.

11. For discussions of Upham, see Carlton Lowenberg, *Emily Dickinson's Textbooks*, ed. Territa A. Lowenberg and Carla L. Brown (Lafayette, Calif.: Carlton Lowenberg, 1986), 98, and Benilde Montgomery, "Emily Dickinson and the Meditative Tradition" (Ph.D. diss., State University of New York at Stony Brook, 1981).

12. Letter 6, according to Johnson's numbering in Thomas H. Johnson and Theodora Ward, eds., *The Letters of Emily Dickinson*, 3 vols. (Cambridge: Belknap Press of Harvard University Press, 1958). Hereafter letters are cited by number, preceded by *L*, parenthetically in the text.

13. I am indebted here and throughout to Louis L. Martz, who describes the Ignatian meditation in *The Poetry of Meditation: A Study in English Religious Literature of the Seventeenth Century* (New Haven: Yale University Press, 1954). See also *The Spiritual Exercises of St. Ignatius Loyola*, trans. Anthony Mottola, introd. Robert W. Gleason, S.J. (New York: Doubleday, 1964).

14. See Appendix A for a transcript of F-40, and Appendix B for a reproduction of the F-40 manuscript. See also the Textual Note for my method of citation.

15. See, e.g., F-1-9, J-323; F-8-11, J-174, which is later repeated as F-21-12; F-25-5, J-1053; F-29-4, J-356; F-9-21, J-199; and F-14-5, J-271.

16. F-40-20; J-1492; F-35-13, J-698; F-28-17, J-573; J-1487. For a discussion of Emily Dickinson's epithets for Christ, see Dorothy Huff Oberhaus, " 'Tender Pioneer': Emily Dickinson's Poems on the Life of Christ," *American Literature* 59 (1987): 341–58, reprinted in *On Dickinson: The Best of "American Literature,"* ed. Edwin H. Cady and Louis J. Budd (Durham, N.C.: Duke University Press, 1990), 139–56.

17. Matt. 7.24–27. Hereafter biblical references are noted in parentheses in the text. All are to the King James Version of the Bible.

18. Donald Davie, *The New Oxford Book of Christian Verse* (New York: Oxford University Press, 1981), xx–xxi, defines Christian poets, as opposed to other religious poets, as those for whom Christ is of central import. So does Miriam K. Starkman, professor emeritus of City University of New York's Graduate Center and director of my 1980 doctoral dissertation, "The Religious Voice of Emily Dickinson," whose definition of the poetry of devotion I have relied upon throughout this book.

19. Thomas à Kempis, *The Imitation of Christ*, trans. and introd. Leo Sherley-Price (Harmondsworth, Middlesex: Penguin Books, Cox and Wyman, 1952), books 3 and 4; *The Works of George Herbert*, ed. F. E. Hutchinson (Oxford: Clarendon Press, 1941). Hereafter references to the *Imitation* and *The Temple* are cited parenthetically in the text.

20. Both synonyms are from Noah Webster, *An American Dictionary of the English Language* (1848

ed.; reprint, Ann Arbor, Mich.: University Microfilms International, 1979). Definitions throughout this study are Webster's.

21. My interpretation of Herbert's "Dialogue" relies heavily upon Helen Vendler, *The Poetry of George Herbert* (Cambridge: Harvard University Press, 1975); Arnold Stein, *George Herbert's Lyrics* (Baltimore: Johns Hopkins University Press, 1968); and Richard Strier, *Love Known: Theology and Experience in George Herbert's Poetry* (Chicago: University of Chicago Press, 1983).

22. Webster's full definition of "circumference" is as follows: "(1) The line that goes round or encompasses a figure; a periphery; applied particularly to the line that goes round a circle, sphere, or other figures approaching these in form . . . (2) The space included in a circle . . . (3) An orb; a circle; anything circular or orbicular."

23. See my 1980 doctoral dissertation, "The Religious Voice of Emily Dickinson" (City University of New York), whose central thesis is that the Dickinson canon must be read holistically as the account of a spiritual pilgrimage through time toward the infinite "Circumference" of God.

24. For a discussion of Emily Dickinson and the emblem, see George Monteiro and Barton Levi St. Armand, "The Experienced Emblem: A Study of the Poetry of Emily Dickinson," in *Prospects 6* (New York: Burt Franklin, 1981), 187–280.

25. According to *Scriptural Meditations on the Rosary*, comp. Daughters of St. Paul (Boston: St. Paul Editions, 1984).

26. My language here and in the following sentence echoes Wolfgang Iser, *The Act of Reading: A Theory of Aesthetic Response* (Baltimore: Johns Hopkins University Press, 1978), and Stephen D. Moore, *Literary Criticism and the Gospels: The Theoretical Challenge* (New Haven: Yale University Press, 1989).

27. See Sewall, *Life*, 153, for Lavinia's comment, and Leyda, *Years and Hours*, 427–74, for Susan Dickinson's unsigned obituary, which is now in Houghton Library's Dickinson Collection, box 9.

28. According to S. P. Rosenbaum, ed., *A Concordance to the Poems of Emily Dickinson* (Ithaca: Cornell University Press, 1964), "Jesus" (and "Jesus' ") appears twenty-one times; "Christ" (and "Christ's") appears twelve times; "Savior" (and "Savior's") nine times; "Redeemer" once; "Rabbi" once; "Son," meaning Jesus, nine times. "Lord" (and "Lord's") appears twenty-six times, and in at least sixteen cases Jesus is clearly intended. "Master" (and "Master's") appears seven times; since "Master" is the variant for "Savior" in J-461, another version of the parable of the ten virgins, and since in J-336 "one that bore her Master's name" is a variation of Rev. 22.4, "Master" signifies Jesus in at least two poems and probably all seven. Added to this list must be the twenty F-40 poems in which he is not named but is the implicit subject, addressee, or speaker, and those poems in which he is given such titles as "Largest Lover," "the Man that knew the News," and so forth. See my discussion of Dickinson's poems on Christ in the section on poems 1 and 2, in Part I of this book.

## Part I: The Composition of Place

1. The parable of the sheep and goats was obviously a favorite of Emily Dickinson's, because she often alludes to it in both poems and letters. In the eighth fascicle's fifth poem, "If the foolish, call them '*flowers*,' " for example, the protagonist concludes with her wish to stand "At that grand 'Right hand,' " the parable's "right hand," where the saved sheep will be placed (J-168). Similarly, the twentieth fascicle's eleventh poem, "Over and over, like a Tune," alludes to "the Justified / Processions / At the Lord's Right hand" (J-367). In the sixth fascicle's fourteenth poem, "I bring an unaccustomed wine," the protagonist concludes that she always bears a cup to slake some pilgrim's thirst "If, haply, any say to me / 'Unto the little, unto me,' / When I at last awake" (J-132), echoing the parable's "Inasmuch as ye did it unto one of the least of these my brethren, ye have done it unto me." Emily Dickinson's most obscure allusion to the parable is in an 1881 letter of sympathy to

Elizabeth Holland after the death of her husband; the poet wrote of Dr. Holland, " 'Inasmuch,' to him, how tenderly fulfilled" (L-729), again echoing Matt. 25.40.

2. The meditator's declaration that all her intentions and actions are directed to Christ's service resembles the Ignatian meditation's opening prayer, in which the meditant prays that "all my intentions, actions, and works may be directed purely to the service and praise of His Divine Majesty." Moreover, her implicit request, in the same poem, that she be among the saved sheep at the Judgment resembles the Ignatian meditation's "second prelude," in which the meditant "ask[s] God our Lord for what I want and desire" (Ignatius, *Spiritual Exercises* 54).

3. See note 5 to the Introduction. Though the order in which Emily Dickinson assembled the fascicles is not necessarily the precise order in which she meant them to be read, reading the fascicles sequentially—that is, in the order, according to *Manuscript Books,* she assembled them—provides unmistakable evidence of an overall narrative development that is summed up in F-40.

## Part II: The Poems of Analysis

1. For a discussion of conceptual deviance, see Samuel R. Levin, *Metaphoric Worlds: Conceptions of a Romantic Nature* (New Haven: Yale University Press, 1988), 37–44.

2. Although biblical scholars no longer believe that Hebrews and several of the New Testament letters were written by Paul, here and throughout I have followed the King James Version of the Bible.

# Selected Bibliography

Alter, Robert. *The Art of Biblical Poetry*. New York: Basic Books, 1985.

Anderson, Charles R. *Emily Dickinson's Poetry: Stairway of Surprise*. New York: Holt, Rinehart & Winston, 1960.

Augustine. *On Christian Doctrine*. Indianapolis: Liberal Arts Press, Bobbs-Merrill, 1958.

Bianchi, Martha Dickinson. *The Life and Letters of Emily Dickinson*. Boston: Houghton Mifflin, 1924.

Bloch, Chana. *Spelling the Word: George Herbert and the Bible*. Berkeley and Los Angeles: University of California Press, 1985.

Burke, Kenneth. *The Rhetoric of Religion: Studies in Logology*. Berkeley and Los Angeles: University of California Press, 1970.

Cameron, Sharon. *Choosing Not Choosing: Dickinson's Fascicles*. Chicago: University of Chicago Press, 1992.

Capps, Jack L. *Emily Dickinson's Reading: 1836–1886*. Cambridge: Harvard University Press, 1966.

Charity, A. C. *Events and Their After-Life: The Dialectics of Christian Typology in the Bible and Dante*. Cambridge: Cambridge University Press, 1966.

Cruden, Alexander. *Complete Concordance to the Old and New Testaments*. Ed. A. D. Adams, C. H. Irwin, S. A. Waters. Grand Rapids, Mich.: Regency, 1949.

Daughters of St. Paul, comp. *Scriptural Meditations on the Rosary*. Boston: St. Paul Editions, 1984.

Davie, Donald. *The New Oxford Book of Christian Verse*. New York: Oxford University Press, 1981.

Drury, John. *The Parables in the Gospels: History and Allegory*. New York: Crossroads, 1985.

Duchac, Joseph. *The Poems of Emily Dickinson: An Annotated Guide to Commentary Published in English, 1890–1977*. Boston: G. K. Hall, 1979.

Eliot, T. S. *The Waste Land*. In *The Norton Anthology of English Literature*, gen. ed. M. H. Abrams. New York: Norton, 1986.

Empson, William. *Seven Types of Ambiguity*. 3d ed. New York: New Directions, 1955.

Farr, Judith Banzer. "Compound Manner: Emily Dickinson and the Metaphysical Poets." *American Literature* 32 (1961): 417–33.

Farr, Judith. *The Passion of Emily Dickinson*. Cambridge: Harvard University Press, 1992.

Fish, Stanley. *The Living Temple: George Herbert and Catechizing*. Berkeley and Los Angeles: University of California Press, 1978.

Franklin, Ralph W. *The Editing of Emily Dickinson: A Reconsideration*. Madison: University of Wisconsin Press, 1967.

———. "The Emily Dickinson Fascicles." *Studies in Bibliography* 36 (1983): 1–20.

————, ed. *The Manuscript Books of Emily Dickinson.* 2 vols. Cambridge: Belknap Press of Harvard University Press, 1981.

Frye, Northrop. *The Great Code: The Bible and Literature.* New York: Harcourt Brace Jovanovich, 1982.

Gelpi, Albert J. *Emily Dickinson: The Mind of the Poet.* Cambridge: Harvard University Press, 1965.

————. "Emily Dickinson: The Self as Center." In *The Tenth Muse: The Psyche of the American Poet.* Cambridge: Harvard University Press, 1975.

Herbert, George. *The Works of George Herbert,* ed. F. E. Hutchinson. Oxford: Clarendon Press, 1941.

Howe, Susan. *The Birth-mark: Unsettling the Wilderness in American Literary History.* Hanover, N.H.: University Press of New England for Wesleyan University Press, 1993.

Ignatius. *The Spiritual Exercises of St. Ignatius Loyola.* Trans. Anthony Mottola. Introd. Robert W. Gleason, S.J. New York: Doubleday, 1964.

Iser, Wolfgang. *The Act of Reading: A Theory of Aesthetic Response.* Baltimore: Johns Hopkins University Press, 1978.

James, William. *The Varieties of Religious Experience: A Study in Human Nature.* New York: Collier Macmillan, 1961.

Johnson, Thomas H., ed. *The Poems of Emily Dickinson: Including Variant Readings Critically Compared to All Known Manuscripts.* 3 vols. Cambridge: Belknap Press of Harvard University Press, 1955.

Johnson, Thomas H., and Theodora Ward, eds. *The Letters of Emily Dickinson.* 3 vols. Cambridge: Belknap Press of Harvard University Press, 1958.

Joyce, James. *Ulysses.* New York: Modern Library, Random House, 1946.

Juhasz, Suzanne, ed. *Feminist Critics Read Emily Dickinson.* Bloomington: Indiana University Press, 1983.

Kermode, Frank. *The Genesis of Secrecy: On the Interpretation of Narrative.* Cambridge: Harvard University Press, 1979.

Levin, Samuel R. *Metaphoric Worlds: Conceptions of a Romantic Nature.* New Haven: Yale University Press, 1988.

Lewalski, Barbara. *Protestant Poetics and the Seventeenth-Century Lyric.* Princeton: Princeton University Press, 1979.

Leyda, Jay. *The Years and Hours of Emily Dickinson.* 2 vols. New Haven: Yale University Press, 1960. Reprint, Hamden, Conn.: Archon Books, 1970.

Lowenberg, Carlton. *Emily Dickinson's Textbooks.* Ed. Territa A. Lowenberg and Carla L. Brown. Lafayette, Calif.: Carlton Lowenberg, 1986.

Martin, L. C., ed. *The Works of Henry Vaughan.* 2 vols. Oxford: Clarendon Press, 1914.

Martin, Loy D. *Browning's Dramatic Monologues and the Post-Romantic Subject.* Baltimore: Johns Hopkins University Press, 1985.

Martz, Louis L. *The Poem of the Mind: Essays on Poetry, English and American.* New York: Oxford University Press, 1966.

————. *The Poetry of Meditation: A Study in English Religious Literature of the Seventeenth Century.* New Haven: Yale University Press, 1954.

Miller, Cristanne. *Emily Dickinson: A Poet's Grammar.* Cambridge: Harvard University Press, 1987.

Miller, J. Hillis. *Tropes, Parables, Performatives: Essays in Twentieth-Century Literature.* Durham, N.C.: Duke University Press, 1991.

Miller, Ruth. *The Poetry of Emily Dickinson.* Middletown, Conn.: Wesleyan University Press, 1968.

Monteiro, George, and Barton Levi St. Armand. "The Experienced Emblem: A Study of the Poetry of Emily Dickinson." In *Prospects 6*, 187–280. New York: Burt Franklin, 1981.

Montgomery, Benilde. "Emily Dickinson and the Meditative Tradition." Ph.D. diss., State University of New York at Stony Brook, 1981.

Moore, Stephen D. *Literary Criticism and the Gospels: The Theoretical Challenge*. New Haven: Yale University Press, 1989.

Nicolson, Marjorie Hope. *The Breaking of the Circle: Studies in the Effect of the "New Science" on Seventeenth-Century Poetry*. New York: Columbia University Press, 1960.

Oberhaus, Dorothy Huff. "Emily Dickinson as Comic Poet." In *Approaches to Teaching Dickinson's Poetry*, ed. Robin Riley Fast and Christine Mack Gordon. New York: Modern Language Association, 1989.

———. "Emily Dickinson's Books." *Emily Dickinson Journal 2*, no. 2 (1993): 58–65.

———. "Emily Dickinson's Poem 698." *The Explicator* 46 (summer 1988): 21–28.

———. " 'Engine against th' Almightie': Emily Dickinson and Prayer." *ESQ: A Journal of the American Renaissance* 32 (1986): 153–72.

———. "In Defense of Sue." *Dickinson Studies*, no. 48 (Bonus 1983): 1–25.

———. "A Reading of Emily Dickinson." In *"Like Season'd Timber": New Essays on George Herbert*, ed. Edmund Miller and Robert Di Yanni. New York: Peter Lang, 1987.

———. "The Religious Voice of Emily Dickinson." Ph.D. diss., City University of New York, 1980.

———. " 'Tender Pioneer': Emily Dickinson's Poems on the Life of Christ." *American Literature* 59 (1987): 341–58. Reprinted in *On Dickinson: The Best of "American Literature,"* ed. Edwin H. Cady and Louis J. Budd, 139–56. Durham, N.C.: Duke University Press, 1990.

O'Keefe, Martha Lindblom. *This Edifice*, pts. 1, 2, and 3, and vol. 3. Copyright 1989 by Martha Lindblom O'Keefe. Four separate typescripts.

Porter, David. *The Art of Emily Dickinson's Early Poetry*. Cambridge: Harvard University Press, 1966.

———. *Dickinson: The Modern Idiom*. Cambridge: Harvard University Press, 1981.

Quarles, Francis. *Emblems, Divine and Moral*. London: Bradbury & Evans, 1845.

Rosenbaum, S. P., ed. *A Concordance to the Poems of Emily Dickinson*. Ithaca: Cornell University Press, 1964.

Rosenthal, M. L., and Sally Gall. "American Originals II: Emily Dickinson's Fascicles." In *The Modern Poetic Sequence: The Genius of Modern Poetry*. New York: Oxford University Press, 1983.

St. Armand, Barton Levi. *Emily Dickinson and Her Culture: The Soul's Society*. New York: Cambridge University Press, 1984.

Sewall, Richard B. *The Life of Emily Dickinson*. 2 vols. New York: Farrar, Straus & Giroux, 1974.

Sewall, Richard B., and Martin Wand. " 'Eyes Be Blind, Heart Be Still': A New Perspective on Emily Dickinson's Eye Problem." *New England Quarterly* 52 (1979): 400–406.

Shakespeare, William. *Twelfth Night*. In *Shakespeare: The Complete Works*, ed. G. B. Harrison. New York: Harcourt Brace Jovanovich, 1968.

Shurr, William H. *The Marriage of Emily Dickinson: A Study of the Fascicles*. Lexington: University Press of Kentucky, 1983.

*Sir Gawain and the Green Knight: A New Verse Translation* by Marie Borroff. New York: Norton, 1967.

Small, Judy Jo. *Positive as Sound: Emily Dickinson's Rhyme*. Athens: University of Georgia, 1990.

Smith, Martha Nell. *Rowing in Eden: Rereading Emily Dickinson*. Austin: University of Texas Press, 1992.

Starkman, Miriam K. "The 'Grace of the Absurd': Form and Concept in W. H. Auden's *For the Time Being*." *Harvard Theological Review* 67 (1974): 275–88.

———. "Noble Numbers and the Poetry of Devotion." In *Reason and the Imagination: Studies in the History of Ideas, 1600–1800*, ed. J. A. Mazzeo, 1–27. New York: Columbia University Press, 1962.

Stein, Arnold. *George Herbert's Lyrics*. Baltimore: Johns Hopkins University Press, 1968.

Stewart, Stanley. *George Herbert*. Boston: Twayne, 1986.

Stonum, Gary Lee. *The Dickinson Sublime*. Madison: University of Wisconsin Press, 1990.

Strier, Richard. *Love Known: Theology and Experience in George Herbert's Poetry*. Chicago: University of Chicago Press, 1983.

Teresa of Avila. *The Interior Castle or The Mansions: Translated from the Autograph of Saint Teresa of Jesus by a Benedictine of Stanbrook*. London: Thomas Baker, 1930.

Thomas à Kempis. *The Imitation of Christ*. Trans. and introd. Leo Sherley-Price. Harmondsworth, Middlesex: Penguin Books, Cox and Wyman, 1952.

Todd, Mabel Loomis, ed. *Poems of Emily Dickinson: Third Series*. Boston: Roberts Bros., 1896.

Todd, Mabel Loomis, and Millicent Todd Bingham, eds. *Bolts of Melody: New Poems of Emily Dickinson*. First and second printings. New York: Harper, 1945.

Todd, Mabel Loomis, and T. W. Higginson, eds. *The Poems of Emily Dickinson*. Boston: Roberts Bros., 1890.

———. *Poems of Emily Dickinson: Second Series*. Boston: Roberts Bros., 1891.

Trawick, Buckner B. *The Bible as Literature: The New Testament*. New York: Barnes & Noble, 1968.

Tuve, Rosamond. *A Reading of George Herbert*. Chicago: University of Chicago Press, 1952.

Underhill, Evelyn. *Mysticism: A Study in the Nature and Development of Man's Spiritual Consciousness*. New York: New American Library, 1955.

Vendler, Helen. *The Poetry of George Herbert*. Cambridge: Harvard University Press, 1975.

Webster, Noah. *An American Dictionary of the English Language*. 1848 ed. Reprint, Ann Arbor, Mich.: University Microfilms International, 1979.

Weisbuch, Robert. *Emily Dickinson's Poetry*. Chicago: University of Chicago Press, 1975.

Wigglesworth, Michael. "The Day of Doom." In *The Norton Anthology of American Literature*. New York: Norton, 1985.

# Index of First Lines

# Index

ED = Emily Dickinson     F, Fs = Fascicle, Fascicles     GH = George Herbert